COMMISSION

Created On Purpose For A Purpose

By Paul Tubach, Jr.

COMMISSION

"COMMISSION" by Paul B. Tubach, Jr. is licensed under a Creative Commons Attribution-NonCommercial-NoDerivatives 4.0 International License

You are free to copy, share and redistribute the material in any medium, format or language as long as the text and content is not altered or misconstrued. Freely it was received... freely it is given. The licensor cannot revoke these freedoms as long as you follow these license terms:

- **Attribution** — You must give appropriate credit, provide a link to the website, and indicate if any changes were made. You may do so in any reasonable manner, but not in any way that suggests the author endorses you or your use. "Attribute this work" as: Paul Tubach, Jr., www.newearthministries.org.
- **NonCommercial** — You may not use the material for commercial purposes, i.e. not for any private, corporate, nonprofit or otherwise financial gain.
- **NoDerivatives** — If you remix, transform or build upon the material, you may not distribute the modified material. The creation or development of any derivatives, secondary workbooks or manuals from this book is reserved solely by the author.
- **No additional restrictions** — You may not apply legal terms or technological measures that legally restrict others from doing anything the license permits.

Paperback ISBN 978-1-949892-25-3
Library of Congress Number - pending
Produced in the United States of America
New Earth Ministries

Scripture taken from the New King James Version. Copyright © 1979, 1980, 1982 by Thomas Nelson, Inc. Used by permission. All rights reserved.

Books and other materials are available online through www.newearthministries.org.

March 2018

Table of Contents

Introduction	xv
Chapter 1: Soul With Spirit	**1**
Soul With Spirit	12
The Flesh Is Weak	18
Mystery of Iniquity	24
Resurrection Clarification	35
The Soul Is Resurrected	36
Eyes Of Our Soul	47
Soul Explanation	50
Eyes For The Mind	54
Sons of God – Through Obedience	62
Minds Decide, Hearts Establish	69
How We Treat Other Spirits	75
Only Three Things – and A Fourth	81
How We Treat Our Body	83
Understanding Why We Are	88
Mercy Explained	93
Goodness and Might	96
Receive Your Commission	100
Created Upright In Rightness	102
Make Me Thy Instrument	109
Chapter 2: The Spirit Within Us	**113**
Strengthened In Our Spirit	118
The Sound Mind!!!	119
Love!!!	124
Power!!!	126
Power In Operation	136
We need the mind of Christ!	151
Death Is A Not-Laughing Matter	154
The Hands Of Governance	157
Unworldly Experiences	162
We Are Spiritual Beings	162

Energeia Thoughts	165
The Power Of Thought	168
The Battlefield Is The Mind!	174
Two Kingdoms In Conflict	181
Weaponized Thoughts	189
Ideology Of Thought	190
Eternity Exists	197
Paradigm Of Co-Existing Realities	200
New Earth Promises	206
On or In	210
The Free Gift	214
Water Into Wine	216
Chapter 3: Spirit (small 's')	**221**
Iscus – Spiritual Attribute Called Strength	223
The Weakened Spirit	226
The Strengthened Spirit	228
Thoroughly Open Heaven	230
Spirit Strengthened With Power	233
Refreshed In Our Spirit	234
Authority To Cast Out Spirits	236
In Closure	241
Chapter 4: The Beatitudes	**243**
Blessed Are The Poor In Spirit	243
The Poor Indicative	248
Tithing To Remind Us	266
The Spirituality Test	269
Blessed Are The Beggars	274
Disciples of Love	284
Blessed Are The Poor	290
Sermon On The Mount	295
Kingdom Opposites	297
Hannah's Prayer	302
Chapter 5: Disciples	**305**
The Gospel Of Grace	309
God's Attributes Given To Mankind	312

Amazing Grace	313
Grace Commands Obedience	314
The Crucible Called Life	316
Trust In The Lord Jesus	322
Disciple Sons and Daughters	323
Sell Everything, Then Follow Me	326
Timothy, My Son	333
Millennial Servants and New Earth Residents	333
Beloved Disciple, Abide In Me	333

The Image Bearer Series

2. Listen – How To Hear God's Voice – better
3. Image – The Revelation Of God Himself
4. Dominion – Our Heavenly Mandate To Occupy Earth
5. Understand – What Jesus Wants You To Know – and Why
6. Commission – Created On Purpose For A Purpose
7. Gateways – Manifesting Heaven In The Midst Of Chaos
8. Here – The Kingdom Of Heaven Is

The Image Bearer Series is based upon Genesis 1:26-28: "Let us make man in Our image, according to Our likeness… and grant them dominion."

"Image" explains 'who' the Lord of Heaven and Earth is, "Understand" explains 'why' we are here, "Commission" explains 'what' man is and 'how' we were created by the Lord, "Dominion" explains 'what' we are supposed to be doing, "Gateways" explains 'how' we are to accomplish our earthly mission, and "Here" explains our eternal destination is actually – Earth.

Many tools were given to mankind that enables us to accomplish our mission objective to have dominion over the kingdom of darkness – and we need to comprehend this truth: earth is our 'Here' – and our 'when' is now! How God created us – and why – is directly related to our sanctification and accomplishing our multifaceted mission for being on earth.

Why are you here – and what's your purpose in life? These books will answer those questions.

When I began writing in August 2012, four drafts were completed within a year, then on Sept. 27, 2013, the Lord spoke to me and said: "You are My writer. Now write!" and then the Spirit directed me to finish draft #4 which became the initial book, *"Regenesis: A Sojourn To Remember Who We Are,"* released in August 2014. Next, the Spirit directed me to work on draft #3 (in reverse order) and then, on October 24, the Spirit told me, "That is not one book with seven chapters – those are seven books." Thus, I have been writing the Image Bearer series under His anointing by hearing His voice and writing what I am directed to write.

Regenesis helped us discover man's true identity, as spiritual beings that are having a human experience, who were created good and upright by God "in His Own image according to His likeness" (Gen. 1:26-27), whereby we have been blessed with many wonderful grace attributes by the Lord to accomplish all that He purposed for man… since the beginning.

Yet for most of us, we've forgotten who we are… and we've forgotten what we are supposed to be doing. Regenesis reminds us who we are, and now, the Image Bearer series is reminding us what we are supposed to do, how we should do it – and more importantly "why" we are doing it.

The Image Bearer series builds upon that knowledge of truth that mankind was created good so as to become what we were created for: to bear His image and imitate Jesus in every respect according to His earthly example – and operate as His heavenly ambassadors for earth.

The heavenly pattern for mankind is: imitate Jesus.
The earthly pattern for this world is: become like heaven.

Who you are is not based upon what you do; "what you do" is based upon "who you are." We get our identity from Jesus. This realigned perspective regarding "who" we are … is to reorient the applecart of faith pointing in the right direction, to focus on Jesus, and to accomplish our primary mission: have dominion on earth – in the name of Jesus.

The numeric order in which the Spirit directed these books: 1,2,8,3,5,4,6,7 was not linear in the least. Let the Spirit guide you in the order He wants you to read them; however, learning how to "Hear God's Voice" is always mission critical to get started on His path for anyone.

On October 24, 2015, the Lord told me to put these books on the internet for free. This was unexpected, and then the Lord whispered to me, "Can you make money on My words? Freely you have received... freely give."

When the Lord tells you what to do, He will also give you His authority, with power and provision, to do all that He commands. We need to embrace this perspective regarding our life on earth in order to understand and comprehend who we are and what we are supposed to be doing. There is much joy and peace living in this manner, and yet... we all make this choice daily to live according to His purpose for His glory – or to live according to our best laid plans. If I can do it – so can you.

Jesus did it, and therefore – "As He is, so are we in this world" (1 John 4:17). I hope you enjoy the Image Bearer series. Grace and peace be yours in abundance.

It's all about Jesus – and God gets the glory!

Glossary of Terms and Definitions

These are some keys to help navigate and understand the scriptures.

Heaven – God's throne, God's home and the permanent place where God's glory dwells
heaven – the spiritual reality of God's kingdom and Christ's presence upon earth
Glory – the fullness of God's presence; the fullness of all God is
Shekinah Glory – the manifest presence of God's Spirit
Christ – the manifest expression of God in Jesus, and regenerate (born anew) men
Jesus – the manifested Living God; Lord of heaven and earth; Lord of Glory; Lord of Hosts
Host – army (a very important term omitted in the NIV and some other versions)
Host of heaven – angels; sons of God and our heavenly brethren (Rev. 19:10)
Host of earth – sons of men, becoming sons of God in the regeneration
Man – the generic term for male and female to connote mankind, humanity, etc.
Earth – the planet; one of three permanent places within the kingdom of God
Hell – the absence of God; one of three permanent places within the kingdom of God; the pit
World – temporary realm on earth under the dominion and operational control of Satan
Satan – Prince of "this world" (formerly known as Lucifer before he rebelled and fell to earth)
Sin – the operating system of this world in opposition to God's sovereignty; separation from God; things done that cause separation
Spirit – the operating system on earth under the Lord's dominion; the Holy Spirit; God's Spirit
Grace – attributes of God's character that are freely given to man

Light – a metaphor implying God's truth
Darkness – a metaphor implying evil – and sinful lies of "this world"
Wickedness – taking credit for what God has done
Evil – using God's glory and power to accomplish your personal agenda
Paradigm – the operating systems of sin or "by the Spirit" on earth
Paradise – the earthly realm in oneness with God apart from sin
Dwelling – a temporary place to live
Abode – a permanent place to live (of existence)
Rest – the permanent state of being where God's presence abides (in your heart and in heaven)
Kingdom of God – all places under the authority of Jesus
Kingdom of heaven – a term used exclusively in the gospel of
    Matthew to describe the kingdom of God as it pertains to
    earth under the Lordship of Jesus Christ

- Life – the source from which all creation exists, and is made alive, as coming from God through Christ Jesus, who is "the Life" and the "author and finisher" of faith (John 14:6; Heb. 12:2)
- Living – those persons spiritually alive with life, who no longer operate in the shadow of Death while sojourning in earthen vessels that will eventually perish for lack of life
- Alive – the spiritual state of being in existence from God's perspective, even apart from the body, and abiding eternally in communion with God's Presence and Spirit
- Dead – the spiritual state of being in existence from God's perspective, but temporarily separated from Him; the eventual disposition of the earthen body without life
- Death – the spiritual state of being permanently and eternally separated from God; the temporary holding place of unregenerate dead that wait there until the judgment

Introduction

Commission is not what you do... commission is about who you are!

This world will try to define you based upon what you do... but that is not who you really are.

Who are you? Why are you are on earth? What's your purpose in life? Why am I the way I am... and why am I going through this hellish existence on earth? Commission is not about what you do... Commission explains basic questions about your identity and what you are supposed to be doing.

Life is a mystery! If your doctrines cannot explain all the "why" questions you've asked, then this book will most certainly cause a paradigm shift in your thought process because the Lord wants you to understand why – but you need new lenses through which to perceive spiritual things from God's perspective.

When people ask: "What do you do?" they are trying to define who you are, but your identity (from a spiritual perspective) was determined by Who made you for a purpose. Your identity is found – in Christ!

This book explains 'how' we were constructed: we are a soul with spirit within a human form. Once we thoroughly understand how – it will become easier for us to see what we're supposed to be doing – and why! Understanding the function of your spirit to assist your soul is essential to comprehend the Lord's commission for you.

You have a commission from God to do something only you can accomplish on this earth... but you must lay down your life in order to receive this commission.

Commissions are given to those who have been born anew by the Holy Spirit and know they are operating under the Lord's authority. We are more than "just" sheep! He sends His disciples on His behalf to do a job for His kingdom. He sends disciples into the kingdom of darkness with the spirit of light within us – to effect a regime change... from darkness to light!

Your commission is greater than you can imagine and this book helps answer many "why" questions you've struggled with. You are an amazing person, and spiritually... you are truly incredible! And yet, you may already know this, but no one has been able to explain it to you... until now.

"Image" explains 'who' the Lord of Heaven and Earth is, "Understand" explained 'why' we are here, "Dominion" explained 'what' we are supposed to be doing, and now "Commission" will explain 'how' we were created by the Lord to accomplish our earthly mission. Many tools were given to mankind that enables us to accomplish our mission objective to have dominion over the kingdom of darkness – and we need to comprehend this truth: earth is our 'here' and our 'when' is now! How God created us is directly correlated to accomplishing our multifaceted mission on earth... as well as our sanctification unto salvation.

COMMISSION

Chapter 1: Soul With Spirit

> "You do not know what manner of spirit you are of" (Luke 9:55).[1]

There have been many opinions regarding which came first: the soul or the spirit. We are living in a period of time when most spiritual leaders now believe we are spiritual beings having a human experience, and for this reason they claim we are a spirit – and that the spirit was given before the soul. I strongly disagree. When we die, our body returns to the earth where it came from, and our spirit returns to God who gave it, so then... what were we beforehand... and what are we afterward when our spirit leaves?[2] What, then, is raised in resurrection... the body, soul or the spirit? This is a good question that will be answered along the way.

The scriptures are clear in saying "God is Spirit" (John 4:24) – and we were created in His Own image according to His likeness, and while this is unquestionably true... God also has a soul (see Isa. 1:14; 42:1; Psa. 11:5; Job 23:13; Lev. 10:38; Matt. 3:17; John 12:27; Heb. 10:38), a mind (Jer. 19:5; 44:21; Rom. 11:34; 1 Cor. 2:16) and a heart (1 Sam. 2:35; Jer. 3:15; 23:20)!

> "Behold, My Servant [*Jesus*] whom I uphold, My Elect in whom My soul delights" (Isa. 42:1).

> "Yes, I will rejoice over them to do them good, and I will assuredly plant them in this land, with all My heart and with all My soul" (Jer. 32:41).

We were created in every aspect in the image and likeness of our

---

[1] Jesus said this to His disciples when they wanted to call down fire upon a village. There are two types of spirits the Lord created (Gen. 2:1): the host of heaven (angels) that can command fire to come down from heaven (Gen. 19:13), and the host of earth (men) who were sent to save men's lives (souls), not kill or condemn.

[2] Consider Elisha when he asked for a double portion of Elijah's spirit. Did Elijah cease to exist because of it? No.

Creator, Jesus Christ, and because we were created by Him (Col. 1:16), our spirit and body belong to Him. When we die, our body returns to the earth (from which it came) and our spirit returns to God (who gave it), so now, follow the linear thought within these scriptures:

> "And the LORD God formed man of the dust of the ground, and breathed into his nostrils the breath of life; and man became a living *being [soul]*" (Gen. 2:7).

> "Then the dust will return to the earth as it was, and the spirit will return to God who gave it" (Eccl. 12:7).

> "His spirit departs, **he returns to his earth**; in that very day his plans perish" (Psa. 146:4).

Our soul was given two partners for our earthly sojourn: our natural body and our spirit.

> "Thus says the Lord, who stretches out the heavens, lays the foundation of the earth, **and forms the spirit of man within him**" (Zech. 12:1).[3]

Let me ask you this question: which came first according to these scriptures – body, soul or spirit? Clearly the soul! And in this order – soul, body, then spirit. The flesh was formed upon us, then our spirit was formed within us. The mystery of man and his purpose on earth will become much easier to comprehend with this understanding firmly planted in your mind.

> "***For You formed my inward parts***; you covered me in my mother's womb. [14] I will praise You, for I am fearfully and wonderfully made; marvelous are Your works, and that my soul knows very well.

---

[3] Most curious is this scripture's omission in Strong's exposition of 'yatsar-3335' of the spirit formed in us by God.

> [15] My frame was not hidden from You, when I was made in secret, and skillfully wrought in the lowest parts of the earth. [16] *Your eyes saw my substance, being yet unformed* "Thus says God the Lord, Who created the heavens and stretched them out, Who spread forth the earth and that which comes from it, *Who gives breath to the people on it, and spirit to those who walk on it*" (Isa. 42:5).[4]

Throughout creation, the spiritual came first, then the material; all things material originated from God's spiritual reality, as all things originating in/from/out of Christ (spiritually) before they were created and formed. "By faith we understand that the worlds were framed by the word of God, so that the things which are seen were not made of things which are visible" (Heb. 11:3; see Col. 1:16), yet one statement by the Apostle Paul seems to contradict which came first…

> "However, the spiritual is not first, but the natural, and afterward the spiritual" (1 Cor. 15:46).

For many years I wrestled with this apparent scriptural contradiction, as if perhaps an error could be found in the scriptures (which I flatly reject), but here it is – an obvious contradiction – unless we interpret what Paul is saying within the material context of our physical and spiritual construction; the natural (body) came first, and afterward the spiritual (spirit)… yet we (our soul) existed "in Christ before the foundation of the world" (Eph. 1:4). Thus, truth has validated and reconciled two differing scriptures and removed any appearance of contradiction.

Now, let me also ask you: to whom does your spirit belong? Your <u>spirit</u> is theoretically "yours" during your earthly sojourn, but your spirit does not belong to you. Your <u>soul</u> is 100% "all you" – *and then* – you were given a spirit to steward while you are in this

---

[4] Hebrew understanding of our soul and spirit often refers to the spiritual aspects of man as "the inward parts."

natural body, but your spirit belongs to God who gave it to you (the reason why God did this will be discussed soon)… and it will return to God at the proper time.

> "For you were bought at a price; therefore glorify God *in your body* **and in your spirit, which are God's**" (1 Cor. 6:20).

> "Or do you not know that your body is the temple of the Holy Spirit who is in you, whom you have from God, **and you are not your own**?" (1 Cor. 6:19).

The breath that God breathed into you – is His breath; He breathed His air into your body and formed His spirit within you (Gen. 2:7) at the same time to animate you as a living '*nephesh*' – a living soul – and thus… "you are not your own."

We are spiritual beings on account of our soul (not our spirit). The spirit within us was "loaned" to us by God to assist our soul and is very significant in helping us perform our assigned tasks on earth, but the soul is who you really are – and the soul is "what" is raised in resurrection (not the spirit).

We are told to glorify God in our body and our spirit, yet we were also created and purposed to glorify God in our soul that produces an increase of glory in the earth with the glory God sowed into our soul (the pearl of great price).[5] That which is of the flesh is worldly, yet that which is spiritual is born of the Spirit to produce more glory in us (by grace) to the praise of His glory.

> "That which is born of the flesh is flesh, and that which is born of the Spirit is spirit. [7] Do not marvel that I said to you, 'You must be born again'" (John 3:6, 7).

---

[5] Read "Dominion" by the author, especially Chapter 14: "The Lord's Dominion"

Our body was given to us as the earth suit for our mission on earth (having been created to do God's will on the earth as the host (i.e. army) of earth – Gen. 2:1, *and then* we were formed of the dust – Gen. 2:7). Then our spirit was given to us by God (formed in us) as a partner for our soul that He purposed to partner with His Spirit to receive spiritual tutoring, guidance and instruction in righteousness; however, before the fullness of this spiritual partnering can occur, we must be born '*anothen*-509' (anew from above) by the Spirit of God. We are spiritual and were made by God, but we need to be born anew (born again) by the Spirit of God.

Apart from this new birth, our mysterious earthly purpose under heaven, to transition our soul from death of life, and this world from darkness to light, is veiled from understanding and comprehension.[6] All is a mystery apart from the new birth by the Spirit!

> "Jesus answered and said to him, "Most assuredly, I say to you, unless one is born again, he cannot **understand** the kingdom of God" (John 3:3; ***oida****: to see, understand, and perceive spiritual things regarding God's kingdom*).

The new birth by the Spirit includes receiving a new heart and a new spirit so that we may live according to the Spirit in righteousness and newness – through truth, change and oneness.

> "I will give you a new heart and put a new spirit within you; I will take the heart of stone out of your flesh and give you a heart of flesh. [27] I will put My Spirit within you and cause you to walk in My statutes, and you will keep My judgments and do them" (Ezek. 36:26, 27).

---

[6] Read "Understand."

In the new birth, the original spirit that was given to us for the life of the soul is replaced by a new spirit… that becomes supercharged by the indwelling Holy Spirit so that we may live dedicated lives according to righteousness.

> "It is the Spirit who gives life; the flesh profits nothing. The words that I speak to you are spirit, and they are life" (John 6:63).

Perhaps the greatest distinction between that which came first (the spirit or the soul) is the scripture from Ezekiel. In the new birth, we are given a new heart and a new spirit, so let me ask this: what happened to "you" during this transaction? "I will give you" indicates something is happening to you, and thus… "a new spirit within you" indicates you are something apart from your original spirit and heart. Clearly, our old spirit was traded out (substituted) for another spirit, as was our spiritual heart, wherein these old things vacated "something" and new things were put into "something." When "spirit-only" followers are confronted with this message, they are quick to say the soul is replaced and a new one is given, yet the scriptures are silent on this tidbit of having two souls (except negatively in James 1:8: *dipsuche*: lit. two-souled; double-minded). Is it possible to believe one way or the other and still be saved? Absolutely! Does any one person know all the answers to God's mysteries? Absolutely not! And yet, we can all take great solace in knowing this: God is in control! Regardless of what we know or think we understand, God remains in control… and the sureness of our hope and salvation is maintained by staying in proper alignment and relationship (intimacy) with Jesus.

Our body has a purpose on earth and our spirit also has a purpose: to glorify God and do His will. So, what is the purpose of the soul? We are taught our soul represents the mind, will and emotion of the inner man that constitutes the essence of who man is, but does this really tell us anything? Not really. We are told we have a soul (or more accurately… we are a soul[7])[8], but what does

---

[7] *"You do not have a soul. You are a soul"* has been attributed to C.S. Lewis,

our soul do and how much influence do we have in managing it? To put it bluntly, your soul is "who" you really are! Your soul is spiritual, your soul is a repository (vessel) for a seed of God's glory placed within you, and your soul existed in God's presence before you were given a spirit or body (which we will discuss soon). Your soul is eternal (Psa. 49:9)!

Does a greater distinction in the scriptures exist between the soul and spirit? Not really, except they are discernible and can be divided from one other by the word of God (Heb. 4:12). This point is <u>very</u> important as truth becomes layered upon truth, so keep this in mind. Many writers in the scriptures reference the spirit of man as one means of describing an invisible spiritual nature within him, which seems to be an indwelling power, character or force compelling him to pursue spiritual matters *and* God's presence… oftentimes with mixed results. Likewise, the term "spirit man" or spiritual man seems to be used interchangeably as being representative for either soul or spirit… or as both when operating in oneness.

In the new birth, we are given a new heart and a new spirit to assist the efforts of our soul to accomplish its earthly mission, which includes the indwelling Spirit's sanctification and renewal process for our mind (note: we are not given a new mind). And yet, the soul and spirit constitutes the inner man (or the spiritual man) within the earthen vessel that is far more important to God than the vessel itself. Thus, the ambiguity surrounding this invisible aspect within us that – we cannot prove or qualify – is why some people disregard any and all spiritual aspects regarding man… as religious

---

yet this must be properly attributed to George MacDonald, who wrote in 1892: "Never tell a child you have a soul. Teach him, you are a soul; you have a body. As we learn to think of things always in this order, that the body is but the temporary clothing of the soul, our views of death and the unbefittingness of customary mourning will approximate to those of Friends of earlier generations." Hannah Peckham, a graduate of Duke University, is credited with this research.

[8] Matthew Henry's Commentary (1662-1714) says of the soul in Genesis 2:7: "It is by it that man is a living soul, that is, a living man; for the soul is the man."

hokum and mere superstition.[9]

Is it the soul or the spirit that makes us spiritual beings? Technically… both! These are two distinct aspects of your invisible spiritual character and nature that defines who you are and determines what you do… which operate in *oneness* of "who" you are, yet they have different functions 'based upon your awareness' as a sojourner having been sent to earth as a former resident of heaven to do God's will.

The body connects you to earthly things, while the spirit connects you to spiritual things. Our soul is the intersect between these two realities: one earthly and the other heavenly (spiritual).

The relationship of the soul, spirit and body helps us to comprehend "three levels of consciousness in all men, that of self-consciousness (through the soul), world-consciousness (through the body) and God-consciousness (through the spirit).[10] The soul's self-consciousness helps us to have knowledge of good and evil, to discern between good and evil, and choose well.[11]

Your soul is the only aspect of "you" that represents "who" you truly are; your soul "is" who you are, both now and eternally… in this life… and the life to follow hereafter! The way you think and the thoughts that determine your will to act – shall continue to operate from the mind of your soul which you currently possess, which is why it becomes mission critical to be transformed by the renewing of your mind (Rom. 12: 1, 2), so that your soul with life eternal will operate with a sanctified mind – and through a yielded will that is obedient to the Lord Jesus.

---

[9] Experiments were conducted in 1901 by Dr. Duncan Macdougall to prove his theory the soul has mass. Variables in his methodology have cast some doubt regarding his findings which indicated the body lost mass (weight) approximately 21 grams at the precise moment of death which he postulated was the weight of the human soul.

[10] Willmington's Guide To The Bible, Q&A section "About Man" #19: "Is man a two-part or three-part being?"

[11] God instructs us "to do well" because sin lies at the door seeking to rule us, but "we must rule over it" (Gen. 4:7).

Life eternal in Paradise will be a place where you have free will and are still able to sin, but your love for the Lord and your devotion to Him will eclipse any desire to trespass into sin. (Jesus lived according to this pattern while upon the earth.) Our probationary time during this season of eternity on earth was determined (as man's second chance after our fall from grace) to examine our heart and mind, to sanctify us, to proof our obedience and test our allegiance – whereby our life 'here and now' becomes a living testimony of our faithful, steadfast allegiance and devotion to serve the Lord Jesus as sons and daughters in His kingdom in the New Earth for all eternity (or not).

The point is: live your life on earth as if you are in heaven now. Don't wait for the angelic resurrection choir – do it now!

Therefore, it is very important to safeguard your soul from contamination and degradation. Your soul is the most important possession (and only possession) you have on this planet. Jesus said:

> "For what profit is it to a man if he gains the whole world, and loses ***his own soul***? Or what will a man give in exchange for his soul?" (Matt. 16:26)

Your soul is what remains of "you" after your body dies and your spirit returns to God. When Jesus was on the cross at Calvary, the last thing He said gives us proof regarding where our spirit goes:

> "And when Jesus had cried out with a loud voice, He said, "Father, 'into Your hands I commit My spirit.'" Having said this, He breathed His last" (Luke 23:46).

This is what all men may expect, for "It is appointed for men to die once" (Heb. 9:27). Our spirit was given to us to assist the life of the soul and become a *living soul* (*nephesh;* Gen. 2:7), and the Spirit breathed the breath of life into us to animate (make alive) this earthly body. Once we (in this body) have accomplished our intended purpose, the spirit which is the life in us, returns to God.

> "For I will not contend forever, nor will I always be angry; for the spirit would fail before Me, and the souls which I have made" (Isa. 57:16).

So, if our soul is the main element regarding who we are as spiritual beings, then this creates some matter of confusion: where does our soul go after death? Technically... it doesn't go anywhere! Our doctrines teach us our soul goes to heaven to be with God, but this is a false heaven doctrine[12]... especially when we consider God is in us, God is always with us, and has promised to never leave us and, thus, we shall (by grace) be with Him in Paradise. If Christ is in us – and we are in Christ – then the absence of our body or spirit does not change anything; we cannot go to be with God – "if" – Christ is already abiding within us. We are "not yet" already there – whereby we are merely waiting for the resurrection to occur that is already resident within us on account of Christ in us (John 11:25). We are already... and... not yet!

Ponder and meditate on that paragraph... before reading any further.

Here is another important point to consider: when Jesus was in the tomb three days, the scriptures teach us He descended into the lower parts of the earth (*Hades*; Eph. 4:9) to set those captives free. How did Jesus go and manifest Himself if He didn't have His spirit? He went as God, yet without His original spirit (that He committed to God) that was given to Him (and likewise us along with the breath of life). Did Jesus go with a body? There is no mention if this happened – or if it didn't. Did Jesus receive another spirit to help His soul descend to Hades? There is no mention if this happened – or if it didn't. And by extension – are we given a new spirit while we wait in Hades or are we given a new spirit in the resurrection or the regeneration? The scriptures are silent on this matter. In the New Earth, however, we will be

---

[12] Read "Here: The Kingdom of Heaven Is" by the author.

one with the Lord – in spirit and in truth – so let me ask you: will we even need a spirit if the Lord is already with/in us? The scriptures are unclear on this matter, so neither will I speculate (nor should we develop theologies that major on minors).

One thing is very clear from the scriptures: God will not let our soul remain in *Hades* (*Sheol*) nor will the soul of the righteous go down to the pit.[13]

> "Therefore my heart is glad, and my glory rejoices; my flesh also will rest in hope. [10] For You will not leave my soul in Sheol, nor will You allow Your Holy One to see corruption" (Psa. 16:9, 10; see also Job 33: 18, 28, 30).

> "O Lord, You brought my soul up from the grave; You have kept me alive, that I should not go down to the Pit" (Psa. 30:3; see also 49:9; 143:7).

Just as God is One **with His Spirit**,[14] likewise – we were created by God as soul **with spirit** to operate in oneness, to accomplish our mission on earth, and to keep us from going down to the pit. The body, however, is merely a vessel to accomplish the tasks ordained for us by God.

> "For God is my witness, **whom I serve with my spirit** in the gospel of His Son, that without ceasing I make mention of you always in my prayers" (Rom. 1:9).

Even while we sleep, our soul is communing with the Lord and receiving spiritual instruction through dreams. One morning, I awoke to find my spirit talking with the Holy Spirit… which

---

[13] IBID; read Chapter 6: "Where Do We Go From Here" to learn about 14 places in the kingdom of God.
[14] "The LORD our God, the LORD is one" (Deut. 6:4). Read "Image" section titled "Father With The Son."

delighted me immensely… and it happened the following morning as well, but not since. Does this mean my spirit does not talk to the Spirit in this manner anymore? Well, read this scripture and discern this yourself:

> "With my soul I have desired You in the night, **Yes**, by my spirit within me I will seek You early; for when Your judgments are in the earth, the inhabitants of the world will learn righteousness" (Isa. 26:9).

Day and night, we are the host of earth having been sent as heavenly ambassadors to accomplish God's plan "in the earth" for "the inhabitants of the world" (read the glossary of terms to see the significant difference for the terms 'earth' and 'world'). Even while resting, <u>my</u> spirit is seeking the Lord by the stillness of my mind (Psa. 46:10).

There are moments of pause in my writings as I meditate (or marinate) regarding the messages the Lord is revealing to me; sometimes days of research and prayer are needed to process the message; and if I get to a point when wisdom and understanding are not enough to reveal the answer, then I am awakened in the early morning hours by the Holy Spirit to guide me and tutor me with answers to the questions I seek so that I may share His truth with others (rather than me spouting off about my opinion).

> "The Spirit Himself bears witness ***with our spirit*** that we are children of God" (Rom. 8:16).

Soul With Spirit

We are soul and spirit… or rather… ***we are soul with spirit within a human form.*** Even though the soul and spirit are nearly identical in operation in regard to our character and personality attributes, they are very different "components" that make up who we are… and they manifest "who" we are differently in regard to God. Contemplate the Magnificat of Mary, for example:

"And Mary said: "My soul magnifies the Lord,
⁴⁷ and my spirit has rejoiced in God my Savior"
(Luke 1:46, 47).

From Mary's song of praise to God, we see the greatest distinction in the purpose of the soul versus the spirit: one magnifies God and the other rejoices in God. The soul magnifies and exponentially multiplies the essential greatness, goodness and wonderful majestic character of God and His marvelous grace attributes – *in us*……
while the spirit rejoices, honors, praises, exalts, celebrates, and glorifies God and His marvelous works, including our redemption and salvation – *through us*.

***When we magnify the Lord in our soul, He becomes bigger than any problem we* encounter.**

In essence, our soul and spirit were given for us to love God and adore Him – in us and through us – because He alone is worthy to be worshipped and adored. If man is given only one test on earth, perhaps this is it: to whom have you dedicated the allegiance of your soul? Stated a little differently: who do you worship and who do you adore the most? Since we will be worshipping the Lord forever as we live eternally in the New Earth, it seems to me a great act of mercy and kindness whereby God allows self-centered goats to winnow themselves, so as not to be put in an eternal place that would be a form of torment to their self-glorifying and self-serving nature.

The soul was *made* (Gen. 1:26 – the expression), then we were *created* upright by Jesus in rightness and goodness, as men of goodwill, according to "His Own" likeness (v.1:27 – the commission), and then we were *formed* of the earth (v.2:7; the manifestation) to multiply goodness and glory upon the earth – and then the spirit was formed in us (Zech. 12:1) in order to help man glorify God and return to Him all the glory we (our soul) produced on the earth – through us. In us *and* through us – this is our manifold reason for being on earth whereby all other reasons are either secondary or superficial to our primary purpose as we have dominion in His name... and give Him all glory.

It's all about Jesus – and God gets the glory! Amen!

The biggest problem we humans have – is the earth suit; it keeps getting in the way of our ability to see our true identity... and thus, the only way we can truly see ourselves is through "His" eyes... by surrendering the "self" to walk in the spirit so the Spirit can give us "new" eyes to see.

If you can perceive this next point, then the remainder of this book will generate much wisdom: the soul consists of the mind and heart. The natural mind and the spiritual soul represent the same thing – the person, yet they operate in different realities. The mind of the soul expresses the thoughts, imaginations, will, determination and intellect of the person, yet the heart produces the emotions and actions – the fruit produced through might and strength to manifest this will. In essence, the expression and the manifestation occur nearly simultaneously in the oneness of the natural and spiritual man – in order to express in us what the Lord purposed to manifest (and effect) through us.

> "I, the Lord, search the heart, I test the mind, Even to give every man according to his ways, According to the fruit of his doings" (Jer. 17:10).

> "But, O Lord of hosts, You who test the righteous, And see the mind and heart..." (Jer. 20:12)

> "As for you, my son Solomon, know the God of your father, and serve Him with a loyal heart and with a willing mind; for the Lord searches all hearts and understands all the intent of the thoughts" (1 Chron. 28:9).

> "I will put My laws in their *mind* [*dianoia*-1271] and write them on their hearts; and I will be their

God, and they shall be My people" (Heb. 8:10).[15]

It is imperative to see this truth: the spirit was given to us by God: A) to come alongside the soul (mind and heart) to walk according to the Spirit in obedience to the Lord... in spirit and in truth; B) to operate in oneness with the Lord as His image bearer; and C) to act as a safety net for the soul. But, from the moment our *mind made a decision* to turn away from the spiritual way to walk according to the worldly way to gratify the natural body (deeds of the flesh), we (at that moment) entered into sin (sometime in our youth) to abandon the heavenly pattern encoded within us to erringly pursue the many cares (schemes) of this world (in the dominion of sin).

> Jesus said: "Watch and pray, lest you enter into temptation. The spirit indeed is willing, but the flesh is weak" (Matt. 26:41).

We were not born in sin, as some teach; we were born into a sinful world whereby we were tempted to act independently of God and thus – by acting independently– we entered into sin as an act of our will (mind). In effect, we traded the divine nature that was encoded within our original spirit (2 Pet. 1:3, 4) to "adopt" the patterns and sinful nature of this world that is opposed to Christ Jesus. Our spirit became corrupted (polluted) by the worldly system that operates according to "sin" and MUST be removed and replaced by a new spirit that operates according to "the Spirit" i.e. according to the operating system of God's kingdom.

When we finally come to our senses and return to the Lord whereby we surrender "everything" of our former self to walk in obedience to the Lord, this, then, is the moment of salvation! We are surrendering not only the former deeds of the flesh but also the

---

[15] *Dianoia*-1271 (*dia*-through, *nous*-mind) is a thorough thinking through, deep meditative thoughts; and occurs in "Love the Lord with all your heart, soul, *dianoia* (mind; understanding) and strength." The spirit is not mentioned! Why? Because the spirit of you... belongs to the Lord!

very control of our body into the Lord's hands! And thus: "It is no longer I who live but Christ who dwells in me." Jesus is now Lord of you – all of you – your soul, spirit and body.

> "I have been crucified with Christ; it is no longer I who live, but Christ lives in me; and the life which I now live in the flesh I live by faith in the Son of God, who loved me and gave Himself for me" (Gal. 2:20).

Your soul (by thoughts of the mind) must make this determination (as an act of your will) to choose between glorifying God through your spirit or glorifying self through your body!

> "For you were bought at a price; therefore glorify God in your body and in your spirit, which are God's" (1 Cor. 6:20).

This conversion to "turn away from the worldly self" that walked according to sin – has to be reckoned dead (and I mean thoroughly dead) – before the walk of faith with a new spirit may begin again in newness. Once this final decision regarding your eternal allegiance to Jesus has been made (by you), *and* the Lord is now sitting enthroned upon your heart, then the Lord will initiate the born anew process through His Spirit which begins by changing out your old spirit that was compromised by the deeds of the flesh – and replacing your hardened heart as well.

> "Then I will sprinkle clean water on you, and you shall be clean; I will cleanse you from all your filthiness and from all your idols. [26] *I will give you a new heart and put a new spirit within you*; I will take the heart of stone out of your flesh and give you a heart of flesh. [27] I will put My Spirit within you and cause you to walk in My statutes, and you will keep My judgments and do them" (Ezek. 36:25-27).

The new spirit (and heart) that are given to us shall assist our soul (mind) in governing the flesh that we surrendered to the Lord; this spiritual transaction with transformation into "newness – through truth, change and oneness" will accomplish many things in the spirit:

- Declare our total allegiance to Jesus Christ and submit our life in obedience to Him – as His servant to serve the Lord and to establish His kingdom on earth
- Nullify the adoption (choice) we made to serve the flesh according to the worldly pattern
- Adopt us into the Father's family as sons and daughters into the Kingdom of God
- Put a new heart and spirit within us whereby we shall be "born anew" by the Spirit of God to become a "new creature (creation)" in the paradigm of Christ
- A new release of the Holy Spirit to abide within us will empower our spirit to strengthen our spirit and be changed through sanctification into newness (and seal us for salvation)
- This new release of the Spirit will also begin the transformation process by renewing our mind through sanctification (Rom. 12:1, 2) so that we may operate according to the heavenly (spiritual) pattern established by Christ Jesus that He demonstrated for us
- We will live according to the spirit – and according to the truth – and we will not return, again, to gratify the desires of the flesh (Gal. 4:9)

Our salvation is assured when we live according to this pattern! Yet many evangelists have created shortcuts to salvation by pulling at the strings of people's hearts through conviction – without them seeking conversion! Having been thoroughly persuaded and convinced by grace to walk by faith (according to the spirit), converts MUST turn away from the worldly system of sin that serves the body (self, ego) by their flesh-focused mind, and furthermore… converts must make a firm declaration to abandon "our desire for this world" – never to return again – and to seek the Lord "in the spirit of our mind." Sadly, we have baptized a great many believers without the slightest regard for conversion – or the sovereignty of Jesus Christ as Lord Almighty.

God loves us and wants us to choose wisely in the mind of our soul –
to operate according to the spirit within us rather than the flesh upon us.

This was the original problem Adam and Eve had, and yet, the subtlety of the deception by Satan was: they were being tempted to get things *they already possessed*. And likewise, so do you! We were all born with a divine nature (spirit) in the similitude of our Creator (in "His Own" likeness), and we were crowned with glory and honor, yet everyone has this same choice to make: either we operate "through the spirit within us" or "out of the flesh upon us." The mind of our soul will direct either the spirit in us to walk by the Spirit and glorify the Lord – or direct the body to gratify carnal desires to glorify our own flesh. This choice is yours alone… and it has eternal consequences!

We are marvelous creatures within creation… sent to govern creation and all created things as His manifest representatives upon the earth. We must accomplish this in communion with Him in oneness of the Spirit through our spirit. Either we live according to the spirit – or we will be unable to understand and comprehend the mystery of man upon the earth – to our own detriment.

The Flesh Is Weak

Most of us are very familiar with the phrase: "The spirit is willing, but the flesh is weak." The word "weak" (*asthenes*-772) 'attributed' by Jesus to the Apostle Paul is a combination of two words (*a*-1-not) and (*sthenos*-4599-strengthen) and literally means: "strengthless." There is a very interesting definition for '*sthenos*' that will greatly illuminate our understanding of man's struggle within this world; it means "to strengthen, i.e. (fig.) confirm (in spiritual knowledge and power)."[16] In other words, the flesh is unable to be strengthened in spiritual knowledge and power... *yet the spirit is*! We really need to thoroughly grasp this concept of the flesh being that part of "who we are" that is literally weighing us down and preventing us from walking in the liberty of the spirit and the empowering of the Spirit to live the life of a saint that is holy, sanctified and set apart – for divine service unto the Lord.

"We are *saints* who are being *sanctified* so as to become a *holy sanctuary*, a people *set apart* unto God, a temple of the Holy Spirit, and a tabernacle for Christ. Let me rephrase the previous sentence by substituting a few Greek words: we are *hagios* (40) who are being *hagiasmos* (38) so as to become a *hagiasmos* (38) *hagion* (39), a people *hagiazo* (37) unto God, as a temple of the Holy Spirit and a tabernacle (permanent dwelling place) for Christ."[17]

We are the *HAGIOS* of God. We do not need a reason... we are the reason we were created – to be *hagios* and host His presence!!!

> "Or do you not know that your body is **the temple of the Holy Spirit** who is in you, whom you have from God, ***and you are not your own***?" (1 Cor. 6:19).

"We were never created, nor were we meant, to be alone. We were created as '*hagios*' to be – and to live – in divine relationship with God. This is our purpose: to be *hagios*. This is our reason for living: *hagios*. Our purpose and our reason for living, as well as the meaning of life, is simply this: *hagios*. We are the reason "why" we were created. We were created as earthen vessels to host the presence of the Divine within us. We are tabernacles for the Holy Spirit of God to dwell in our midst – in oneness with us – and with oneness flowing through us."[18]

---

[16] Strong's Concordance.
[17] Excerpt taken from "Listen" section titled "Logos Words To Hear."
[18] Excerpt taken from "Understand" section titled "Understand This."

And yet… the weakness (strengthlessness) of our flesh was formed upon us even as our spirit was formed within us (with God's power operating through our spirit) so that these two aspects (elements or instruments) of who we are, that seem diametrically opposed to one another, are perfecting within us something of great value: they are sanctifying our soul. We can no sooner crawl out of our flesh than we can jump around in our spirit; these two elements of "who" we are – are perfecting the work of God in us and through us to sanctify us and prepare us for eternity (as well as other purposes known to God). This is the "push me, pull you" dynamic tension that exists within every one of us that strives to be holy before the Lord according to the spirit within us, BUT the flesh wages war against the spirit man for some mysterious reason the Apostle also struggled to comprehend: the mystery of iniquity.

> "For the good that I will to do, I do not do; but the evil I will not to do, that I practice. [20] Now if I do what I will [purpose] not to do, it is no longer I who do it, but sin that dwells in [the flesh of] me. [21] I find then a law, ***that evil is present with me***, the one who wills to do good. [22] For I delight in the law of God according to the inward man. [23] But I see another law in my members [body], warring against the law of my mind, and bringing me into captivity to the law of sin which is in my members. [24] O wretched man that I am! Who will deliver me from this body of death?" (Rom. 7:19-24).

Who will deliver us? Paul explains in Chapter 8: the answer is the Holy Spirit!

Paul stated eloquently the dynamic tension of sanctification whereby we must rely upon the empowering of the Spirit through our spirit to strengthen the spirit within us against the weaker member placed upon us. And thus, we were given the body of flesh for yet another spiritually good reason: to remember God in our times of testing and to call out to Him in our humility and abasement. Back in 2010, I was at the top of my professional "suit and tie" game when, suddenly, I made a bad decision in my mind which I regard as a Nebuchadnezzar moment. What happened after that decision became a cascade of personal failures that put an end to that career. During the years prior to this event, I had become a very pompous, proud, arrogant, smug, conceited, self righteous "jerk" who was very proud of "his" accomplishments... which was the problem: I was claiming God's blessing and hand of favor on my life – as mine – as my own doing. I took credit for my intellect, my creativity, my determination, my resourcefulness, and my "abilities" that were gifts given to me by the Lord... therefore, I needed to be greatly humbled by Him to learn the truth.

> "God resists the proud, but gives grace to the humble." (James 4:6).

The pride that our natural man struggles with, so as to put our best face on for the world to see whereby we give the appearance to others that we "got it all together," is a fake and counterfeit façade; this worldly system knows we are faking it, as does the heavenly system we were sent to implement. We were sent here as the weaker things of God to manifest the power and might of God in the face of His enemies (another reason why we are here)... which our pride and fleshly arrogance seeks to hide behind the mask of religious hypocrisy. We may look righteous... but our spirituality is only skin deep!

We are being sanctified and made holy, and the net result of this sanctification for our soul *by* our body *and* spirit is: humility... the humbling of our soul.

And yet, the message we hear on Sunday is for saints to be perfect and holy just as God is perfect and holy – and yet God is Spirit who is without materiality or substance and without the limitations of the flesh – and yet Jesus is God who manifested Himself and came to earth as our Example, clothed in the flesh of humanity, whereby He accomplished perfectly everything that God wants to accomplish in us and through us... by being strengthened and empowered by the Spirit who dwells within us. This is the salvation message of freedom in Christ that is afforded to us: in the spirit, we are set free from the limitations and the bondage of the flesh – and the opinions of others – and our self perception – that has temporarily imprisoned us in this world of sin and corruption within a natural body. Once we have been set free from the bondage of fake masks upon our natural man, this then is when the spirit man is able to rise up (*anabaino*-305- ascend)[19] and become what God intended us to be – along with all our warts and glaring imperfections that are used by others to humiliate us and denigrate us as "less than" people within this world that is consumed with perfecting outward appearances… while the inner man suffers from depression, anxiety, abandonment, and other psychoses' that our troubled soul endures without benefit of knowing the clue (answer) to our depraved spiritual condition:

WE NEED JESUS!

THE HOLE IN OUR SOUL NEEDS JESUS!

Our spirit and flesh were placed alongside one another, as strength and weakness (or perhaps strength in weakness – or perhaps power under restraint – i.e. humility) to sanctify our soul.

The Apostle Paul was very familiar with the weakness of the flesh and its inability to operate in righteousness for holiness. Paul had within his own flesh "~~an infirmity~~" (<u>a weakness;</u> *astheneia*-769, from *asthenes*-772; see below) that somehow prevented him from greater works which some suspect was bad eyesight or some malady sustained from numerous injuries resulting from preaching the good news near hostile people with rocks opposed to the gospel of grace, but I suggest the weakness was simply this: the body of flesh itself. Paul wanted to experience even more supernatural and miraculous events which he knew man was capable of (such as Peter walking on water), such as his heavenly visit "into Paradise and [he] heard inexpressible words, which it is not lawful for a

---

[19] Word study on ascend '*anabaino-305*' in "Kingdoms" (book #9) section titled: "Onward, Inward then Upward" (to our high calling in Christ Jesus).

man to utter," so Paul prayed three times asking the Lord to deliver him "lest I should be exalted above measure by the abundance of the revelations, [and then] a thorn in the flesh was given to me" (2 Cor. 12:7; which I believe the thorn refers to Judaizers that followed him to torment him wherever he went to preach the gospel of grace and truth)…

> "And He [the Lord] said to me, "My grace is sufficient for you, for My strength is made perfect in weakness [*astheneia*]." Therefore most gladly I will rather boast in my ~~infirmities~~ [weaknesses – *astheneia*], that the power of Christ may rest upon [1981] me" (2 Cor. 12:9).

Literally: My *dunamis* (miraculous power) in *astheneia* weakness (i.e. within the body of flesh) is *perfected* (*teleioo*-5048; divine character consummated and completely accomplished in us according to grace wherein Christ's character has been fully and perfectly formed in us).

Man's greatest obstacle to perceiving the heavenly reality that surrounds us and exists within us – is the weakness imposed by the earth suit which was formed upon us… which also sanctifies us.

"Rest upon" in this instance is the word '*episkenoo*-1981' which means: "to spread a tabernacle over; to tent upon; abide with; to cover" and comes from '*skenoo*-4637' "to occupy (as a mansion)" from "*skenos*-4636; a hut or *temporary residence*, i.e. (fig) the human body (as the **abode** of the spirit… and used metaphorically of the body as the **tabernacle** of the soul, 2 Cor. 5:1, 4."[20] Strong's stated it perfectly!

Our body is the tabernacle of the soul. And our body is the abode of the spirit where the Lord abides (John 14:23). The word '*mone*' (abode) which was spoken by Jesus in John 14:2; "In my

---

[20] Strong's Concordance.

Father's house are many *(mone) abodes*" (also translated "*mansions*") are literally: many dwelling places.

> "For we know that if our earthly house, this tent [4636-temporary tabernacle], is destroyed, we have a building from God, a house not made with hands, eternal in the heavens. ² For in this we groan, earnestly desiring to be clothed with our habitation which is *from* [*ex*; from-out-of] heaven" (2 Cor. 5:1, 2).

Our soul is "the expression" of who we are, and our body and spirit are manifest expressions of what we are, who we are and what purpose God commissioned us to fulfill. Think of your spiritual and physical construction as three gloves, with your spirit inflated within you and your body formed upon you… functioning as tabernacles for the soul and spirit.

Our earthly body is just a temporary perishable tabernacle (tent), and the initial spirit that was given to assist our soul is also temporary… until the day our soul makes a "*permanent*" decision to build a "*permanent*" house (abode) for the Lord to abide within our new heart (Ezek. 36:26) where eternity resides (Eccl. 3:11) as we exist as a new creation (creature) within the kingdom of God (2 Cor. 5:17). Why were we given these temporary perishable instruments? How come the Lord didn't just perfect us according to grace while we existed in His presence in heaven with Him? Those are excellent questions that are explained in the mystery of iniquity.

Mystery of Iniquity

> "For the good that I will to do, I do not do; but the evil I will not to do, that I practice" (Rom. 7:19).

Evil exists in the world… yet for one good reason: sanctification. Just as our body with many members is able to do good in the world, it has an inherent weakness that causes it to stumble into sin; and while our spirit is able to strengthen the inner man and also discipline our body to become subordinate (bring into bondage, subjection) to the spirit (1 Cor. 9:27), it seems the flesh upon us wages war against the soul within us for an unknown reason, and thus, the mystery.

Let me propose this: if everything in the universe was good, then there would be no knowledge of it unless the presence of some counterpart is able to create a distinction; the invisible presence of evil helps us to perceive the invisible evidence of goodness. "Good" is a relativistic term, as is "hot" – it is irrelevant unless it can be contrasted by cold or other varying degrees of hot (like coffee, molten lava or the sun). Likewise, all terms have corresponding opposites to help us comprehend a system of values and judgments, such as love/hate, full/empty, light/darkness, joy/sorrow, hope/despair, faith/unbelief, healthy/sick, fast/slow, rich/poor… and so on.

The living organism placed upon us is confined to this physical reality with its system of values and judgments, yet the spirit within us is not constrained by the limitations of time, space, place… or eternity. The spirit is constrained only by life/death.

The dynamic tension between the living organism placed upon "the soul with spirit" creates a mysterious union of Mr. Hyde upon Dr. Jekyll for one season of eternity on earth for this reason: our soul's sanctification. Why did the Lord intentionally create us to function in this manner? This is the mystery of iniquity and the mystery of sanctification (combined) that is at work upon us and within us to proof our allegiance to Jesus. Why did the Lord ordain this? This is an excellent question that you must ask Him yourself. It is my 'opinion' that this was done as the most loving and kind way of reconciling the kingdom after the war in heaven broke out (Rev. 12:7). Rather than judging us in that moment, the Lord purposed that *we would judge ourselves* based upon the litmus test of life on earth to determine our allegiance to Jesus *and* our willful obedience to love Him *and* serve Him despite having the presence of evil all around us. We are being tested… and it is <u>we</u> who judge our selves worthy or unworthy of redemption!

We are on probation[21] (having been sent from heaven) to attend class whereby you determine your future place in the kingdom of God (of which there are at least 14)[22] based upon your deeds of righteousness and your faithful obedience to Jesus – or the lack thereof. We are in class to learn at least three things: 1) to love the Lord and one another, 2) to remember our three-fold purpose on earth[23], and 3) to remove all seeds of doubt.

Jesus is our Teacher and earth is the classroom. "He has shown you, O man, what is good" and the Lord also inspired His holy prophets to write down all the information we need to "do justly, love mercy and walk humbly" such that "we are all without excuse" when it comes to passing the test (or not). More significantly, the Lord our God (Jesus) sent the promise of the Holy Spirit as our Paraclete to come alongside us and tutor us while we are in class. How awesome is that!!! The test is open Book and a Tutor has been provided to help us pass the test! Every time we encounter a new situation or circumstance that is beyond our ability to remain steadfast, all we need to do is open the Book (Bible) and then ask the Holy Spirit to guide us into all truth and righteousness… so that we may continue to endure and persevere in faith – by grace.

Seems simple enough, right?

Neither the body nor the spirit is inherently good or evil; they are both instruments the Lord has given us (our soul) to assist us in our classroom experience (i.e. a hammer can be a tool or a weapon). How we choose to utilize these instruments – and whether we decide to ask/seek/find and utilize other tools and gifts of the Spirit to help us overcome all obstacles of faith (and also the attacks of

---

[21] Term was used by Matthew Henry: "We must aim at the glory of God in all. We must glorify Him on the earth, which He has given unto the children of men, demanding only this quit-rent; on the earth, we are in a state of probation and preparation for eternity." Matthew Henry's Commentary on the Bible, St. John, Ch. 17:1-5; II.(2).[1].3.2; p. 1153.

[22] Read "Here" to learn about "I go to prepare a place for you" as one of fourteen places in the kingdom.

[23] Our three-fold purpose: dominion, sanctification, glorification.

the enemy) – is your choice. It's all ON YOU! We were all given the same tools in our initial toolbox to resist the devil and the temptation to sin, but when the enemy turns up the heat against you, do you withdraw from grace to walk according to the flesh, or do you cry out to the Lord to strengthen your spirit with additional tools of grace to become the "mighty" warrior and over-comer the Lord created you to be?

During our formative years as children, we were unable to know let alone perceive the danger we were up against. We acted like little children – every day was play – and we trusted implicitly. Parents are especially going to appreciate this next point: remember when your little blessing from the Lord did something really bad and you asked them why they did it, and their reply was, "I don't know." Perhaps you asked a second time only to receive the same reply. And putting them on time out didn't help them come up with an answer they could articulate at that age, so, what caused them to do it? "Mommy, the weakness of my flesh overpowered my spirit which caused me to trip over the threshold of offense into sin" is most likely *not* the answer you received, but it is more likely the correct response. Truly, they don't know why they did it; they know they did it, and after receiving instruction they know that it was wrong, but they know not why. Some deeds and activities that look inviting at an early age are shunned later on by social norms – for good reason. Likewise, some adults screw up and they don't know why either; however, "I don't know" is not an acceptable answer for adults with responsibilities. We MUST take responsibility when we screw up rather than play the blame game to find a scapegoat.

And yet, this is exactly what the Apostle Paul is confirming to us: he didn't know why he did the things he *purposed not* to do. A mysterious "something" was at work against him within his members (body) which waged war against his mind that confounded his reason and intellect.[24]

> "For the good that I will to do, I do not do; but the evil I will not to do, that I practice. [20] Now if I do what I will [purpose] not to do, it is no longer I who do it, but sin that dwells in [the flesh of] me. [21] I find then a law, ***that evil is present with me***, the one who wills to do good. [22] For I delight in the law of God according to the inward man. [23] But I see another law in my members [body], warring against the law of my mind, and bringing me into captivity to the law of sin which is in my members" (Rom. 7:19-23).

This dynamic tension between the inward man (soul with spirit) that is spiritually connected to a heavenly paradigm governed by Jesus – is being tested and perfected by the outward man (our members, i.e. the body of flesh where sin resides that was taken captive to the law of sin) which is connected to the worldly paradigm governed by Satan. The sanctification "push me, pull you" test for our soul is pass-fail… and the first test of faith as believers becoming disciples is to make our flesh subordinate to our spirit that is yielded to the Lordship of Jesus Christ.

> "For he who sows to his flesh will of the flesh reap corruption, but he who sows to the Spirit will of the Spirit reap everlasting life" (Gal. 6:8).

This is an extremely important scripture to comprehend! The Greek says: "sowing to the spirit of the Spirit" actually makes more sense. We are supposed to partner with the Spirit to produce the fruit of righteousness, so… when we "sow to the spirit" within us rather than the flesh upon us, we will reap "of the Spirit" everlasting life rather than corruption by partnering with this world. Whatever we sow into, our soul shall reap the fruits thereof

---

[24] I was reminded recently of a show with Flip Wilson and his famous one-liner, "The devil made me do it" which made for great TV humor, but the truth is… the devil doesn't make us do anything… we act upon his suggestions.

– either through the spirit within us or the flesh upon us. ***Whichever one you feed… is the one that wins.***

Sexual perversion and sinful deeds done by the body of flesh are outward indications that our flesh-focused soul remains captive to the kingdom of darkness. Salvation with life eternal "of the Spirit" has yet to occur; repentance is needed!

Our body and spirit belong to God, yet we are cautioned in this respect: no man can serve two masters. We are psychotic in every respect to think we can serve God in our spirit yet crave carnal things with our body, yet we witness this in church all the time.

The main problem within the institutional church today is this: it correctly teaches us we are blinded by sin and need Jesus, but during our first Sunday school lesson we get re-indoctrinated into the paradigm of sin by teaching after teaching about the doctrine of sin and thus we become blinded again by focusing our attention on sin (or a fatalistic sinful nature) dwelling in us…

… but what converts really need to be taught is the doctrine of grace, the work of the Holy Spirit that empowers us to resist temptation and overcome sin, and the supremacy of Christ as our new focus in life! We need to be set free from our bondage to the law of sin and the operating system of sin to walk in the liberty of the Spirit!!! We need to be taught grace and truth in Faith 101!

Iniquity is also translated "lawlessness" (*anomia*-458) as "one who acts contrary to law."[25] Where did this lawlessness originate? Lawlessness did not originate with man, nor did it originate in the Law; iniquity originated with Lucifer "And iniquity was found <u>IN</u> him" (Ezek. 28:15) and this is the only instance in the entirety of scripture where iniquity was found "in" anyone. Satan (formerly Lucifer) stole glory belonging to God in an attempt to become like God Himself, started a war with God in Heaven, was cast down where he took the glory of the earth captive, then he established

---

[25] Strong's Concordance.

the kingdom of darkness with those angels that were thrown out of Heaven with him, and then he sought after the offspring of God (sons of men) to take them captive as well. Mankind was sent to earth by the Lord as the clean-up crew to overthrow Satan and the kingdom of darkness, but Adam and Eve were tempted to do the same thing on earth Satan did in heaven: take God's glory "lawlessly" and act independently of Him. Satan is "the man, and the destroyer of nations" through whom sin entered into this world, "the man who made the earth tremble, who shook kingdoms, [17] who made the world as a wilderness and destroyed its cities" (Isa. 14:16, 17). Adam and Eve were his first victims – and you and I are among billions more deceived by this destroyer of souls.

The earth suit formed upon man is a "type" of life support unit and biohazard protective suit against Satan – combined. The body is temporary, was created with weakness and is expendable. When the body operates in subordination to our spirit according to the will of our soul (as predetermined and purposed by God), then the earth suit works well and can be protected by our spirit, but when carnal desires and "lawless" opportunities to trespass into sin are offered as temptations by Satan – *and we act on them* – then we have "entered into" sin. Mankind was sent into Satan's dominion of sin as the Lord's manifest representatives and redeemers for the earth, as "lights" sent into the world of darkness, but when we tripped over the threshold of offense, we freely "entered into" sin. Neither sin nor iniquity entered into us (our soul or spirit); we entertained iniquity (lawlessness) by thoughts in our mind resulting in our heart's actions whereby our members (body) became captive to Satan's dominion of lawlessness – in sin.

Sin resides within our earthen body (members; Rom. 7:23), but never "within" us (our soul).[26] **The flesh cannot be strengthened under duress from spiritual attacks, but the spirit can**! And it must… because our soul depends on it!

---

[26] Contrary to Catholic Doctrine, which teaches "the slightest stain upon their souls" will prevent them from entering into God's presence, is rooted upon the premise that sin can be attached to our soul. Baltimore Catechism (Book 4).

Keep this foremost in mind: God is dwelling in us and with us and He is cohabitating alongside us within this earthen vessel. God and Satan cannot be manifested in the same place; either we will love the one and hate the other... but we cannot manifest both within our tabernacle. The divine nature in us (our spirit; 2 Pet. 1:4) hosts God's presence, so I ask: why do we teach more about having a sinful nature upon us (in our members) rather than the divine nature within us?

Our spirit can be strengthened and empowered by the Spirit of God dwelling within us to resist temptation and overcome Satan's lies and deceptions to avoid lawlessness. This is God's plan for all men. We were sent by the Lord as the cleanup crew to redeem the earth, but we trespassed into sin and our original mission on earth became compromised – which then became a rescue and recovery operation for the souls of men... with heavenly assistance. "The spirit is willing, but the flesh is weak" – and this relationship as two instruments given to our soul was predetermined on purpose for a divinely good reason: man needed a Savior!

Many stories with this theme are woven into the Bible and recorded to help us understand and remember what we are supposed to be doing on earth (Job, Ruth, Joshua, Gideon, Daniel).

We are on probation in a classroom environment (earth) to help us remember who we are and what we are supposed to be doing. If there is "one" golden thread throughout all the books I write, then this is it: we need to remember! We need to remember – and understand – who we are so that we may live according to the Spirit and get back to doing the plan of God "on earth as it is in heaven."

Life on earth is not fair... but God is just! Be obedient to Jesus and your soul will continue to live eternally (Psa. 49:9). Earth is a dragnet and our spirit was given to us to help us overcome Satan's snare of death on earth in order to remain in life... and Jesus is the Life (John 11:25; 14:6).

The sanctification process is not easy; if it were, then everyone would be saved, whereby Jesus warned:

> "Because narrow is the gate and difficult is the way which leads to life, and there are few who find it" (Matt. 7:14).

Consider what happened when King Saul rebelled against the Lord and did not obey His word:
"the Spirit of the Lord departed from King Saul" (1 Sam. 16:14-23), and then the Lord sent an evil (KJV) spirit to torment him (they were commanded from heaven, but they were not 'sent' from heaven). Our understanding taught to us in church regarding God is unable to comprehend this event because "God would never cause evil" and yet (as another example) the Lord sent Israel into lands inhabited by wicked people to kill them (which is a type of evil from the perspective of those being killed) because God judged them unworthy of His kingdom (and another example being the Great Flood). Back on point: King Saul requested David play worship music to drive away the evil spirit, and once again, we are left with an interesting scenario – a paradox: the evil spirit sent by God and the goodness of God are both manifested in the same place to seemingly war against one another. Goodness prevailed in that moment, but Saul did not elect to remain in that goodness because his spirit was not upright within him.

Good and evil are oftentimes "co-manifested" in the same place at the same time.

Everything God does is always for our good, which sometimes includes suffering (Rom. 8:28).

When a proud man is being crushed and humbled by the Lord, does not this person consider those effects against him as evil or malevolent? When we encounter a catastrophic loss, do we not ask ourselves: "What did I do to deserve this?" The natural man upon us is unable to judge rightly[27], yet the spirit within us is able to judge rightly (unless it has adopted the worldly pattern that is blinded by sin rather than the paradigm of Christ).

Which brings me to another perception regarding how the kingdom works: how do we determine if something is good or evil? Since God is good and everything God *made* is good, then where did evil come from? Simple: the Lord Almighty (Jesus) *created* it!

> "I form the light, and create darkness: I make peace, and *create* evil: I the Lord do all these things" (Isa. 45:7; KJV).

The mystery of iniquity (simply stated) is: God created us with weakness to be susceptible to lawlessness.

The Lord is testing us… but the proofing of our soul to determine our steadfast devotion and allegiance to Jesus – is done by us. It is you who will bear witness either for or against yourself on the Day of Judgment. "Did you do all that I told (commanded) you to do?"

Iniquity, it seems, is our tendency to sin – willingly and willfully – knowing the consequences, yet choosing to do it anyway (King David with Bathsheba is a prime example). Man has a weakness in this regard despite the knowledge of doctrines, ordinances, parental instruction or the conviction of the heart by the Holy Spirit. We were all born with a weakened (fill in the blank) that is susceptible to the law of iniquity (lawlessness) in our members (i.e. the body of flesh).

Iniquity… is less about our weakness to avoid sin… than our willingness to enter into it without forethought of repentance!

---

[27] The term "nature" in 1 Cor. 15:44 is '*psuchikos*-5591' (from '*psuche*-5591-soul') "constitutes a person who yields everything to the human reasonings of the soul, not thinking there is need of help from above." Strong's.

Consider, now, the initial generations of man upon the earth: Adam begot Seth and Seth begot Enosh. Even before Seth was born, he had two brothers (Cain and Abel) that nearly ended the many generations of man, but once Enosh was born through Seth, the grandson of Adam created a foothold to assure the dominion of man upon this world through many generations to come. The name Enosh (583)[28] comes from the Hebrew word '*enowsh*-582' means: "a mortal," is translated "man" 520 times and, occurring in Job and the Psalms, "it suggests the frailty, vulnerability and finitude of "man" as contrasted to God."[29] **Enowsh suggests the weakness of man to describe him as "a weak and dependent creature**,"[30] and it is from this time forward in human history that "men began to call on the name of the Lord" for divine assistance (Gen. 4:26) because our adversary, the devil, seeks to obliterate man from the earth.

Man was created "*with*" weakness and is susceptible to temptation by Satan to act lawlessly in opposition to God!

> Jesus said: "The spirit is willing but the flesh is weak" (Matt. 26:41)

We get strength and empowering through our spirit – from the Holy Spirit. The Lord placed our spirit and body alongside our soul for the sanctification and perfection of our soul… as strength (spirit) in weakness (body)[31] … and also as a testimony against powers and principalities that rebelled against God (Eph. 3:8-10). Everything that is happening to us is in regard to: 1) perfecting our soul in righteousness and holiness through sanctification by the Spirit, 2) doing the will of the Lord, and 3) having dominion over "this world" and the enemies of God.

---

[28] Enosh is literally spelled Enowsh; also spelled Enon.
[29] Strong's Concordance.
[30] IBID; study on Jehovah, *YHWH* (3068).
[31] The idea that the body is our strength and the spirit is weak constitutes a false doctrine by "the destroyer of souls."

> Now then "... work out your own salvation with fear and trembling" (Phil. 2:12).

In the judgment of the living, we may be asked only one question: "Did you learn to love?" Our entire classroom experience is about love, our obedience to the Lord... and living in meekness.

The mystery of man is: sanctification. Sanctification is a process whereby we are being transformed back into sons of God, again. This process is often painful and messy. So now, if you agree with this understanding as to the mystery of iniquity, then that is wonderful. Now allow me to propose another mystery for your consideration: since Jesus said we will be like angels in the resurrection (Matt. 22:30) – what were we before we came to earth? (Clue: do research on the term "sons of God.)

And now, let us consider... "what" is raised in resurrection?

Resurrection Clarification

> "There is one glory of the sun, another glory of the moon, and another glory of the stars; for one star differs from another star in glory. [42] ***So also*** is the resurrection of the dead. ~~The body~~ It is sown in corruption, it is raised in incorruption. [43] It is sown in dishonor, it is raised in *glory* ['*doxa*' honor]. ***It is sown in weakness, it is raised in power***. [44] It is sown a natural body, it is raised a spiritual body. There is a natural body, and there is a spiritual body" (1 Cor. 15:41-44; ~~stricken~~ words were added by commentators. The correct translation for σπείρεται "it is sown" (which also occurs three more times) was reintroduced by the author in v.42).

"What" was sown in weakness which will be raised in power? The operative word in this scripture is "IT." Now ask yourself...what is the topic the Apostle Paul is discussing? Is it glory, the resurrection, or the body? He is talking about glory! ***There is the glory of the natural body and there is the glory of the spiritual body, and this later type of glory pertains to the resurrection.*** And yet, somehow, our bible translators are fixating upon the resurrection of the natural body, just as those with whom the Apostle is attempting to educate. "What" was sown in weakness, or perhaps reworded slightly, "what was sown into our weakness (i.e. the natural body)?" How can something that became sinfully antagonistic to Christ (our body) be raised incorruptible? Impossible! This message is not about the body being raised in resurrection, but rather... "it" is about the soul (as one type of glory) being raised in resurrection **with** God's glory (the glorious seed of "it") that was sown into our soul (the pearl of great price) which was placed "within the weakness of the flesh" that will be raised "in power" incorruptible – whereby a new spiritual body will be superimposed upon our soul (that comes to us '*ex*' *from out of* heaven).

The word "glory" in verse 43 '*doxa*-1391' can also be translated as "dignity, glorious, honor, praise, worship" and since '*doxa*' is also translated "honor" as spoken of by Jesus in John 5:41, 44 (2x); esp. 8:54 (3x), the most likely meaning by Paul to contrast "dishonor" is "honor."

The soul is raised in the resurrection with glory, just as Christ was also raised in glory and in power (Rom. 6:4; 1 Pet. 1:21), and likewise, the souls of men – through faith in Christ – will also 'be raised in glory and in power.' If God's glory is attached to it, then it will be raised and saved; if not, then it will be cast into fire and burned.

The soul is resurrected, not the body... nor the spirit![32]

---

[32] There are many believers that were taught our spirit is raised in resurrection, so I ask: where do the scriptures mention the "salvation of your spirit"? When the Lord tells us to love the Lord with all that is within us, He mentions: heart, soul, mind and strength. Why is our spirit omitted? Because our spirit belongs to God! The soul is who we are, the soul is what is saved, and our soul will be raised in resurrection glory, not the spirit or the body.

> "Therefore we were buried with Him through baptism into death, that just as Christ was raised from the dead by the glory of the Father, even so we also should walk in newness of life" (Rom. 6:4).

"Jesus seeded His glory into us to produce more glory, and we were sent to earth with His authority and power to operate under His authority and power to have dominion over the earth."[33]

Our soul with the seed of God's glory is "it" which will be raised in resurrection[34]... never to be corrupted by any desire to sin against the Lord ever again... even though we shall continue to have free will with life eternal in Paradise.

> "Though now you do not see Him, yet believing, you rejoice with joy inexpressible and full of glory, [9] receiving the end of your faith—***the salvation of your souls***" (1 Pet. 1:8, 9).

If Christ be in you... you will be raised with Christ.

> "If then you were raised with Christ, ***seek those things which are above***, where Christ is, sitting at the right hand of God" (Col. 3:1).

Did Jesus ever teach about the resurrection of the body? No! Did the Apostles ever teach about the resurrection of the body? No! The "resurrection of the dead" is what they preached, not the resurrection of the body. The Nicene Creed (c.325) mentions "the resurrection of the dead;" however, the Apostle's Creed mentions "of the body" as does the Athanasian Creed[35] whereby some after-

---

[33] Excerpt from "Dominion" chapter 9: "Christianity is not a religion," p.99.

[34] This answers the question from page #1: what will be raised in the resurrection? The soul!

[35] "He ascended into heaven, He sits at the right hand of the Father, God Almighty, from whence He will come to judge the quick and the dead. At His coming all *men will rise again with their bodies* and shall give account for their own works. And they that have done good shall go into life everlasting; and they

life alterations to the Nicene Creed were erringly made.[36] And this confusion remains in the church to this day.

Some of this confusion is understandable because Jesus was raised bodily in resurrection as the firstfruits of many brethren (1 Cor. 15:20), yet this happened for at least two reasons: 1) to fulfill scripture "Nor will You allow Your Holy One to see corruption" (Psa. 16:10); and 2) to authenticate the resurrection will happen as promised by Jesus (1 Cor. 15:12). Just as Jesus was raised in glory, likewise, so shall we (but without the earthly body).

"Glory is the fullness of all that God is – and glory is all that God is. We do not become more of what he has… we become more of who He is."[37]

Sadly, and regrettably it seems, we spend more money and time planning for our burial and "after life celebrations" with elaborate marble monuments neatly placed within pastoral cemeteries alongside millions of other rotting corpses who likewise cared more for their lifeless body abiding in death… rather than spending a couple bucks to purchase a good bible and attend a bible study to actually learn the truth so as to take care of their soul – after the resurrection.

"The Parable of the Unjust Steward was the Lord's way of teaching us to consider where we are going after this life… and to plan ahead! Jesus "praised" the unjust wicked steward who had more sense than sons of light to plan ahead, because he storehoused goods of unrighteous mammon in the place where he was going (which wasn't a good place)"[38] and yet we give no thought to how we (the saints of God) will be living eternally with an empty storehouse without any righteousness credited into our account.

---

that have done evil into everlasting fire." Athanasian Creed (perhaps 700 A.D.)

[36] In 381, the Third Ecumenical Council formally reaffirmed the Nicene version and declared that no further changes could be made, nor could any other creeds be adopted. Thus, the Apostle's Creed is inferior to the Nicene Creed.

[37] Excerpt from "Dominion, chapter 14: "The Lord's Dominion."

[38] Excerpt from "Dominion" section titled: "Living Tabernacles for the Divine."

"Well done" will not be what faith-merchants selling heaven will hear, nor will death-merchants selling life insurance policies to finance eternal bliss graveyards. Anathema! The institutional church has been selling something we were never promised (Heaven) hoping to attain something we already possess by faith: "The kingdom of God is within you" (Luke 17:21).[39]

A spiritual body will be superimposed upon that which is raised in resurrection (i.e. your soul) – if you have been judged worthy to attain life eternal in Paradise, which comes to us – '*ex*' – from out of heaven. We were sown like wheat seed upon the earth to produce an increase of glory upon the earth (by our soul) and to disperse the darkness with the lamp within us (through our spirit); and in the resurrection, we will become like our glorious Savior – raised in glory – as life-giving spirits in glory (1 Cor. 15:45).

There are many types of glory in everything…

> "So also *is* the resurrection of the dead" (1 Cor. 15:42).

"All the dead" with life according to faith will be judged in the resurrection. The souls of the faithful will exist in Hades[40] awaiting that day "and come forth—those who have done good, to the resurrection of life, and those who have done evil, to the resurrection of condemnation (John 5:29); yet the souls in unbelief and rebellion (who have counted themselves as unworthy of judgment) will continue to remain in "Death" (Rev. 1:18) awaiting that day when they are thrown into hell's fire.

> "But those who are counted worthy to attain that age, and the resurrection from the dead, neither

---

[39] Read: "Here: The Kingdom of Heaven Is" by the author.
[40] Hades is not Hell. Hades is the temporary holding place of the dead; Hell is a permanent place 'without' the presence of God. Read Chapter 6 in "Here: The Kingdom of Heaven Is" to learn about "many places" within the kingdom of God.

> marry nor are given in marriage; ³⁶ nor can they die anymore, for they are equal to the angels and are sons of God, being sons of the resurrection" (Luke 20:35, 36).

The reason many will object to this truth is because they have been sold a false-heaven doctrine that includes the resurrection of the body – into Heaven, no less. And if our spirit is already abiding in heaven with God on account of Christ's righteousness (as "spirit-only" doctrines teach), then why give a rip about what your soul does after you've made your profession of faith at the altar? (Once saved, always saved… only applies to being saved from the place called "Death" – having passed from "death to life" – to wait in Hades for the judgment of the faithful).

And yet, we care far more about what happens to our body than what happens to our soul!

The resurrection (of our soul) happens so that an inquisition (a rigorous spiritual accounting) can be conducted (to make a determination and render a judgment) by Jesus (our Judge) regarding what was required of you… to see if you are counted worthy of life eternal in Paradise – or not! Which also includes seeing if you were a good steward of God's resources – or not!

"What does the Lord require (*darash*-1875) of you?" (Micah 6:8) means: "to seek, inquire, ask, require" and implies making an inquest, performing a rigorous examination of everything that was said and done, and with it "often has the idea of avenging an offense against God"[41] (see Gen. 9:5). Where is this inquiry and rigorous examination performed in the Day of Judgment? Well, it isn't done in Heaven (God's throne)! The words "Hades" and "Sheol" will help us understand what happens to our soul after our body dies. Jesus said:

> "So it was that the beggar died, and was carried by the angels to Abraham's bosom. The rich man also

---

[41] Strong's Concordance.

died and was buried. ²³ And being in torments [391] in Hades, he lifted up his eyes and saw Abraham afar off, and Lazarus in his bosom" (Luke 16:22, 23)

"The word (*basanos*-391) translated "torment" implies, "through the notion of going to the bottom." This word means "touch-stone, which is a black siliceous stone used to test the purity of gold or silver by the color of the streak produced on it by rubbing it with either metal." [42] The application of this word implies gold and silver (the works of men) are being tested and questioned by the touch-stone to authenticate and verify the quality and character of the metals being tested. And this definition corresponds to the Hebrew word Sheol meaning: "to inquire; to request, to demand."

"Hades, then, "through the notion of going to the bottom" and Sheol, "the inquiry that demands a response" represent the same place where man waits, is questioned and therefore must give an answer (an accounting) for everything that we have said and done in regards to our life on earth. This is not the place of judgment (at least not yet)… this place is like a courtroom, where a time of formal hearing and interrogation for every person occurs… and may also be regarded as prison (as a temporary holding place to wait for the formal hearing of your case)."[43]

All those (according to faith) will be waiting for the resurrection and the judgment of the dead in Hades (except martyrs; Rev. 20:4); some will receive new clothing for their spiritual being (i.e. our soul, the spirit-man within us) to enter into Paradise, but some (such as hypocrites) will be cast naked into outer darkness (Matt. 8:12; 22:13; 25:30).

---

[42] Word study on torment '*basanos*' (G931) only occurs three times, twice said by Jesus, Matt. 4:24, as well as 'tormentors' (G930) in Matt. 18:34.
[43] Three paragraph excerpt from "Here: The Kingdom of Heaven Is" section titled "What Happens in Hades" p.67.

"For in this we groan, earnestly desiring to be *clothed* (1902-*ependuomai*)[44] with our habitation which is *from* (*ex-out of*) heaven, ³ if indeed, having been *clothed* (1746), we shall not be found naked. ⁴ For we who are in *this tent* (4636)[45] groan, being burdened, not because we want to be unclothed, but further *clothed* (1902), that mortality may be swallowed up by life" (2 Cor. 5:2-4).

(Verse 4 word diagnostic from the Greek) "For indeed we groan the [one] being in the tabernacle (4636-temporary tent) being burdened, inasmuch as we do not wish (**to ekduo-**1562 but **to ependuomai-**1902) **to put off but to put on over**[46] in order that the mortal may be swallowed up by the life" (2 Cor. 5:4).

"Paul is very specific about his word choices. Our future "*clothing*" (1902, occurs only twice) – "to be clothed upon, caused to be put on over"[47] refers to our future, eternal habitation-body, as coming from "out of" heaven to be put on us. Let me say this again: our future body for our future residence is "from out of" heaven. And "if indeed, having been clothed" (1746, '*enduo*' – to enter into, get into), having put on the new man (Eph. 4:24; Col. 3:10), our new (resurrection) "habitation" which is from out of heaven will be "put on over" us as new-earth men. We do not go into heaven to get this house (habitation, dwelling) – it comes "out

---

[44] (1902-ependuomai)(2x) from 1909 (epi- is a **superimposition**, over, upon) and 1746 (enduo-to enter into, get into) with the idea of slipping into and superimposing over/ upon a new outer garment or clothing.

[45] (4636-tabernacle) Tent: a hut or temporary residence; temporary tabernacle (same as in verse 1).

[46] (1562-ekduo) to sink out of, strip, take off from, unclothe; figuratively, of putting off the body at death (the believer's state of being unclothed does not refer to the body in the grave but to the spirit, which awaits the "body of glory" at the resurrection." Strong's Concordance.

[47] Strong's Concordance.

of" heaven – and is superimposed onto us. Is this starting to make sense now?"[48]

We slip out of the natural body when we die, and then a spiritual body is superimposed upon us (the spiritual being –soul – that is raised in resurrection) by the Spirit after the judgment. You are "It" – a spiritual being (a soul with spirit) that wears different clothing (tents) during different seasons of eternity on earth.

And yet, our bible translators fixate on a bodily resurrection. Anathema!

At this point, many may be asking this question: do we receive this spiritual body when we die or at a later time? A new spiritual body will be given to us sometime after the judgment and the resurrection happens, but we don't need a body in order to exist (except here on earth). That's our biggest problem... the earth suit keeps getting in the way of our ability to perceive and understand who (and what) we truly are.

The liberating truth of the gospel is that we will no longer be constrained (burdened) once our natural body perishes... when mortality is swallowed by immortality. Our soul will be set free from the confines of this corruptible body whereby those counted worthy with the life of Christ dwelling in them will be given a glorious incorruptible body with life eternal in Paradise.

What these bodies will look like is somewhat veiled at the moment, yet Jesus told us we will be like angels. And yes, there is gap of time between the death of the body and the resurrection where we wait in a temporary holding place (Hades), but if Christ is in you and you have been clothed in Christ, then the "life" is already in you and the wait shouldn't be that bad. Jesus promised those who host His presence that He will never leave us nor forsake us. Sadly, those who trust in religion rather than Jesus will never know the guarantee of this promise.

---

[48] Excerpt from "Here" section titled: "Men Are Spiritual Beings."

Your body is just a "thing" that was placed over and upon your soul that the Lord gave you to steward, to take care of – and to use for His glory to advance the kingdom of heaven on earth.

Don't let your "thing" get in the way of perceiving "who" you really are!

Adam and Eve didn't need to clothe their body in Paradise, but when they tripped over the threshold of offense and stumbled into sin and their original glory faded, then they realized… "Oh * * * *, I have a body. Quick, give me something to cover this thing up!" Not even the Lord wanted to look at it, so He sewed animal skins for them to wear.[49] The natural body is beautiful, but the spiritual body we will receive in the resurrection will be absolutely "glorious"!

> "And if Christ is in you, the body is dead because of sin, but the Spirit is life because of righteousness" (Rom. 8:10).

> "For he who sows to his flesh will of the flesh reap corruption, but he who sows to the Spirit will of the Spirit reap everlasting life" (Gal. 6:8).

Our eternal business on earth is not to focus on the body or to perfect the temporary tent through proper diet and exercise (though good stewards will do these things), but rather, to safeguard the pearl of great price (God's glory) that was sown into our soul to accomplish perfectly God's plan for us by being strengthened in our spirit – and by operating in oneness with the Spirit.

> "…that He would grant you, according to the riches of His glory, to be strengthened with might through His Spirit in the inner man" (Eph. 3:16).

---

[49] And thus we have another name for Jesus: *Jehovah Taphar,* the Lord & Tailor (Strong's H8609).

The inner man (our soul) has a body formed upon us and a spirit formed within us. When Adam and Eve were in the garden, they were naked yet not ashamed because they had another garment placed upon them; they were clothed (crowned) with glory and honor. This garment of glory is what the disciples saw when Jesus was transfigured, and this is what we shall be in the resurrection, but as for now… this glory was taken captive by Satan when we exchanged our glory and our divine authority when we acted lawlessly by taking from the tree of knowledge and acting independently (in rebellion) to do our will rather than His. We traded the glory garment of praise and honor with authority – for second-rate coveralls of condemnation and death.

When we declare our steadfast obedience to Christ, a wonderful spiritual dynamic happens: we become clothed "in Christ Jesus." Jesus is now our robe of righteousness, our full armor of God and our mantle of authority to accomplish the will of God on earth.

> "I will greatly rejoice in the LORD, my soul shall be joyful in my God;
> For He has clothed me with the garments of salvation,
> He has covered me with the robe of righteousness,
> As a bridegroom decks *himself* with ornaments,
> And as a bride adorns *herself* with her jewels" (Isa. 61:10).

Beloved… how do you see and perceive yourself? If you continue to say, "I am just a wretched sinner saved by grace," then you are perpetuating Satan's deception! When angels and demons see you, they no longer see you… they see Jesus. And the glory which you had before the world was… will be returned to you in the regeneration, but until that day happens, you are being sanctified to become again what you were beforehand: sons of God.

You are the redeemed of the Lord… and it's time to wake up and walk according to your high calling in Christ Jesus! Awaken and arise!!! You are sons and daughters of God that are being sanctified in holiness and righteousness – in preparation for eternity.

Consider this: Jesus is God; Jesus was God the entire time He was on earth and He lived a perfect life in holiness and righteousness, and yet... **Jesus sanctified Himself**. (John 17:19). His body, just like yours and mine, is the "element" or "instrument" that is being used by God to sanctify us in righteousness and holiness... yet the main difference being Jesus didn't need to be sanctified, but He said this to teach us the purpose of the body. *The mystery of man on earth is sanctification within earthen vessels* – and therein we are to be sanctified by the truth... and we were given the earth suit for this reason: to live as *hagios*, being sanctified in the weakness of flesh yet not surrendering to the lawless desires and cravings of the flesh, so we may return home as *elohims* – as sons and daughters of God Most High!

Consider, now, what Micah says that unifies many of these terms and concepts:

> "But truly I am full of power by the Spirit of the Lord, and of justice and might" (Micah 3:8).

May we walk humbly and reverently as we love God, and love one another as we host God's Presence and Spirit within us as we have dominion on the earth. Life is a test – and the earth suit is one instrument of the Lord's sanctification unto salvation to see if we will focus our affection to give glory to the body upon us or... to give God the glory through the spirit within us.

We have a choice to make within our mind (soul) either to promote the spirit or the body. Adam and Eve were experiencing life on earth in spirit-directed oneness with the Lord until they acted independently of God to focus on gratifying the body (deeds of the flesh)... and they exchanged their glory and honor for the garment of sin and heaviness. When they fell from grace (out of fellowship with the Spirit), it was then, in that moment, that they saw their nakedness and hid from the Lord. And the same is true with all men today. Everyone on earth has this choice to make: either remain in fellowship toward the Lord in spirit – or turn away from the spirit-directed life to walk according to the flesh-directed life.

Life on earth is a test. It is pass or fail. You are on probation to see what you will do with the glory God entrusted to you. There is no greasy-grace curve or sliding scale for shoulda-coulda-woulda. Either you love the Lord Jesus will ALL your heart, soul, *dianoia*[50] and strength,[51] **and** you love your neighbor as instructed by Christ, **and** you walk according to the spirit with the Spirit of Christ abiding within you... or not. If you believe this is the truth of God, then do it by grace according to faith.

Faith is not what you believe to be true – but doing what you believe is the truth. Faith is the assurance and the certainty <u>with</u> the conviction that compels us into action to imitate Jesus.

> "... for whatever is not from faith is sin" (Rom. 14:23).

Eyes of Our Soul

What are you seeing with your eyes? Whatever you look at is the result of one thing: what your soul (mind) directs your eyes to look and seek. This is a conscious determination by your mind to look and see what you are seeking after. Many of us have heard the words of Jesus regarding plucking out our eye if it causes us to sin, so I would like to clarify this point: Jesus is very literal, but Jesus is not commanding us to mutilate the body. Let me explain...

---

[50] The Greek word '*dianoia*-1271' (translated mind) "means: **understanding**, a thorough thinking through, the exercise of the mind; deep thought, meditation (Eph. 1:18; 4:18; 1 John 5:20). *We are told to love the Lord with all our heart, soul and 'dianoia'* (Matt. 22:37; Mark 12:30; Luke 10:27). Other references include (Eph. 2:3; Col. 1:21; Heb. 8:10; 10:16; 1 Pet. 1:13; and esp. 2 Pet. 3:1); "imagination" (Luke 1:51)." Excerpt copied from "Understand" by the author.
[51] Since the heart and the mind are representative of the soul, it may make more sense to translate *dianoia* as "understanding" which (BTW) was a NT term inserted into the OT text (Deut. 6:5).

The soul (mind) makes decisions all the time to focus either on the things of the spirit or the things of the flesh. In this regard, our eyes are able to see within two paradigms: physical and spiritual. From this perspective, consider your eyes as "representative" of these two realities: one being spirit and one being flesh. If we have made a final determination in our soul to walk in the spirit, we will therefore not seek after sinful desires to gratify the flesh and BOTH our eyes are good and full of light; however, if your mind is focusing on something that is sinful in nature – then either change your mind – or remove the lens. If you cannot change your mind (which is a rhetorical statement), then the phrase mentioned by Jesus above: gouge out your eye, is the drastic and overly dramatic way of trying to curb your insatiable desire for the sinful things of this world. The eye is merely the lens through which our soul (mind) directs the focus of our attention and affection. If your eye is causing you to forfeit life eternal because your focus is on worldly sinful things, then get rid of your eye. Ok, now think about that phrase for a moment: is your eye causing the problem… or your mind? Indeed, it is your soul (mind) that is causing the problem, not your eye, so the statement by Jesus must be interpreted as sarcasm[52] and must not be interpreted literally. Either get rid of the desire for worldly stuff by changing your mind (soul)… or gouge out your eye. So, now, which one are you going to choose *if* your eternal destination were dependent upon your choice at this very moment? Gouge your eye or change your mind? You have ten seconds to make this choice.

> "And if your eye causes you to sin, pluck it out and cast *it* from you. It is better for you to enter into life with one eye, rather than having two eyes, to be cast into hell fire" (Matt. 18:9; see also Matt. 5:29; Mark 9:47).

Did Jesus say He wanted you to be partially disabled with only one eye in order to enter the kingdom of heaven… or was the message

---

[52] Sarcasm indicates the opposite of what a person literally means. *Sarcasm* comes from the Greek words "*sarx*-4561- flesh" and "*asmos*-to tear or rip" *meaning* "to tear the flesh" which is an interesting play on words by Jesus.

for us to change the focus of our mind?

OK, times up! It's been ten seconds, so what choice did you make? If you think I am being rhetorical, then perhaps you are being insincere with God and are playing games in your mind with your eternal destination. In Russian roulette, you have a one in six chance of losing, but with the Lord of Heaven... the failure rate is 100% if you continue to walk in disobedience.

Through the instrumentality of the eye, the soul will see whatever the heart desires (and the desires of the heart were planted there by thoughts of the mind). Whatever you love in your heart will direct the focus of your soul's attention because they operate in oneness... in sin as well as in grace.

Do not think this next question arbitrary: do you claim to walk by grace but live according to sinful passions? How, then, is it possible for you to live with one good eye and one bad eye yet claim to see clearly enough to discern spiritual matters – with distorted vision? How is it possible to walk in wisdom and understanding to perceive greater things with one eye darkened? How is it possible to see spiritually (according to the spirit of your mind) with one eye corrupted by sin – with perhaps a beam protruding out of it?

In the Sermon on the Mount, Jesus is teaching us to change the focus of our soul (our mind's attention *and* our heart's affection) to focus our eyes on the spirit-directed life that is aligned with the Spirit of Grace and Truth. Seek Jesus. Follow Jesus. Imitate Jesus. Obey His commandments. Become His disciple! Abandon all that worldly crap, change your mind and refocus your attention on this:

> "But seek first the kingdom of God and His righteousness, and all these things shall be added to you" (Matt. 6:33).

Soul Explanation

By now, there are some who can see a conflict in the manner in which they were taught about the soul as being mind, will and emotion. Well, the soul is the mind and heart – and the spirit is the enabling. Apart from the spirit, the soul is unable to express itself in spiritual realities – and apart from the body, the soul is unable to associate itself in earthly realities.

The Hebrew and Greek are renowned for very specific words to convey concrete meanings; the Greeks had four words for love, eight for doubt, sixteen for understand, eight for wash, and so on. And there are some words that are notorious for great diversity of meaning and interpretation, like the Hebrew word '*nephesh*- 5315' typically translated "soul." There are 735 occurrences of this word which has been translated as: soul (475x), life (117x), person (29x), mind (15x), heart (15x), creature (9x), body (9x), himself (8x), yourselves (6x), dead (5x), will (4x), desire (4x), man (3x), themselves (3x), any (3x), appetite (3x), miscellaneous (47x) such as beast and ghost. And there may be other terms used by modern day translators as well.

Strong seems to have a biased understanding of what the soul is and what it does. He writes: "*Nephesh* means soul; self; life; person; heart" without any mention of the mind whatsoever, yet his initial word diagnostic reads: "a breathing creature (i.e. animal of (abstract) vitality; used very widely in a literal, accommodated or figurative sense (bodily or <u>mentally</u>). *Nephesh* is translated 'mind' as often as heart, but Strong does not include it in the meaning of *nephesh*, yet introduces a new term: "self." Thus, believers have become familiar with the soul being associated with the heart and the self, yet I will show you the mind and heart (both) represents the soul of man.

> "As for you, my son Solomon, know the God of your father, and serve Him with a ***loyal heart and with a willing mind***; for the LORD searches all hearts ***and*** understands all the intent of the thoughts. If you seek Him, He will be found by you; but if

you forsake Him, He will cast you off forever" (1 Chron. 28:9).

A loyal [perfect-KJV] heart and a willing mind represents the soul operating in oneness and in concert with one another (and the spirit) to accomplish the will of the Lord – in us and through us.

The word "heart" (*lebab*-H3824) which occurs 252 times in the Old Testament means: "heart; mind; midst. Heart can refer to the organ… or the inner part or middle of a thing. *Lebab* can be used of the inner man, contrasted with the outer man. *Lebab* is often "compounded" with the soul for emphasis (2 Chron. 15:15)."[53]

Within this context, it is important to consider the manner in which Hebrews understood the soul '*nephesh*' of man. "The best biblical definition is found in Psalm 103:3 "all that is within" a person."[54] "The Hebrew system of thought does not include the opposition of the terms "body" and "soul," which are really Greek and Latin in origin. The Hebrew compares/contrasts "the inner self" and "the outer appearance" or, as viewed in a different context, "what one is to oneself" as opposed to "what one appears to be to one's observers."[55]

In this regard, nearly all Hebrew references to heart and soul are synonymous for the inner man that constitutes the thinking, feeling, will and emotion of "the person within us" without creating conflicting ideas of whether the heart is able to think, understand and comprehend (based upon 58 verses that link the heart to think/thought/understand) as opposed to these functions being relegated only to the faculties of the mind. The heart and mind were created to operate in tandem oneness with one another even though they perform distinctly different functions (in us versus through us).

---

[53] Strong's Concordance.
[54] IBID. Study on nephesh.
[55] IBID.

> "But Jesus, *knowing* [*oida*-1492-understanding, perceiving] their thoughts, said, "Why do you *think* [*enthumeomai*-1760-to reflect on, ponder] evil in your hearts?" (Matt. 9:4).

There are teachers past and present that take sides preferring either the mind or the heart (one that is rational and corrupt while the other is deceitful and corrupt), and yet... both the mind and the heart were created good with goodness to operate in oneness of the Spirit, yet were permitted as an act of our will to become corrupted by "this world."

The goal of this teaching is not to create a dichotomy that separates the functionality of the soul without the spirit, or the mind without the heart, but rather... to see the spirit within us as a precious gift from God that was given to help us (i.e. the soul with spirit/heart that operates in oneness) whereby we live according to the plans God predestined for us as sojourners from heaven... as spiritual beings operating under the guidance of the Holy Spirit... as sons and daughters living according to goodness, by grace.

Let me ask you this: where does the body get its initial breath? From the Lord (Gen. 2:7). How does the living creature (man) continue to breath? Is it not by nerve impulses from the brain?

Let me show you some KJV scriptures along with the original language that I believe may be responsible for some of our misinterpretation (and ergo the solution) regarding the nature of the soul and the spirit as the essence of *and* the manifestation within – mankind:

> "For as he thinks in his ~~heart~~ *nephesh* [soul/mind], so is he" (Prov. 23:7).

Bible translators made a choice to translate *nephesh* as heart instead of mind (for whatever reason does not really matter). The mind is the primary means whereby we think and decisions are made by our soul to either seek after the things of the spirit or to seek after the things of the flesh. Whatever we think upon and focus our attention upon... is what we treasure and, thus... what we think is what we become; what we think becomes our reality. The eyes, in this respect, become the lens (that work in tandem with our mind) through which our soul operates as the "focus-directed, object-seeking" gatekeeper to either gaze upon heavenly (spiritual) things or earthly (fleshly) things. The literal translation is:

> "As man acts as the gatekeeper of his soul, so he becomes" (Prov. 23:7).

Whatever we behold – we become.

As the gatekeeper for your soul, you are admonished to guard it and protect it from corruption and worldly influences... and the spirit within us is intended to assist us in this effort. Whatever you allow to pass through your gateway (your heart) – you become – either spiritual or worldly.

You are soul with spirit, so then, what is your purpose for being on earth? Well, this answer is three-fold: 1) you are *'hagios'* to glorify the Lord *in* your soul and *through* your spirit, 2) you were given a commission with dominion (God's authority with power) to do a spiritual job on earth (which will be revealed to you by the Spirit when the time is right)... and 3) you are living one season of eternity on earth in preparation for eternity hereafter either in the New Earth... or in the Pit. We would do well to consider the implications of life eternal either with true riches ... or with eternal torment in hell's fire.

> "I will put My Spirit within you and cause you to walk in My statutes, and you will keep My judgments *and do them*" (Ezek. 36:27).

This is a good word of encouragement! The Spirit was given to help us to walk in uprightness.

Eyes For The Mind

The eye is typecast with the mind (or soul) in many scriptures, such as:

> "Who has put wisdom in the mind? Or who has given understanding [998] to the ~~heart~~ ***mind*** [7907]" (Job 38:36).[56]

Within this context, the eyes become the "observatory" or lens (windows to observe) whereby the mind (soul) is able to "separate mentally and distinguish" between things seen (and perceived) as either worldly or spiritual… so as to understand with the mind and walk in wisdom with understanding according to the manner in which we were created – as *hagios* in uprightness.

> "The spirit of a man is the lamp of the Lord, searching all the inner depths of his *heart*" (Prov. 20:27).[57]

> Jesus said: "The lamp of the body is the eye. Therefore, when your eye is good, your whole body also is full of light. But when your eye is bad, your body also is full of darkness" (Luke 11:34).

We were given two types of eyes for the journey: physical and spiritual. The eye is the lamp for the physical body (and mind) of man to focus on whatever our soul desires, and our spirit was given to us by the Lord to operate within us as "His" lamp for the

---

[56] Mind – the first mention is [inward 2910 + parts 1506], "inmost thought" i.e. the spiritual faculties within the inner man. ***Mind*** – the second mention (erringly translated 'heart' in the KJV) is '*sekviy*-7907' "observant (i.e. concretely) the mind; from 7906-observatory" and is used in context with '*biynah*-998' "understanding, wisdom, knowledge; from the root word '*biyn*-995' to separate mentally or distinguish; understand." Strong's Concordance.

[57] Heart (translated belly-KJV) is '*beten*-990' meaning: "to be hollow; belly (31x), womb (31x), body (8x)." Thus, body (or being) may be a better translation within this context, since men are earthen vessels. Strong's Concordance.

spiritual man, which was designed to redirect and refocus the desires of our heart, soul, mind and strength – solely on Him.

The lamp of the body is the eye… the lamp of the soul is the spirit.

You have waded through deep waters and patiently endured many scriptures with me thus far – and now I want to show you something truly exciting by following this line of reasoning:

- Jesus is the Light of the world – and Jesus is Lord of Heaven and Earth
- Jesus said: "You are the light of the world" – and Proverb 20:27 teaches us the spirit in man is the lamp of *the Lord*
- "Now the Lord [Jesus] is the Spirit; and where the Spirit of the Lord is, there is liberty" (2 Cor. 3:17)
- The spirit within us is the lamp from Jesus to disperse the darkness of this world – and the lamp of the body for man is the eye to help the soul (mind) discern good from evil
- The lamp (spirit) within us (that the Lord placed there) is able to turn the reins of man (the thoughts of our mind) to know the truth and walk therein according to the spirit

The spirit within us is the light (lamp) that was given to us by the Lord that is being strengthened by the Spirit of God that changes our focus (way of seeing things) and renews our mind … so that we may operate as sons of light… in order to transform this darkened world into the kingdom of Christ with two good eyes full of light.

You are sons of God and sons of light! This is "who" you really are!

> "While you have the light, believe in the light, that you may become sons of light" (John 12:36).

The spirit within man is the lamp of the Lord's light that He is using to disperse the darkness.

> "You are all sons of light and sons of the day. We are not of the night nor of darkness" (1 Thess. 5:5).

The spirit was given by God as a spiritual instrument to partner with and help the soul (the gatekeeper of our mind) to illuminate our life like an observatory, in tandem with the word of God, for us to correctly see, discern, distinguish and perceive every choice made by our soul (mind) as either godly in righteousness – or as disobedience in unbelief. When we walk according to the Spirit – in spirit and in truth, we will not gratify the desires of the flesh (Gal. 5:16).

> "If we live in the Spirit, let us also walk in the Spirit" (Gal. 5:25).

> "There is therefore now no condemnation to those who are in Christ Jesus, who do not walk according to the flesh, but according to the Spirit" (Rom. 8:1).

If the Lord is not the primary focus of our soul and spirit (lamp), then our inward parts will become darkened. Therefore, keep your mind focused on Jesus – or else you will focus your eyes on worldly desires that our body's crave and, thus, risk spending eternity in hell's fire.[58]

> "And the man said to me, "Son of man, ***look with your eyes*** and hear with your ears, ***and fix your mind on everything I show you***; for you were brought here so that I might show them to you. Declare to the house of Israel everything you see" (Ezek. 40:4).

---

[58] Within this context, the body was given to man in order to sanctify him and test his resolve.

> "And you, son of man—will it not be in the day
> when I take from them their stronghold, their joy
> and their glory, ***the desire of their eyes, and that on
> which they set their minds***" (Ezek. 24:25).

Consider these scriptures to help cement this concept of – eyes for the mind (of your soul):

> ***"My eyes bring suffering to my soul*** [*nephesh*]
> because of all the daughters of my city" (Lam. 3:51;
> translated heart-KJV).

> "And among those nations you shall find no rest,
> nor shall the sole of your foot have a resting place;
> but there the LORD will give you a trembling heart,
> ***failing eyes, and anguish of soul*** [*nephesh*]" (Deut.
> 28:65; *sorrow of mind*-KJV).

> "I also will do this to you: I will even appoint terror
> over you, wasting disease and fever which shall
> ***consume the eyes and cause sorrow of*** ~~heart~~ ***soul***
> (*nephesh*)" (Lev. 26:16).

When we focus our eyes on things that are inconsistent with our mission and calling in life, our soul suffers in anguish with sorrow, but when our soul is upright within us, our soul is able to complete our heavenly mandate to have dominion using the "things" God has entrusted to us.

> For God has given man the ability to see,
> distinguish and separate between worldly sinful
> things and goodly spiritual things with his mind …
> and to produce wisdom and understanding in his
> soul that glorifies the Lord, *but* we have followed
> after many schemes… to our own peril (author's
> message).

At this point, there are many astute students of the scriptures that are seeing a trend: the soul (mind and heart) was created by God to operate in oneness with their spirit in order to achieve their mission objectives (have dominion) and fulfill their commission granted by the Lord.

And yet there is a deeper lesson to be mined from sifting this truth: we were created like our Creator to operate in a manner consistent with the Godhead we adoringly love and serve. Our heavenly Father is the soul (mind-and-will) of the Godhead who alone knows the appointed times and seasons; and our heavenly Savior, Jesus Christ, is the spirit (heart-and-emotion) of the Godhead who is able to manifest Himself and show us how much Elohim loves us.

God [*Elohim*] so loved the world that *YHWH* sent Himself as Emmanuel, as an only begotten Son – "For unto us a Child is born, unto us **a Son is given**; and the government will be upon His shoulder. And His name will be called Wonderful, Counselor, Mighty God, **Everlasting Father**, Prince of Peace" (Isa. 9:6).[59]

"The creative thoughts of God and the creative power of His word always precede creation. In this manner, "word is two-fold: λόγος ἐνοιάθετος – word conceived; and λόγος προφόρικος – word uttered. The λόγος ὁ ἔσω and ὁ ἔξω, ratio and oratio – intelligence and utterance."[60] And this explains why Jesus is called "the Word of God."

The Father is "*ratio*" (the Soul of God) who expresses His will by the thought of His intellect.[61] The Son is "*oratio*" (the Spirit of

---

[59] To understand the complexity of this statement, read "Image" by the author. Yes, the whole book!!!

[60] Excerpt taken from Matthew Henry's Commentary on the Whole Bible, an exposition on John 1:1; Volume VI, p. 848; MacDonald Publishing Company, McLean, Virginia.

[61] Jesus did not credit the "Father" with the following terms: compassion, kindness, mercy, feel, grieve, passion, heart of, remorse, weep, joy, glad, rejoice. These terms, however, are attributed to the Godhead, as well as to Jesus.

COMMISSION

God)[62] who manifests the heart and emotions of God by every word (*logos*) and every utterance (*rhema*) revealed of/from God... as the Word of God (John 1:1-5).

We were created in God's image according to "His Own" likeness – as soul with spirit, to be a representative likeness of Jesus upon the earth... to the praise of His glory.

> "Behold! My Servant whom I uphold, My Elect One in whom My soul delights! I have put My Spirit upon Him; He will bring forth justice to the Gentiles" (Isa. 42:1). "And suddenly a voice came from heaven, saying, "This is My beloved Son, in whom I am well pleased" (Matt. 3:17).

"When it comes to words and pattern languages, there is always a thought that precedes the utterance, and this is especially true with man as well. The Divine conversation with man and all creation originates in 'ratio' before an 'oratio' utterance, which we clearly see expressed regarding the '*logos*' and '*rhema*' of God; a Divine thought (*logos*) is followed by an utterance (spoken and unspoken *rhema* words). Within the context of creation, we see the thoughts of God to "make and orchestrate" all things according to His will and plan, whereby the manifestation of His thought is followed by all things being created and formed by the hand of Christ our Creator."[63]

This is why every word spoken by us is important – and every careless word will be judged by the Lord. We are sons and daughters of God Most High when every thought we think and every word we utter either brings praise and glory to God... or we dishonor the Lord our God.

The soul and spirit of man was created by God "in His Own image

---

[62] "The Lord is the Spirit" (2 Cor. 3:17) – and Jesus is God who is Spirit (John 4:23).
[63] Excerpt from "Listen" section titled "Origin and Source."

according to His likeness." In this regard, man was created with a divine nature in the similitude of our Creator, Jesus Christ.

> "Grace and peace be multiplied to you in the knowledge of God and of Jesus our Lord, [3] as His divine power has given to us all things that *pertain* to life and godliness, through the knowledge of Him who called us by glory and virtue, [4] by which have been given to us exceedingly great and precious promises, that through these ***you may be partakers of the divine nature***, having escaped the corruption that is in the world through lust" (2 Pet. 1:2-4).

The divine nature is none other than the spirit God formed within us.

> "For what man knows the things of a man except the spirit of the man which is in him? Even so no one knows the things of God except the Spirit of God" (1 Cor. 2:11).

The mystery of man on the earth is sanctification in earthen vessels. We were created by the Son of God to become sons of God… wherefore the body is one of the Lord's instruments either for our sanctification and salvation… or an instrument for our own condemnation and judgment.

So I ask: do you know what manner of spirit is within you? The spirit in man, which was given to him by God, is an instrument placed alongside his soul to assist his efforts in attaining spirituality, whereby man is: A) given a new spirit in the new birth to live as a new creation (Ezek. 36:26), B) our spirit can be added to in greater measure (Elisha asked for a double portion of Elijah's spirit; 2 Kings 2:9), C) can be increased to accomplish God's purposes according to God's commission to balance (measure and equalize) his spirit to the task set before the saint under a commission (Prov. 16:2), D) as well as placing the guarantee of the Holy Spirit alongside our spirit in the new birth to live according to the Spirit-directed life – and – accomplish greater works (Ezek.

36:27).

> "He who has knowledge spares his words, and a man of understanding is of a calm [excellent-KJV] spirit" (Prov. 17:27).

A spiritual man with understanding in his mind will operate calmly because of the calm spirit within him to help manage his affairs… rather than the rowdy flesh upon him. Self control is one of the gifts of the Spirit, and the Spirit alongside our spirit enables our spirit-man to operate according to self control… if that is your choice.

> "But you are not in the flesh but in the Spirit, if indeed the Spirit of God dwells in you. Now if anyone does not have the Spirit of Christ, he is not His. [10] And if Christ *is* in you, the body *is* dead because of sin, but the spirit *is* life because of righteousness" Rom. 8:9, 10).[64]

When your spirit is partnered with the Spirit, your actions will testify the Spirit is operational within you. Likewise, if Christ is in you according to faith, then you will cease to allow your body to have operational control of your soul (because of its tendency toward sin), but now you will live out of your spirit within you because – the spirit is life… because of righteousness.

The whole point of this book is: to illuminate your mind to see the choice set before you: either live out of the flesh upon you or the spirit (which is life) within you. However, it's your choice how your soul decides to manifest itself – either as flesh or spirit. Jesus said of us: "That which is born of flesh, is flesh, but that which is born of Spirit, is spirit" (John 3:6).

---

[64] The author believes this is one instance when the word spirit (small 's') was intended: "but the spirit is life." An identical word is found in John 3:6: "born of the Spirit, is spirit" (small 's').

> "But he who is joined to the Lord is one spirit with Him" (1 Cor. 6:17).

So I ask again: choose this day if you plan to live out of the spirit within you or the flesh upon you. The flesh is limited in its capability and is destined for corruption, yet the spirit in man is able to continue in life eternal – and – accomplish miraculous and supernatural deeds and exploits in the name of Jesus. How do you want to be remembered… by deeds of the flesh or by deeds according to the spirit?

The grace we need to live each and every day is apportioned to us without measure by the Spirit of Grace; the Spirit alongside us enables us to live according to the spirit within us to accomplish – and endure – many things. However, this mystery has yet to be revealed to me: how I can operate – out of my spirit – at all times. At some future time, I shall write about it, but until then, I perceive it has much to do with an increase of faith, favor and focus (vision).

> "For as many as are [born and] led by the Spirit of God, these are sons of God" (Rom. 8:14).

Sons of God – Through Obedience

> "For you are all sons of God through faith in Christ Jesus" (Gal. 3:26).

Perhaps man's greatest challenge is to realign the deeds of the outer man with the original goodness of the inner man, which can only happen through our sanctification by the Spirit.

> "Truly, this only I have found: that God made man upright, but they have sought out many schemes" (Eccl. 7:29).

If we could simply perceive one another as soul with spirit – with God and His goodness dwelling in us rather than focusing on their outward appearance or their deeds of iniquity (sins) performed through the unregenerate man, we may become "more like God" in this respect – as not being judgmental... and infinitely more merciful!

Consider what manner of man the Lord was looking for when He eliminated the family of Eli from the priesthood:

> "Then I will raise up for Myself a faithful priest who shall do according to what is *in My heart and in My mind*. I will build him a sure house, and he shall walk before My anointed forever" (1 Sam. 2:35).

Knowing *and* doing what is "In My heart and in My mind" in oneness with the Spirit is what the Lord is looking for!!! The Lord wants us to know His thoughts and know His ways! To think (or ponder in our heart) that man is *not* able to operate in this manner – is the threshold of religious fatalism and satanic deception. *We were created in His likeness to become a likeness of Him* – as gateways of goodness – and thus, the thoughts of the righteous man is delightful to Him, but the thoughts of the wicked and unrighteous man is thoroughly offensive and repugnant to the Lord.

> "Let the wicked forsake his way, and the unrighteous man his thoughts; let him return to the LORD, and He will have mercy on him; and to our God, for He will abundantly pardon. [8] "For My thoughts are not your thoughts, nor are your ways My ways," says the LORD" (ISA. 55:7, 8).

If our thoughts are wicked, our heart should convict us; but if our heart is wicked, then the actions of our body will convict us. "Let the wicked forsake his way" and diligently seek the Lord... so that "we" in oneness of soul with spirit... are able to "glorify God in your body and in your spirit, which are God's" (1 Cor. 6:20).

> *"**Beloved, I beg you as sojourners and pilgrims, abstain from fleshly lusts which war against the soul**"* (1 Pet. 2:11).

The sons of Eli had become morally offensive to the Lord and abused the office of the priesthood by taking advantage of people's offerings, polluting the sacrifices, having carnal relations with women in the doorway of the tabernacle and – most of all – dishonoring the Lord! Feel the heart of Jesus as He speaks these words to Eli:

> "Why do you kick at My sacrifice and My offering which I have commanded *in My* dwelling place, and honor your sons more than Me, to make yourselves fat with the best of all the offerings of Israel My people?' [30] Therefore the LORD God of Israel says: 'I said indeed that your house and the house of your father would walk before Me forever.' **But now the LORD says**: 'Far be it from Me; for those who honor Me I will honor, and those who despise Me shall be lightly esteemed. [31] Behold, the days are coming that I will cut off your arm and the arm of your father's house, so that there will not be an old man in your house" (1 Sam. 2:29-31).

"But now" is how the Lord typically "disregards" obsolete promises with "new" messages and updated promises. The God Who never changes… does change His mind![65] The Lord told Samuel He would build him a "sure house" (above) and the Lord asked David a similar question (2 Sam. 7:5), yet David went down a different path to please the Lord by building a physical structure rather than a home for the Lord in his heart:

> "Now it came to pass when the king was dwelling in his house, and the LORD had given him rest from all his enemies all around, [2] that the king said to

---

[65] See Exodus 32:14; Jeremiah 18:7-10; 26:3; Jonah 3:10; and also Gen 18:26-32.

Nathan the prophet, "See now, I dwell in a house of cedar, but the ark of God dwells inside tent curtains." ³ Then Nathan said to the king, "***Go, do all that is in your heart***, for the LORD *is* with you." ⁴ But it happened that night that the word of the LORD came to Nathan, saying, ⁵ "Go and tell My servant David, 'Thus says the LORD: "***Would you build a house for Me to dwell in?***" (2 Sam. 7:1-5).

The Lord made a sarcastic statement because the Lord knew what David purposed in his heart to do. "Would you build a house for me to dwell in" as if God needed a building while they roamed in tents, as if the Lord needs a physical house when He fills the cosmos with His glory, but David did what was in his heart anyway… so he purposed to build a temple rather than a permanent abode for the Lord within his heart.

"Thus says the Lord: "Heaven is My throne, And earth is My footstool. Where is the house that you will build Me? And where is the place of My rest?" (Isa. 66:1).

The message given to Eli against the priesthood that dishonored the Lord and disrespected the offering is the same message that I sense the Lord is bringing to the institutional church today: "Stop polluting My house with vain teachings and crafty messages that tempt My indignation and cause My children to go astray by following shallow doctrines! What need do I have with buildings? You are My building; you are My sanctuary; you are My Holy Temple! You are an earthen tabernacle I created to host My presence. You are My Church… My bride! Build a permanent house for Me with a willing soul – within a steadfast heart – that is pleasing to Me that focuses your attention and affection upon Me – that does ALL My will – in spirit and in truth. Your soul is at peace when I enter the place of My rest within your heart-home!"

"Do you not know that you are the temple of God and that the Spirit of God dwells in you?" (1 Cor.

3:16).

The eternal question is: will you purpose with your soul (in your mind by an act of your will) to build a permanent resting-place *in your heart* for the Lord to abide?

> "Jesus answered and said to him, "If anyone loves Me, he will keep My word; and My Father will love him, and **_We_** will come to him and make **_Our_** home with him" (John 14:23; *emphasis* by the author).

"Where is the house will you build for Me" (Isa. 66:1). "What house will you build for Me?" (Acts 7:49). These scriptures are asking the same question to all of us: Are you going to build a permanent house (abode) in your heart (spirit) for the Lord – or not?

> "God, who made the world and everything in it, since He is Lord of heaven and earth, does not dwell in temples made with hands" (Acts 17:24).

God does not dwell in temples made by human hands…
God dwells in temples that have human hands!!!
Selah.

The soul creates a permanent dwelling place <u>in your heart</u> (house/abode) for God to abide.

At 3 A.M. the next morning, the Spirit awakened me to teach me this:

"When our body dies, our spirit returns to God… only to return to us once again as a living stone incorporated within a city prepared by God… as the bride of Christ… which is the New Jerusalem" that comes down to us from out of Heaven onto the New Earth in the regeneration.

[Note: I was woefully unprepared for that revelation.]

> "… you also, as living stones, are being built up a spiritual house, a holy priesthood, to offer up spiritual sacrifices acceptable to God through Jesus Christ" (1 Pet. 2:5).

To be in the spirit and operate according to the Spirit is the closest thing we have on earth right now – as a foretaste of life eternal in Paradise.

This helps us to comprehend one mystery regarding man: what happens to us when we die. Our body returns to the earth from which it came, our soul waits in Hades until the Day of Judgment[66] and our spirit returns to God from whence it originated until the day of redemption in the regeneration… which comes back to us as a living stone in the New Jerusalem (which explains why "we" appear to be resident in two eternal places at the same time).[67]

> "For thus says the High and Lofty One Who inhabits eternity, whose name is Holy: "I dwell in the high and holy place, **with him** who has a contrite and humble spirit, to revive the spirit of the humble, and to revive the heart of the contrite ones" (Isa. 57:15).

What house for the Lord are you building in your heart? What true riches through deeds of righteousness in Christ's name are being credited into your account for your use when your soul gets to the other side?

> "I, the Lord, search the heart, I test the mind, even to give every man according to his ways, according

---

[66] Hades is not Hell. Hades is the temporary holding place of the dead. Read "Here" chapter 6 for greater detail.

[67] This also explains why some people are able to have "out of body" experiences. Our spirit, by grace, is able to move about unencumbered by our body – unlike our soul that is obligated to remain within the body at all times while the body is alive, which explains the "spirit normal" occurrences mentioned at the beginning of this section.

> to the fruit of his doings" (Jer. 17:10).

Is attaining heaven your only focus in life… or serving the Lord Jesus in spirit and in truth?

> "That which is born of the flesh is flesh, and that which is born of the Spirit is spirit" (John 3:6).

We are spiritual beings having a human experience for one season of eternity on earth – and we MUST be born anew by the Spirit! We are being tested and proofed as sons and daughters on probation to determine if we are going to dedicate our full obedience and allegiance to the Lord by glorifying the Lord *in* our soul and *through* our spirit – or – to determine if we will continue to glorify the "self directed man" within the body of flesh we were given. Either glorify the Lord with your spirit or serve yourself in your body… the choice is yours.

Therefore, keep your soul's attention and your heart's affection focused on this:

> "But seek first the kingdom of God and His Righteousness [Jesus], and all these things shall be added to you" (Matt. 6:33).

> "For you were bought at a price; therefore glorify God **in your body and in your spirit, <u>which are God's</u>**" (1 Cor. 6:20).

The Spirit of God is with us, in us and operating through us; our spirit is being empowered by the Spirit of God and our soul is being instructed to produce more glory – in us and through us – and our body, likewise (which is God's), will glorify God by manifesting His deeds of glory through us (His body) on earth.

Your body belongs to God![68] **Your spirit belongs to God!**

---

[68] Contrary to the pro-abortion narrative, a woman's body *does not* belong to her; and her murderous choice is evil.

These are "His things" which He gave you as instruments to be used by you (your soul) – to glorify God! **"You are not your own"** (1 Cor. 6:19). You were bought (redeemed) at a price! If this is news to you, then this is great news if you live by it according to faith. Believe it, live according to the truth... and magnify the Lord in your soul!

> "For whoever desires to save his life will lose it, but whoever loses his life for My sake will save it" (Luke 9:24).

The life within you is His, your body is His, your spirit is His, your breath is His, and God is dwelling within you, so now... when are you going to surrender yourself and become a willing partner with Him as an agent of change... instead of being part of the problem?

> "Now may the God of peace Himself *sanctify you completely*; and may your whole spirit, soul, and body be preserved blameless at the coming of our Lord Jesus Christ" (1 Thess. 5:23).

> Amen.

Minds Decide, Hearts Establish

Before we look at a very significant scripture, let me reiterate something I've been saying throughout this book: our soul consists of two parts: mind and heart. We were made like our Maker to express thoughts through the mind of our soul – and we were created like our Creator to manifest these thoughts in word and deed through the heart of our soul.

The expression precedes the manifestation.

Thoughts (*expressions* in the mind) *precede* words and deeds (*manifestations* by the heart).

> "My mouth shall speak wisdom, and the meditation

of my heart shall give understanding" (Psa. 49:3).

The following scripture (below) is unique among biblical passages because it has a dual message, and while this is not uncommon, the reason for this is because two different words are found among biblical texts (check the footnote in your bible for the NU-Text and M-Text). Both words have been inserted into verse 18 so we can see the dual message.

> "... that the God of our Lord Jesus Christ, the Father of glory, may give to you the spirit of wisdom and revelation in the knowledge of Him, ^{18} the eyes of your [1271 – understanding – heart] being enlightened; that you may know what is the hope of His calling, what are the riches of the glory of His inheritance in the saints, ^{19} and what *is* the exceeding greatness of His power toward us who believe, according to the working of His mighty power" (Eph 1:17-20).

The word '*dianoia*-1271' (which is the term Strong's cites; '*dia*' through + '*nous*-3563' mind) means: through the mind, representing "deep meditative thought" is translated – mind (9x), understanding (3x), imagination (1x); the word '*kardia*-2588' (Engl. cardio) means: heart. Even though there is a distinct difference between these terms, the meaning and intent is consistent in regard to the functionality of the soul because, as Strong's continues with *kardia*, "the heart, i.e. (figuratively) the thoughts or feelings (mind); also (by analogy) the middle"... represents the center for "man's entire mental and moral activity."[69] In other words, the heart – as the middle (or center) of our being (soul) – makes manifest the thoughts and feelings (expressions) of/from the mind. Bingo!

Our soul is the core of our being, having both mind and heart that represents the "hidden person of the heart" (1 Pet. 3:4) which

---

[69] Strong's Concordance.

constitutes "the real man."[70] Our heart represents the core of our being (soul), however, the word "enlighten" (*photizo*-5461; Eph. 1:18) deals with the mind, which means to shine, brighten up and illuminate (i.e. truth) and is derived from the word (*phos*-5457) meaning, "to make manifest; expressing light as seen by the eye; and metaphorically, as 'reaching the mind.'" Truth must reach the mind and be assembled – to create an expression – before it can become manifest and operational "with understanding" in – and through – the heart.

> "Who has put wisdom in the mind? Or who has given understanding to the heart?" (Job. 38:36).

When our mind is unable to *suniemi* understand, then our heart has nothing to *suniemi* either.

> Jesus said: "When anyone hears the word of the kingdom, and does not *understand* it [4920 – *suniemi,* to put together mentally, to comprehend], then the wicked one comes and snatches away what was sown in his heart. This is he who received seed by the wayside" (Matt. 13:19).

The Spirit wisdom and understanding gives grace to men (xxx) ... but who puts understanding in the heart? Let me return to a previous scripture above – "Lest they should understand [in their mind] *with* their hearts and turn" (Matt. 13:15). If this scripture had said "should understand *in* their heart" rather than "*with*" their heart, an entirely different meaning would have been conveyed. The mind and heart need to operate in oneness. For example: a person focused on feelings and emotions will place the heart superior to wisdom with truth; drama is oftentimes the net result. A person focused on the intellect will struggle with intimacy; lack of mercy and showing compassion is oftentimes the net result.

One small seemingly insignificant word (in) is monumental in

---

[70] IBID.

meaning and substance! So I ask: who put understanding in the heart? A: you! Your thinker put understanding in your knower (either consciously or subconsciously), then your knower helps your thinker choose wisely. Our conscious *with* co-perception of mind and heart oneness is the balance we need in order to make good moral decisions, to understand the message of truth, to operate with justice and mercy toward one another, and to walk humbly before God with an upright heart. (Micah 6:8)

> "As for you, my son Solomon, know the God of your father, and serve Him with a loyal heart and with a willing mind; for the Lord searches all hearts and understands all the intent of the thoughts. If you seek Him, He will be found by you; but if you forsake Him, He will cast you off forever" (1 Chron. 28:9).

The heart, as the center of our being, manifests the thoughts and intent of our being, and the hearts' primary purpose is to host God's presence "as the Center at the center" of our being. Our heart, then, becomes the tangible "secret place" wherein we foster an intimate relationship with Jesus and, through faith, proceed to build a spiritual house for the Lord to abide (Isa. 66:1; Acts 7:49; John 14:23), and in this regard… our heart becomes the spiritual home we will inhabit in eternity (because eternity already exists in our heart; Eccl. 3:11). It is critically important to understand this point: you are building your eternal *oiketerion* – habitation house and dwelling place – right now, through faith.

Home is where your heart is!

Is Jesus the Center of your center? Is Jesus the Focus of your being?

Going back to the initial paragraph (above), we need to see the operation of our soul as the dual operation of heart with mental understanding (and vice versa), which Jesus mentions in Matthew and Mark and which John elaborates on by quoting Isaiah 6:10:

"For the hearts of this people have grown dull. *Their* ears are hard of hearing, And their eyes they have closed, Lest they should see with *their* eyes and hear with *their* ears, Lest they should understand [4920] with *their* hearts and turn, So that I should heal them" (Matt. 13:15).

"And to love Him with all the heart, with all the understanding [4907], with all the soul, and with all the strength, and to love one's neighbor as oneself, is more than all the whole burnt offerings and sacrifices" (Mark 12:33).

"He has blinded their eyes and hardened their hearts, Lest they should see with *their* eyes, Lest they should understand [3539] with *their* hearts and turn, So that I should heal them" (John 12:40).

A mind that lacks understanding is perhaps the greatest purveyor of doubt and unbelief. There are seventeen Greek words in the scriptures that are translated "understanding" and even more that describe knowing, knowledge, perception and comprehension: [71], [72]

- 'Suniemi' (4920) to put together mentally, to comprehend, be wise, to consider, to unite perception with what is perceived (Luke 24:45; Matt. 13:15)
- 'Sunesis' (4907) a mental putting together (from 4920); intelligence; understanding; (Gnosis (1108) denotes knowledge by itself and apprehension of truths; Sophia (4678) denotes wisdom as exhibited in action by power of reasoning; Sunesis denotes critical, apprehending the hearing of things; Phronesis (5428) practical, suggesting lines of action)

---

[71] All words found resulting from a study on UNDERSTAND in Strong's Concordance and Vines Expository.
[72] Excerpts from "Understand" section titled "Understand The Word."

- 'Noieo' (3539) from 3563-*nous*, to comprehend, to perceive with the mind (as distinct from perception by feeling); think, exercise the intellect, understand (Matt. 15:17; 16:9, 11; 24:15; John 12:40; Rom. 1:20; Eph. 3:4; Mark 7:18; 8:17)

Our spiritual and physical construction is impossible to comprehend apart from the regenerate mind that operates according to newness – through truth, change and oneness. Apart from truth that is revealed to us by the Spirit of Truth, there are some specific aspects of hearing by the listener who seeks to comprehend words spoken … yet is unable to grasp the meaning and intent of the message because… they are spiritual words that can only be understood by a renewed mind (Rom. 12:2). A diligent, born again listener, however, will hear the message and seek to comprehend the message, and thus… receive revelation truth with wisdom and understanding.

The eyes of our understanding (soul) represents the tandem operation of the mind "with" heart in oneness of purpose and effect, which compliment the means wherefore we were created as "the salt of the earth" to inhabit earth. Our soul is having a human experience that is being tested and proofed (authenticated) to resolve our eternal determination and *'oiketerion'* habitation – in this life and the life hereafter. We shall continue to live eternally in whatever *oiketerion* we have built with our heart during this life – either for better or worse.

The spirit that God placed within us (to complement our soul) is the "light of the world" which the Holy Spirit enlightens to build the kingdom of heaven upon the earth, yet is negatively used by unregenerate minds to build or destroy kingdoms that are hostile to God and His purposes.

> "Now He who establishes us with you in Christ and has anointed us *is* God, [22] who also has sealed us and given us the Spirit in our hearts as a guarantee" (2 Cor. 1:21, 22).

The heart is that principal component of our soul that hosts God's presence, builds a house for the Lord to tabernacle within us, and the Spirit is the seal in our heart that authenticates and guarantees our soul (mind and heart) is destined for salvation.

Therefore, guard your heart. Guard the good treasure in your heart.

> "A good man out of the good treasure of his heart brings forth good; and an evil man out of the evil treasure of his heart brings forth evil. For out of the abundance of the heart his mouth speaks" (Luke 6:45).

Jesus said:

> "For where your treasure is, there your heart will be also" (Luke 12:34).

His word is the final authority on this subject.

How We Treat Other Spirits

There is much evidence for the essence of something within man that is revealed by what is manifested through him. There are some (atheists, for example), who say it is impossible to prove that God exists. I disagree. There are, however, some who live life in such a manner that proves their point: God is nowhere to be seen or found as evidenced by the life they manifest.

> "And my soul shall be joyful [1523] in the Lord; it shall rejoice in His salvation" (Psa. 35:9).[73]

> "I will greatly rejoice in the LORD, my soul shall be joyful [1523] in my God" (Isa. 61:10).

---

[73] Joyful '*gool*-1523' means: "to spin around" gleefully with exceedingly joyful gladness. Strong's Concordance.

Can the evidence of joyful glee be found in you? Can people tell if there is any goodness in you? Since you are reading this book, I certainly hope so. There are some who seem to lack a spirit of goodness within them, and though we may not be willing to call it evil or an unclean spirit, when a person's life exudes such negativity, hate and moral depravity so as to give no indication that God is within them nor the spirit of goodness is within them nor the Spirit of God is guiding them, then my advice is simple: bless them anyway. They belong to God… and it's up to God to change what needs to be changed within them… not good intentions or outward interventions by us. We are to be good examples… not good interventionists. Be the good example you expect others to be. Follow Jesus and imitate Jesus. People learn more by observation and imitation than by good advice.

What comes out of a person through their heart reveals the thoughts of their mind (soul). For it is through the gateway of our heart, being manifested by the deeds of the body, wherein the true thoughts of our mind are revealed. Our gatekeeper (the mind of our soul) makes this happen.

How we treat others is a good indication of our spiritual "understanding" of God. If you are (angry, timid, arrogant, fearful, manipulative, generous, kind, stingy, controlling… fill in the blank) toward people, this is a good indication of how you feel toward God based upon how you perceive Him. You may strenuously reject this notion, but this is probably due to the spirit of religion that has tricked you into thinking there is a church-life and a secular-life; your holy thoughts toward God on Sunday are exemplary… and then you put God in the box and go about the other 6.92 days a week living your life independent of God – and then treat others however you want to. When you want to produce God-talk, you put on your church-face to speak a word of truth, but when the table is turned how quick we are to defend our worldly attitudes and secular opinions to justify our self-centered-kingdom preferences.

God is everywhere… and God is within everyone. *How you treat other people is exactly how you treat God… because you are subjecting God (who dwells in them) to your treatment of that person. If we truly grasped this concept, the world would be more humble, meek, kind, merciful and forgiving toward one another… except for one thing: this world is mercy-less.*

"Do unto others as you would have others do unto you" is "The Golden Rule" we have taught our children (Matt. 7:12; Luke 6:31) which is a Christianized version of "Eye for an eye, and tooth for a tooth," <u>but now</u> I say to you, "***Do unto others as you would have God do unto you***" is more precisely to the point Jesus was making: "But I say unto you, love your enemies, bless them that curse you, do good to them that hate you, and pray for them which despitefully use you, and persecute you" (Matt; 5:44-KJV; Luke 6:28). Why Jesus commanded us to treat other people in this manner seems mysterious… unless we comprehend our reason for being on earth (being commissioned to have dominion against the kingdom of darkness) is to save souls, not destroy them like our adversary. Therefore, Christians must rise above the status quo of "this world" by doing good toward our enemies even as we encounter suffering and persecution whereby our acts of goodness will serve as a testimony against evil.

God dwells (temporarily) in everyone – even our enemies! If you want mercy, kindness, forgiveness or any other grace attribute "from God," then show mercy, kindness and forgiveness toward one another… especially your enemies! (Matt. 6:14, 15) We are hypocrites to think of God in one manner… yet treat people another.

Treating everyone the way we would like to be treated is not going to take back enemy territory! Treating other people better than we are treated contradicts the kingdom of this world that treats us as less-than (inferior, insignificant, insecure) people. We are the host (army) of earth that was sent into the dominion of Satan to disperse the darkness and, like all armies engaged in warfare – casualties are expected. To think that God does not want us to suffer or encounter persecution goes against three things:

1. The gospel of Christ – "You will be persecuted" on account of Christ (John 15:20)
2. Christ Himself – or do you think you are better than Christ who suffered for us as the Commander of the Army of the Lord
3. Christ's commission for man – to have dominion on earth against our enemy who seeks to kill us and prevent us from taking back (redeeming) the land

The painless, suffer-less, sacrifice-nothing gospel that the church preaches cannot answer this question: why does humanity suffer? There is a very good reason why (which the doctrine of sin cannot adequately explain), but the church prefers rapture to escape all end times suffering and persecution rather than coming against God's enemies in righteousness and truth. Suffering isn't fair! Suffering isn't convenient! Solomon in Ecclesiastes wrestled with this dilemma, as did Job. We are engaged in a spiritual war and we will encounter suffering as part of the human condition – not because of something bad *we did* whereby God is avenging an injustice, but rather – because evil decided to wage war against God and everything that belongs to God. And since we are God's children, evil is coming against us even as we avenge the injustice done against the Lord. Christians are especially hated and persecuted by Satan because we are the Lord's children and, therefore thus, we are an enemy of Satan's dominion of evil.

The primary reason we experience human suffering is due, in part, to our original commission as members of the Host of Earth in the Army of the Lord, and secondarily – because of our willing participation in the rebellion against God (our fall from grace). Stopping your participation in the rebellion will not diminish your suffering because Satan's dominion still considers you an enemy combatant – and darkness must endeavor to compromise your commission by deceiving you and tricking you to embrace many lies of the enemy… so as to remain slaves to sin (in the kingdom of darkness)… in order to utterly destroy every human being. As you continue to grow deeper in your faith and commitment to Jesus as

His disciple, you will *not* encounter bliss and tranquility… but rather, increased persecution, suffering and injustice.

The first trick of the enemy is to convince us we are wretched human beings; secondly, we are worthless and unworthy to be called His beloved; and thirdly, we are less-than creatures – having been created on purpose for a purpose to come against God's enemy yet without any remembrance of who or what we really are. The enemy must continually compromise our true identity in order to compromise our mission against him and his kingdom of darkness.

> Jesus said, "Or what king, going to make war against another king, does not sit down first and consider whether he is able with ten thousand to meet him who comes against him with twenty thousand?" (Luke 14:31).

We are the army of earth that are being sanctified into disciples and are being recruited by the Lord for combat (Rev. 16:14; 17:14). Consider, now, that those who suffer persecution and even martyrdom for the sake of Christ will receive a new commission in the New Earth and made rulers by Christ Jesus over kingdoms, nations, cities, and tribes in the kingdom of God.

> "Blessed are those who are persecuted for righteousness' sake, for theirs is the kingdom of heaven. [11] "Blessed are you when they revile and persecute you, and say all kinds of evil against you falsely for My sake. [12] Rejoice and be exceedingly glad, for great is your reward in heaven, for so they persecuted the prophets who were before you" (Matt. 5:10-12).

We often think of our great reward in heaven as being riches and great wealth, but this is a misnomer; our great reward in heaven is being entitled to wait under the altar in Heaven as those counted worthy to suffer for the sake of Christ and, having been martyred, will be part of the first resurrection of the dead to rule and reign with Christ for a thousand years (Rev. 20:4). Wow!

Why do we suffer on earth? By now, I think you understand the reason: because Jesus created us and this world hates Jesus.

Now let me ask you this: why did the Messiah have to suffer? The OT scriptures indicated a Messiah would come, but it did not clearly indicate He would suffer (except in retrospect). So, why did Jesus have to suffer? Our doctrines teach us "to fulfill the scriptures" but let me remind you "Who" the "Voice" of the Old Covenant was; Jesus is the Word of God and He spoke God's messages to the prophets who wrote what they heard from the Messiah Himself. Jesus knew He was going to suffer and die long before His disciples did, but when He tried to explain this to them, Peter rebuked Him for saying it (yes, Peter rebuked God; Matt. 16:22; Mark 8:32). So now, let me ask you again: why did the Messiah have to suffer? Even though He came as a conquering King, He became exactly like us (as a man) to become our heavenly example and show us: in this world… we will suffer like Him… if we belong to Him.

> "For to this you were called, because Christ also suffered for us, leaving us an example, that you should follow His steps" (1 Pet. 2:21).

We suffer, not so much because of what we have done, but because of what we are capable of doing against Satan to vanquish the kingdom of darkness by the sword of truth. Our suffering is the message found in Job: we have an adversary that wants to obliterate us from the face of the earth. We are like sheep led to slaughter as a living testimony of the Truth of God abiding in us.

> "For, in fact, we told you before when we were with you that we would suffer tribulation, just as it happened, and you know" (1 Thess. 3:4).

Christ died for us – aught we not suffer the same as Him on account of Him? Jesus is our Lord – aught we not desire to become like Him in every regard? Jesus taught us suffering for righteousness sake is the way of the cross for all "sons of God" in this world.

> "But we see Jesus, who was made a little lower than the angels, *for the suffering of death* crowned with glory and honor, that He, by the grace of God, might taste death for everyone" (Heb. 2:9).

The point is:

> "For as many as are led by the Spirit of God, these are sons of God. [15] For you did not receive the spirit of bondage again to fear, but you received the Spirit of adoption by whom we cry out, "Abba, Father." [16] The Spirit Himself bears witness with our spirit that we are children of God, [17] and if children, then heirs—heirs of God and joint heirs with Christ, ***if indeed we suffer with Him, that we may also be glorified together***. [18] For I consider that the sufferings of this present time are not worthy to be compared with the glory which shall be revealed in us" (Rom. 8:14-18).

This is our great profession: "if" we become like Him in this world and we suffer with Him, then we will be raised in resurrection to become like Him – in glory! "As He is – so are we in this world!" As we abide with Him – so like Him we yearn to become! When we suffer – on account of our faithful obedience to Christ our Lord – great will our reward in heaven be!

Only Three Things – and A Fourth[74]

There are only three things I desire: 1) to know Jesus – 2) *and* the power of His resurrection – 3) *and* the exceeding greatness and glory that resides in Him – as He dwells in me:

---

[74] Section copied from "Image."

> "... and be found in Him, not having my own righteousness, which is from the law, but that which is through faith in Christ, the righteousness which is from God by faith; [10] *that I may know Him and the power of His resurrection,* ***and the fellowship of His sufferings***, being conformed to His death, [11] if, by any means, I may attain to the resurrection from the dead" (Phil. 3:9-11).

4) *And fourthly… the fellowship of His suffering.* This is not a popular topic, but it is extremely important for disciples to comprehend. This worldly paradigm hates humans because we were created by the Lord! Suffering in this world is to be expected – especially by those who bear His image!!! Suffering with persecution is what happens when we encounter this world that is violently opposed to Christ Jesus (Matt. 11:12) which may also include "being conformed to His death." We were sent to earth in order to execute a regime change from darkness to light.

If you are not experiencing suffering or persecution as a Christian (and I'm not talking about first world suffering, like your cell phone battery died, you got a dent in your Mercedes or you don't like eating chicken two days in a row), then ask the Holy Spirit why… if you really want to know, that is. Everyone has a cross to carry – and every cross is unique to every person.

> "For I consider that the sufferings of this present time are not worthy to be compared with the glory which shall be revealed in us" (Rom. 8:18)… "but rejoice to the extent that you partake of Christ's sufferings, that when His glory is revealed, you may also be glad with exceeding joy" (1 Pet. 4:13)… "and also a partaker of the glory that will be revealed" (1 Pet. 5:1).

Some may ask: why do innocent children need to suffer? And this question is typically followed by: "if God were a loving God, there would be no suffering in this world." In the New Earth, there will be no more suffering or pain, but during this phase of eternity on earth... there will be pain and suffering, so if you don't want suffering in this world, then you (not God) must stop it from happening. Don't fix it – change it! If you aren't changing it, then _you_ are the problem!

The Lord gave us authority to have dominion over the earth and the dominion of Satan, and it is "we" who were sent here and commissioned by the Lord to bring an end to this evil regime. If you want to eliminate suffering, then you must put an end to it, so I say to you... stop blaming God for not doing something that _you_ are supposed to be doing! The Lord gave you authority and power and dominion... and much responsibility as well. It is your responsibility to put an end to suffering. So I ask: would you still have a job if you consistently failed to do what your employer told you to do? I think not.

Suffering is the way of the cross whereby our soul are being sanctified by choosing to focus on the spirit within us rather than the body upon us.

And yet... we as members in the church are overly fixated on gratifying the physical body.

How We Treat Our Body

The way we treat our body is another indicator of the spiritual reality within us. If we treat our body with disrespect by polluting it with detrimental things (like alcohol, drugs, cigarettes, too much food, too many pharmaceuticals), or by calling too much attention to it with jewelry, bling and ornamentation, or by failing to properly maintain it with proper diet and exercise, then what people see "in our body" is the first clue to what is happening "in our soul." These are outward indicators of what is troubling our soul. Physicians and nurses are now (possibly) able to look at physical symptoms as a superficial (surface) problem to what ails us within. Not all diagnosis plaguing our physical body are manifestations of inner struggles, but many are. We are not to judge one another by the outward appearance (as judging a book by its cover), since we are all in transition from what we were... to becoming who we really are... but a person that abuses their own body oftentimes is wearing a garment over their soul that gives us an indication of what's going on inside. Self control is a gift by the Spirit ... as reason is for our intellect.

Does it not seem odd that the American church makes members feel guilty when they do not fast, but is erringly silent on gluttony and obesity?

Think of your body as a living organism that was placed upon your soul... as a temporary garment that belongs to God... that you must steward, take care of and give an account to Him!

Now think of the Jewish temple as an archetype of our person: our outer court (body) is the worldly interface, the inner court is our soul and spirit, and the most Holy Place is the tabernacle wherein we construct "the secret place" for the Lord our God to permanently abide as we host His Presence in our heart. Perhaps the main problem is this: the inner court is empty most of the time... and our physical bodies are "acting out" various psychoses' because there is a huge empty hole in the middle of our being that desperately wants to be restored and made "whole." This hole was intentionally constructed within us by One person for only one Person: by the Lord Jesus to rule and govern our life upon our heart-throne – by grace and truth – through the spirit. We are merely "becoming" whatever we have beheld in our heart.

Everything we do on earth, including the operational use of our body, comes into alignment with the things of God – through the spirit. *As the soul thinks and dictates, thus our heart manifests the inward reality through our outward man.* When the soul within you operates according to goodness, grace and glory, *then* your heart will manifest the following attributes: love, peace, meekness, humility, gentleness, kindness, self control, and longsuffering along with joyfulness and thanksgiving to God (and the greatest of these is love – 1 Cor. 13:13). A healthy heart within us will manifest these attributes.

> "But the fruit of the Spirit is love, joy, peace, longsuffering, kindness, ***goodness***, faithfulness, gentleness, self-control. Against such there is no law" (Gal. 5:22).

> "Even so, every good tree bears good fruit, but a bad tree bears bad fruit" (Matt. 7:17).

An unhealthy heart having been compromised by our mind seeking after the cares of "this world" will manifest the opposite of God's grace attributes. Recently, a brother in Christ with whom I have had many deep spiritual conversations with, made a request of me; days later, the Spirit compelled me to seek him out to offer some assistance... and I was verbally abused by him. The Spirit educated me in the days afterward that he suffers from what the clinical world calls a "passive-aggressive" personality, and then the Spirit went on to say, "We are called to be meek, humble... but *not* aggressive... which is anger vented outward according to the spirit of domination, not dominion." There is much to be learned under the tutoring of the Holy Spirit!

Oftentimes... the hidden nature or spirit within a person is manifested only under stress; dire circumstances and extreme situations will cause "some spirits" within us to boil to the surface. We must not make excuses when this happens, either for ourselves or for others in their humility; we must recognize it and take ownership of it and then: "humble yourselves" (James 4:10; 1 Pet. 5:6).

> "But I fear, lest somehow, as the serpent deceived Eve by his craftiness, so your minds may be corrupted from the simplicity that is in Christ" (2 Cor. 11:3).

The goodness within us is there because God (who is good) put it there. One of my favorite personal quotes is: "The only good in me – is the good God put there." ***When we supplant our life with***

all the attributes of God (grace) in our mind and heart, then we will produce godly fruit that is consistent with grace (i.e. the attributes of God). If your desire is to be godly, then think godly thoughts and act god-like by imitating Jesus according to His likeness. Our highest calling in life is to imitate Jesus, establish His kingdom upon the earth ***and*** give God all the glory for the goodness we manifest. If you want to live in peace – then this is the means to do so:

> "Let this mind be in you which was also in Christ Jesus" (Phil. 2:5).

In simplicity… if you think like Jesus… you will act like Jesus. Thinking one way yet acting another is hypocrisy, as if trying to live according to a double standard by standing between two ways (1 Kings 18:21). The reason why first century converts were called Christians is because their conduct was noticeably different *and exceptional* when compared to others still operating according to worldly standards – and thus – a new term was introduced in the marketplace to designate this new way and standard of living. When Christ's truth becomes operational within you, it will change your manner and character and the way you act – because, now, you think like Jesus! His truth compels us to think differently and, thus, we act differently.

> "Only let your conduct be worthy of the gospel of Christ, so that whether I come and see you or am absent, I may hear of your affairs, that you ***stand fast in one spirit, with one mind*** striving together for the faith of the gospel" (Phil. 1:27).

Every good gift and every perfect gift comes down to us from God (James 1:17). The Lord Jesus is the "Goodness Interventionist" of this world who was sent to save this world – by grace and truth. And we were sent here as gateways of grace to be His manifested "upright change agents with goodness" in the name of Christ our Lord. We are on this earth to usher in a regime change from darkness to light by the truth of God and thus… save many souls alive… with the goodness God placed within us *and* is manifesting through us.

We were created upright in rightness and goodness, and called "very good" by God Himself. This is how we were created and this is how we are supposed to act toward one another as we maintain a personal relationship with God by hearing His voice, but many of us stopped listening to the Voice of Truth, we put God in a box labeled 'religion' and then we proceeded to get as much good for our personal benefit… even at the expense of our less fortunate brethren.

Since God created us this way (good and upright), then what does God require of us?

> "He has shown you, O man, what is good; and what does the LORD require of you, but to do justly, to love mercy, and to walk humbly with your God" (Micah 6:8).

And Jesus took these three commands and refined them into two:

> "The first of all the commandments is: 'Hear, O Israel, the LORD our God, the LORD is one. [30] And you shall love the LORD your God **with all your heart, with all your soul, with all your mind, and with all your strength.**' This is the first commandment. [31] And the second, like it, is this: 'You shall love your neighbor as yourself.' There is no other commandment greater than these." (Mark 12:29-31).

Being good is only half the message; doing good in the name of the Lord to advance His kingdom and His agenda, which includes loving one another and taking care of them, is the basis of our spiritual obligation and loving devotion to Jesus… as sojourners on earth. When we fully understand and comprehend that we were created good such that ***goodness is who we are*** and not what we do, we will stop trying to do good – and become the goodness we were created to "be."

Being a good person – is oftentimes the phrase people use to justify themselves when the conversation "Are you saved?" or the topic of heaven comes up. When clarification is sought, they typically respond using "their" standard for good: they do not murder, steal or cheat. Well, that basic standard was spiritually encoded within all of us, yet our application of this standard to live according to goodness has become watered-down by our personal interpretation of goodness as it pertains to looking out for "number one" and the "I'm not as bad as so-and-so" comparison to extremely violent individuals. That standard is not the heavenly standard used to measure goodness: Jesus is!

Understanding Why We Are

How we perceive ourselves – and our reason for being on earth – has a dramatic affect on the manner in which we live, and relate to (love) one another and relate to God. Do we live "justly?" Do we love "mercy?" Do we walk "humbly" with our God? (Micah 6:8) These terms will be paramount to comprehend more truth as we move into the next section.

Let's start by defining the terms "good" and "justly" from Micah:

- Good [OT] (*towb*-H2896) "good, favorable, festive, pleasing, pleasant; well; better; right; best;" and good [NT] in a variety of senses: (*kalos*-G2570) "beautiful, good, excellent in its nature and characteristics" and (*agathos*-G18) "that which, being good in its character or constitution, is beneficial in its effect."

- Justly (*mishpat*-H4941) "a verdict (favorable or unfavorable) pronounced judicially, esp. a sentence of formal decree; abstract – justice; **mishpat means judgment**" and is translated (421x) as "judgment (296x), manner (38x), right (18x), cause (12x), ordinance (11x), lawful (7x) plus 39 other occurrences with nine other terms, including justly (1x)

> "For God will bring every work into judgment [*mishpat*], including every secret thing, whether good or evil" (Eccl. 12:14).
>
> "You shall not pervert the judgment of your poor in his dispute" (Ex. 23:6)

The Lord created us good so as to do justly (do right, judge rightly) toward one another. Now let's consider the terms "mind" and "strength" from Mark – and an interesting correlation can be found that results in revelation:

- '*Dianoia*-1271' (translated mind) means: "***understanding***, a thorough thinking through, the exercise of the mind; deep thought, meditation (Eph. 1:18; 4:18; 1 John 5:20). *We are told to love the Lord with all our heart, soul and 'dianoia'* (Matt. 22:37) and strength (Mark 12:30; Luke 10:27).[75]

- '*Ischus*-2479' (translated strength) means: "forcefulness; denotes ability, force, strength;" as "strength afforded by power" and "it describes the full extent of power wherewith we are to love God."[76]

This "tent" or "tabernacle put upon us" is what the Lord referred to regarding Paul's weakness; "strength within weakness" is afforded to us by God's miraculous power that is working within us as we remain steadfast and fervent in our love and devotion to the Lord our God – in humility. Our strength is literally His power given unto us (our spirit) to love Him – which includes His power to love one another. This power is God's power by God's grace (His attributes and His empowering by His indwelling Spirit) that is given to strengthen us so we may accomplish our mission on earth – to have dominion over His enemies *and* save other souls alive. Does this last sentence resonate with your understanding of life on

---

[75] Excerpt copied from "Understanding" and mentioned previously in this section; definitions from Strong's.
[76] Strong's Concordance.

earth?

> "Whom have I in heaven but You? And there is none upon earth that I desire besides You. ²⁶ My flesh and my heart fail; but **God is the strength of my heart** and my portion forever" (Psa. 73:25, 26).[77]

It is interesting to note: the fullness of understanding (*oida*-1492; John 3:3) and empowering (*dunamis*-1411) is made available <u>only</u> through the new birth by the Spirit after we have made a full confession <u>with</u> conversion to serve Jesus as Lord of your heart and soul.[78] And thus, we are able to the see this empowering that is promised to us:

"You *shall* love the Lord" with *all* your heart and soul – with ***dianoia*** and ***ischus*** – with ***understanding*** that comes after being thoroughly persuaded and convinced by the gospel of Christ to live according to the truth… and ***might*** with the Spirit's supernatural *dunamis* power operating within us to strengthen us in our weakness (the earthly abode). In this regard, it is God's grace that initiates and performs this operation – in us and through us – according to His miraculous power to the praise of His great goodness, grace and glory!

Love the LORD your God – "with all that is within you" – ***with all your heart, with all your soul, with all the understanding of your soul (mind), and with all the might of your spirit (heart).***

"Might" is perhaps a better translation for Mark 12:30, as it is more closely aligned with Deut. 6:5, which is '*me'od*-3966.' As an adverb, it means "very, greatly, exceedingly," and as a noun it

---

[77] Strength (*tsur*-H6697) can mean "a rock or boulder large enough to serve as an altar." Strong's Concordance.

[78] The phrase "heart, soul, mind, strength" is a New Covenant term for an Old Covenant concept that referenced only the heart and soul (Deut. 10:12; 11:13; 13:3; 26:16; 30:2, 6, 10; Joshua 22:5; plus others) except in Deut. 6:5 which the Lord Jesus referenced as the first commandment: "heart, soul, strength" as it appears in Matt. 22:37.

implies *absolutely everything you've got within you* – i.e. exceedingly great strenuous effort with mighty determination. Only one person in the Old Testament (that I have been able to find thus far) has been credited with using "might" within this context: Josiah (2 Kings 22:1-23:25). This person single-handedly removed ALL articles put in the temple made for Baal and Asherah, the idolatrous priests, graven images, high places, altars, and eliminated all evil practice, perverted persons, sorcery and all abominations, and executed ALL the priests that performed these rituals during the most massive revival and spiritual clean-up in Israel's history. "Might" is how the Lord wants us to operate – and "By His Spirit" – He will enable us with His power to perform it.

> "Not by [human] might nor by [human] power, but by My Spirit,' Says the Lord of hosts" (Zech. 4:6).

In fact, the Lord purposed for this type of "mighty ones" to fill His earth with the fullness thereof! Deut. 6:3 says, "That you may increase mightily [*me'od*]." And thus, "these are the mighty ones" that the Lord is calling TODAY and activating for duty right now so that He can release more glory, power, grace and goodness in this final season to initiate the kingdom age – through His mighty-empowered-humble ones. Are you willing to step forward and become part of "this mighty generation" that you were destined for – or is "all in" too much of a commitment for you to make at this time or is "humble yourself" too self abasing for you at this time?

Beloved one – He created you for this very purpose! This is your moment in history! And your spirit within you is testifying to these words you are reading because they are literally exploding within your heart right now. Seek Him – and ask Him what His desire is for you. Ask Him for your commission. It's time to let your light shine and displace the kingdom of darkness with the truth of Jesus Christ – which He desires to manifest through you!

Not 'might do it' or maybe – but by your determined MIGHT as an act of your will strengthened by His SPIRIT, we are to do the Lord's will on earth <u>*as we walk humbly with our God*</u>!

The term "humbly" (*tsana*-H6800) means: "to humiliate" as does "humble" (*tapeinoo*-G5013) "to make low or bring low; to bring to a humble position."[79] This is the same word used in "humble yourselves" (James 4:10).

> "When pride comes, then comes shame; but with the humble [*tsana*] is wisdom" (Prov. 11:2).

From personal experience I've learned: if you do not humble yourself and put to death all manner of pride within you (that operates according to the flesh), the Lord will humiliate you. Consider how the Lord of Heaven and Earth willingly and obediently humbled Himself, put on flesh, and accomplished perfectly the will of God – whereby He serves as our Great Example.

> "And being found in appearance as a man, He [Jesus] humbled [*tapeinoo*] Himself and became obedient to the point of death, even the death of the cross" (Phil. 2:8).

Putting our best face forward in "this world" is contradictory to what the Lord did – and what He desires for us. If becoming a fool for Jesus is going to accomplish perfectly the Lord's purposes on earth through our humiliation, then this can be done willingly (yielded unto Him as a living sacrifice) or it can be done the hard way. This is the Lord's planet – and His plan triumphs!

> Jesus said: "And whoever exalts himself will be humbled, and he who humbles himself will be exalted" (Matt. 23:12). "Therefore whoever humbles himself as this little child is the greatest in the kingdom of heaven" (Matt. 18:4).

> "Therefore humble yourselves under the mighty hand of God, that He may exalt you in due time" (1 Pet. 5:6).

---

[79] Strong's Concordance.

We are all like sheep having gone astray by seeking other pastures to pursue our own will and agenda, and yet the Lord is faithful and merciful to receive us back to Himself "if you seek Him with all your heart and with all your soul" (Deut. 4:29). Understanding and might will be added to your heart and mind after that, but– first and foremost – we must humbly seek the Lord with the fullness of our heart's affection and our mind's attention.

Truly, all we need… is to "be" <u>thoroughly</u> willing… and God will enable us by His power!

Mercy Explained

> "What does the LORD require of you, but to do justly, to love mercy, and to walk humbly with your God" (Micah 6:8).

My direction from the Lord throughout these books was not to consult man's wisdom or the teachings or commentaries of others, but rather to wait upon the Holy Spirit to guide me and bring understanding in regard to the scriptures… and this is my intention even now. My pastor at Family Worship Center in St. Augustine, Florida brought a remarkable word about mercy one Sunday morning that I felt compelled (by the Spirit) to research and, if possible, locate a citation for it. Through the internet, I found one citation with perhaps the best description about mercy that hopefully will bless you as much as it has me (note: this message will be vitally important when we get to the next session about the Beatitudes, especially "mercy" in Matt. 5:7).

"English language dictionaries are of limited help in understanding this mercy's biblical usage. In English "mercy" is normally used to mean showing compassion, forbearance, pity, sympathy, forgiveness, kindness, tenderheartedness, or liberality or refraining from harming or punishing offenders or enemies. These synonyms give us some insight on this word; they all express how a merciful person might act. However, none of them specifically pictures what biblical mercy is because the scriptural concept is virtually untranslatable into a single English word.

"The Greek word used in Matthew 5:7, *eleemon* [1655] means essentially the same as its English counterpart, "merciful." However, in all likelihood Jesus spoke in Aramaic, and the idea behind His statement about mercy come from Old Testament—that is, Hebrew—usage and teaching. The word He would have used is the Hebrew and Aramaic *chesed*.'

'William Barclay's *Daily Study Bible* commentary on Matthew regarding this word states:

'It does not mean only to sympathize with a person in the popular sense of the term; it does not mean simply to feel sorry for some in trouble. *Chesedh* [sic], **mercy, means the ability to get right inside the other person's skin until we can see things with his eyes, think things with his mind, and feel things with his feelings** [bold italics by the author]. Clearly this is much more than an emotional wave of pity; clearly this demands a quite deliberate effort of the mind and of the will. It denotes a sympathy which is not given, as it were, from outside, but which comes from a deliberate identification with the other person, until we see things as he sees them, and feel things as he feels them. This is *sympathy* in the literal sense of the word. *Sympathy* is derived from two Greek words, *syn* which means *together with*, and *paschein* which means *to experience* or *to suffer*. *Sympathy* means *experiencing things together with the other person*, literally going through what he is going through. (p. 103)

'Much easier said than done! Having a sense of another's feelings to this degree is very difficult to do because we are normally so self-concerned, so aware of our own feelings, that sensitivity for others to this depth often requires a great effort of the will. Normally, when we feel sorry for someone, it is an exclusively external act because we do not make the effort to get inside another's mind and heart until we can see and feel things as he does. It is not easy to walk in another person's shoes.

'The world, from which we have all come, is true to its nature; it is unmerciful. The world prefers to insulate itself against the pains and calamities of others. It finds revenge delicious and forgiveness tame and unsatisfying.

'This is where we all begin. Indeed, all too often in the church, worldliness is hardly dormant, revealing itself in acts that show some degree of cruelty. Usually, these cruelties are delivered verbally, but all too frequently, brethren simply ignore the real needs of others.

'The mercy Jesus teaches is not humanly derived. He says in Matthew 6:14, "If you forgive men their trespasses, your heavenly Father also will forgive you." This occurs, not because we can merit mercy by being merciful or forgiving of others, but because we cannot receive the mercy and forgiveness of God unless we repent. We cannot claim to have repented of our sins if we are unmerciful towards the sins of others.

'The truly merciful are too aware of their own sins to deal with others in sharp condemnation, so they constrain themselves to deal humbly and kindly with those in need. Nothing moves us to forgive others like the amazing realization that God has forgiven *our* sins. Mercy in God's children begins by experiencing His forgiveness of them, and perhaps nothing proves more convincingly that we have been forgiven than our readiness to forgive.

'Recognizing God's mercy is a key element in motivating our expressions of mercy. Too many people today, even in the church, possess a "welfare mentality." They go through life with little or no gratitude, thinking they deserve the handouts of governments or private citizens. Ingratitude is vital to understanding this because, as long as one is unthankful, his thoughts will center on himself. The merciful person is sensitive to others' needs and takes action to supply them. An ungrateful person, though, insulates himself from others' pains because he is too focused on his own perceived miseries.'"[80]

"Grace removes guilt; mercy removes misery."[81]

Wow!!! With this definition of mercy, let us consider how Jesus, our God and Savior, came to earth and got inside human flesh, *as Mercy Incarnate*, to experience everything that we go through, which He did in meekness and lowliness, and humbling Himself became obedient even unto death on a cross.

> "For we do not have a High Priest who cannot *sympathize with* [touched with the feeling of-KJV] our weaknesses, but was in all points tempted as we are, yet without sin" (Heb. 4:15).

The Mercy from Heaven became clothed in humanity to teach us the truth, as the Righteousness of God manifested before men… so that we may have peace with God!

> "Mercy and truth have met together; righteousness and peace have kissed" (Psa. 85:10).

Thank you, Jesus, for loving us so much… that You came to earth to prove it! Amen!

Goodness and Might

> "He has shown you, O man, what is good" (Micah 6:8).

"Goodness" is in us because God is in us, but that is not the problem; living according to goodness is more likely the problem, as something we try to "do" instead of "be."

---

[80] Citation on mercy, Forerunner Commentary, John W. Ritenbaugh. http://www.bibletools.org/index.cfm/fuseaction/Topical.show/RTD/CGG/ID/7132/Eleemon.htm

[81] Strong's Concordance; study on 'eleios-1656.'

If goodness is part of our character and essential nature, then being good and doing good should be "natural" for us… and yet it isn't. Why? Well, theologians have been asking and answering that question for nearly 6,000 years and it seems we are no closer to the solution than when we first began searching for answers. I believe it has to do with our understanding of the "spirit" within us and our voluntary obedience of living under the guidance of the Holy Spirit.

I believe we were born with a temporary spirit that guides us until the time we decide to turn our full allegiance over to Jesus and follow His Spirit… whereby we are given a new heart and new spirit that is devoted to serving Jesus and doing God's will (not ours). The temporary spirit was for the temporary dwelling place (heart-house), but when we become "born anew" by the Spirit of God, a permanent abiding place is established within us whereby we are being conformed into the image of Christ our Creator according to His likeness. At that moment, a spiritual shift has taken place within us to begin our transformational process back into "sons of God." This process takes time… and gets harder and harder along the path of discipleship… so endure and don't give up! Persevere… and don't ever give up!

"Christ is being formed in us, by grace through faith, until Christ is fully formed within us and newness of the Spirit is birthed through us to become a new creation "in" Christ upon the earth (whereby we are being formed, conformed and transformed into the image of Christ by the Spirit of Christ)."[82]

> "Everyone who is called by My name, Whom I have created for My glory; I have *formed* him, yes, I have made him" (Isa. 43:7).
>
> "My little children, for whom I labor in birth again until Christ is *formed* in you" (Gal. 4:19).

---

[82] Excerpt from "Image" section titled "Christ In Us."

> "For whom He foreknew, He also predestined to be **_conformed_** to the image of His Son, that He might be the firstborn among many brethren" (Rom. 8:29).
>
> "I beseech you therefore, brethren, by the mercies of God, that you present your bodies a living sacrifice, holy, acceptable to God, which is your reasonable service. ² And do not be conformed to this world, but **_be transformed_** by the renewing of your mind, that you may prove what is that good and acceptable and perfect will of God" (Rom. 12:1, 2; the word transformed '_metamorphoo_' is also translated "transfiguration" in reference to Jesus' appearance being changed).

Therefore, our initial salvation experience that comes by the Spirit's conviction of our heart to enter into faith is the first step of sanctification… through which we are being saved. We must continue in faith and do as the Spirit teaches us to continue in sanctification… or we forfeit the grace of God by choosing to walk out of His hand into disobedience. Sanctification is oftentimes painful and messy, and yet… so is childbirth! We are (metaphorically speaking) being birthed into the kingdom of God from out of the kingdom of darkness and into the light of God's love, truth, mercy, grace… whereby our soul and spirit are set free to walk in the freedom of the Spirit… for God's glory.

Sadly, it seems, our evangelistic salvation messages only take us to faith (first base) – yet avoids the message of sanctification and the "new birth" (second base) and the message of discipleship and suffering (third base). Pardon the baseball analogy, but you cannot advance "Home Plate" from first base, and yet this is precisely what our salvation messages teach. Why? Because we know that discipleship involves the total surrender of our life in obedience to Christ who abides within us to become a bondservant of Jesus – even if – this includes suffering or martyrdom. Preachers make a good show on Sunday by selling Heaven (which we were never promised) and rejoicing in the beauty of our salvation when would-be converts come forward in the altar call, but if they mention suffering for the sake of Christ, well... the offering plate may be negatively impacted... as indeed, it should!

Follow this line of thinking:

- Our body was formed upon us (Gen. 2:7)
- Our initial spirit was formed within us (Zech. 12:1)
- Then a new spirit is given to us in the new birth by the Spirit (Ezek. 36:26, 27; John 3:3-8) – and we are given a new heart as well
- The Holy Spirit transforms our mind to operate in newness– through truth, change and oneness of the Spirit (Rom. 12:1, 2)...
- ... Until we are **conformed** to the image of Christ (Rom. 8:29) and Christ is fully formed in us (Gal. 4:19)...
- ... With God abiding within our permanent abode (John 14:23) – *in our new heart*
- Thereby completing the *metamorphoo* (metamorphosis; transformation) of sons of men "back into" sons of God that are now waiting for the resurrection that already resides within them on account of Christ ("I Am the Resurrection") who dwells within them

Our salvation is a present-active-continuous process from-out-of temporary into eternity.

Jesus wants us to become transformed (*metamorphoo*) by the renewing of our mind that becomes radiant and brilliant... like Him... that operates with revelation truth!

"Once the mind of man has been renewed, sanctified, and '*metamorphoo*' transformed by the Spirit of truth, it will operate in revelation splendor by grace and glory, with truth and understanding – with the appearance of lightning as it flashes across the sky. The mind of the new man that operates in newness of the Spirit will become radiant and operate according to revelation, yet the mind of the old man shall continue to operate under demonic influence. Yes, the mind of the old man is "demonic" in nature! You may bristle at this comment, so allow me to state this differently: the wisdom of this world shall continue to corrupt the mind of the old man to remain demonic in nature rather than divine and radiant with revelation.

> "This wisdom does not descend from above, but is *worldly*, sensual, demonic" (James 3:15; *italicized* word '*epigeios*-1919' corrected by the author).

"Saints, this world is demonic, sensual and sinful because the prince of darkness has corrupted it with lies, confusion, doubt and fear resulting in unbelief in order to pervert truth in our mind and thwart faith from taking root in our heart. We were all born through water into this demonic world of darkness and sin, yet we have a way of escape: be born anew through the Spirit and be saved… from death into life… through faith in Jesus Christ."[83]

Receive Your Commission

The commission the Lord desires for us is predicated upon our willingness to be tested and proofed beforehand. By grace, the Lord has given His authority to us as adopted sons and daughters according to faith, but He will withhold His power until we can be trusted to use it for kingdom purposes – rather than selfish motives. Within this context, soldiers are not given a commission until they have successfully passed Basic Training and are prepared to do as they are commanded – as well as to think in the same manner as their commanding officer.

"When the Father's Presence permanently abides within us, we likewise can cease from our labors and enter into His rest because this salvation phase of our life with the Father is now complete; we are no longer striving… now we abide in Him as He abides in us! We have been saved, preserved in Christ and have been sealed for redemption by the Holy Spirit! Next begins the "dominion with a

---

[83] Excerpt copied from "Gateways" section titled: "Thoughts, Purposes and Plans."

commission" phase of our life on earth whereby the Holy Spirit begins sanctifying us, changing us, renewing us, **transforming** us and manifesting Himself through us to save other souls alive and take back what the enemy has stolen from the Father. Our efforts from this point forward are done for our Father's glory through Christ Jesus our Lord by the empowering of the Holy Spirit. It is no longer you doing it – it is now *Elohim* doing it… in you, with you and through you, to the glory of the Father."[84]

"Where is the house that you will build Me? And where is the place of My rest" (Isa. 66:1). Their place of rest is now residing within the heart-home we built and consecrated for Them to abide in, which successfully completes the Lord's plan of salvation for us – and now Christ *commissions* us to have dominion over His enemies – with His authority residing in us and His power flowing through us by the Spirit of God. Wow, indeed!"[85]

"The kingdom of God is within you" (Luke 17:21).

"We have been saved – in order to receive a commission from Christ – to complete the work of Christ – to have dominion upon the earth – with God abiding in us – in the name of Jesus – for His eternal glory."[86]

The nature of our spirit is spiritual, and yet there are two aspects of the spirit: it can be divinely inspired by God and it can be negatively influenced by evil. The old spirit that became corrupted and polluted by the things of this world must be replaced in the new birth, but woe upon us when we return again to the meagerly and beggarly ways of this world to operate, once again, according to the worldly pattern of sinful activities performed in our mind and heart (Gal. 4:9). Woe indeed! The Spirit will hold us in contempt!

---

[84] Excerpt copied from "Image."
[85] IBID.
[86] IBID.

Our spirit can be divinely inspired or demonically influenced. The kingdom of God is comprised of two kingdoms: the kingdom of heaven where Jesus is Lord – and the kingdom of darkness where Satan rules. And because the kingdom of God "is in you" – you are able to build one kingdom or the other (heaven or hell) in your heart – and it is through your heart that you are influencing this world either for good or for evil.

Beloved, whatever kingdom you build in your heart – is the one you will spend eternity in.

This message has been stated and restated several times within this chapter using a variety of formats to help everyone understand and perceive the spiritual reality within us that has been misconstrued by the "Once saved, always saved" false salvation theology… which gets people eager for Heaven and onto first base… without any thought of follow-up to teach sanctification or discipleship or operating according to the kingdom of heaven. They want grace without any sacrifice… and the Spirit within us grieves.

That which is good is from above – worldly is from below

> "For you were once darkness, but now you are light in the Lord. Walk as children of light [9] (***for the fruit of the Spirit is in all goodness, righteousness, and truth***), [10] finding out what is acceptable to the Lord. [11] And have no fellowship with the unfruitful works of darkness, but rather expose them" (Eph. 5:8-11).

> "Do they not go astray who devise evil? But mercy and truth belong to those who devise good" (Prov. 14:22).

Created Upright – in Rightness

God created us upright and very good to operate in uprightness and produce righteousness in the earth. The good that we accomplish upon the earth is because God placed His good spirit within us, and therefore, we became gateways for God's goodness to flow through us. This becomes a very important point: the good in us is God's goodness being revealed in us and through us for the praise of His glory, not ours.

> "Teach me to do Your will, for You are my God;
> Your Spirit is good. Lead me in the land of
> uprightness" (Psa. 143:10).

The will of God for mankind is to love the Lord and love one another, and thus, we are here to help one another as we get through this probationary phase of eternity. Our interest to help others ahead of our own self-interest is one aspect of meekness... and the other is (most importantly) establishing the preeminence of God in our life as our number one priority. The good deposit within us is how God designed us to live in uprightness, but when we use this goodness to better our "self" at the exclusion and detriment of others is what the Law warned us about, yet could never teach us apart from the tutoring of the Spirit in divine wisdom *with* understanding... and with mercy!

> "Is the Spirit of the Lord restricted? Are these His
> doings? Do not My words do good To him who
> walks uprightly?" (Micah 2:7).

And yet, the blessing of the Promised Land was not because Israel walked in uprightness before the Lord, but rather... as a reproof against the wickedness of the nations they were sent to displace and conquer. This point is most important to remember: we were sent to earth to have dominion over the deeds of wickedness in this world and institute the kingdom of goodness and righteousness for God's glory... and fill the earth with His glory being released through us. Yet it seems we prefer to build our own kingdoms... and produce deeds of wickedness instead.

> "It is not because of *your* righteousness or the
> uprightness of your heart that you go in to possess
> their land, but because of the wickedness of these
> nations that the Lord your God drives them out

> from before you, and that He may fulfill the word which the Lord swore to your fathers, to Abraham, Isaac, and Jacob" (Deut. 9:5).

Abraham was already a mighty nation within the land of his father, Terah, yet the Lord commanded him to leave his father's house and come out of his father's land to become a new type of nation upon the earth… as a God-focused, Spirit-directed, spiritual nation called out, set apart and consecrated to do the Lord's will. Yet in the course of time, Israel forgot who God is, and forgot the will of God, and forgot His majestic character within them, and they forgot the promises made to Abraham as well.

We are sojourners on a journey to remember the promises and the testimony.

> "Do good, O Lord, to those who are good, and to those who are upright in their hearts" (Psa. 125:4).

The problem we have today resonates with the same problem since ancient times: we see with the eyes, and we judge with our intellect… yet fail to perceive the spiritual reality all around us through our heart and mind.

At work within us is our spirit (which belongs to God) that is helping our soul endure many trials, but at some point… our soul (by unclean thinking and ungodly thoughts) compromised our spirit by partnering with many spirits associated with those thoughts… which are inconsistent with the character (nature) of Christ. When the lamp (spirit) within us partners with spirits of darkness, the lamp does not go out, per se, but the darkness overtakes the light and diminishes the effective ability of our spirit to be "the light of the world."

And Solomon said: "You have shown great mercy to Your servant David my father, because he walked before You in truth, in righteousness, and in **uprightness of heart** with You; You have continued this great kindness for him, and You have given him a son to sit on his throne, as it is this day" (1 Kings 3:6). Then the

Lord said:

> "Now if you walk before Me as your father David walked, **in integrity of heart and in uprightness**, to do according to all that I have commanded you, _and if_ you keep My statutes and My judgments..." (1 Kings 9:4).

This is an interesting word from the Lord who regarded David as a man "in integrity of heart and in uprightness" even though David plotted in his heart (i.e. schemed) to have carnal relations with Bathsheba (i.e. coerced and raped her) and commit adultery; he lied about it and then attempted to conceal the illegitimate child by having Uriah (the husband) intentionally killed in battle (i.e. murdered). This is the same man whom God said is, "A man after My own heart" (Acts 13:22). The facts don't add up! And yet, the fact of this man who stumbled into sin is somehow different because – he kept an open place in his heart for the Lord to dwell. David knew he was doing wrong and when his sin was revealed to him, he repented... and asked the Lord to forgive him.

Perhaps the hardest thing for spiritual leaders to uphold is the high regard people put upon them. When a leader stumbles and their iniquity is revealed, it often has devastating effects upon them and they leave the ministry in shame... never to return again. If this sounds like something that happened to you, then consider your calling from the Lord and ask Him: "Did You revoke it?" Ask the Lord "in a humble and contrite spirit" what He wants you to do and consider this story:

"There was an executive for a large corporation that routinely handled large financial transactions. One day, the executive discovered that he had mismanaged over a million dollars that resulted in a substantial loss to the company. In shame, the man walked into his boss's office and told him what he had done, and just before turning to leave... he handed his boss his letter of resignation and then went toward the door. Nearly outside the office, now, the executive heard his boss call him back into the office wherein the manager asked him, "Do you know what you did wrong?" Yes, the executive replied. "Will you ever make that mistake again? No, the executive replied. Then the manager handed the letter of resignation back to the executive and told him to get back to work. Completely stunned and shell-shocked, the executive asked: "Why?" The manager replied, "The loss has already occurred. It was a million dollar lesson you needed to learn and this experience is more valuable now to the company that losing a valuable employee." Well, the executive stayed with the company and made millions upon millions for the company after that!"

We all make mistakes, but it is easier for a man with an upright heart to get back up and continue in rightness than it is for a man whose spirit is not upright within him. The church needs to consider this lesson as many ministers with tarnished reputations are going to be reactivated for duty in this new season of greater grace, greater works and greater glory because… they will never make "that" mistake again. Their humility will testify on their behalf.

> "For a righteous man may fall seven times and rise again, but the wicked shall fall by calamity" (Prov. 14:16).

The Lord is seeking sons and daughters who will worship Him in spirit and in truth, with loyal and contrite hearts, whose spirit is upright within them. A great harvest of souls is on the horizon and "war-scarred" veterans of the pulpit and other ministries as well are being activated for duty for the Third Great Awakening. Settle your account with the Manager of Heaven and ask Him what He has purposed and planned for you. It may be that He has an "upgrade" in mind for you. Consider, now, the Psalm written by David, whereby we may learn much by his life:

> "LORD, who may abide in Your tabernacle? Who may dwell in Your holy hill? [2] ***He who walks uprightly, and works righteousness, and speaks the truth in his heart***; [3] He who does not backbite

with his tongue, nor does evil to his neighbor, nor does he take up a reproach against his friend; ⁴ In whose eyes a vile person is despised, but he honors those who fear the LORD; he who swears to his own hurt and does not change; ⁵ he who does not put out his money at usury, nor does he take a bribe against the innocent. ***He who does these things shall never be moved***" (Psalm 15).

Let the Lord's mercy, grace and forgiveness wash over all of us, especially those I've mentioned.

> King David said: "I know also, my God, that You test the heart and have pleasure in uprightness. As for me, in the uprightness of my heart I have willingly offered all these things; and now with joy I have seen Your people, who are present here to offer willingly to You" (1 Chron. 29:17).

Many years later, David was on the battlefield alongside many men much younger than himself and nearly lost his life, "Then the men of David swore to him, saying, "You shall go out no more with us to battle, lest you quench the lamp of Israel" (2 Sam. 21:17). Perhaps David remembered his disastrous failure when he had a choice to make: either go out to battle like all other kings… or contemplate a sinful act with a married woman (1 Chron. 20:1).

The mystery of iniquity is not that sin happens <u>by</u> us, or that sin happens <u>to</u> us, but rather… ***sin does not define us***! Sin does not compromise our identity! ***Sin compromises our mission***! The doctrine of sin (which is a manmade doctrine to explain why men sin) is feeble in its attempts in blame-casting and minimizing man to continually punish and restrict the upright spirit within man who needs only to acknowledge sin, repent from it and get back on tract by moving away from it… in order to be "who" the Lord defines you to be.

"The enemy will continue to attack us, not because of what we've done in our past, but rather… to prevent us from walking into the destiny God purposed for us… which the enemy knows infinitely more than we do because our manifest destiny is to their peril, not ours!"[87]

Our true identity is found "in grace."

Don't let your destiny be in bondage to your history.

There is a significant distinction between persons as either operating in rightness with an upright heart – or operating in unrightness whose heart is not upright within them. If your heart is loyal, faithful, steadfast, upright and subordinate in all things to the Lord's sovereignty in your life, then now it's time to ask the Lord what He thinks rather than listening to the opinion of others.

- "My words come from my upright heart; my lips utter pure knowledge" (Job 33:3).
- "My defense is of God, who saves the upright in heart" (Psa. 7:10).
- "For look! The wicked bend their bow, they make ready their arrow on the string, that they may shoot secretly at the upright in heart" (Psa. 11:2).
- "Be glad in the Lord and rejoice, you righteous; and shout for joy, all you upright in heart!" (Psa. 32:11).
- "Oh, continue Your lovingkindness to those who know You, and Your righteousness to the upright in heart" (Psa. 36:10).
- "The righteous shall be glad in the Lord, and trust in Him. And *all* the upright in heart shall glory" (Psa. 64:10).
- "But judgment will return to righteousness, and all the upright in heart will follow it" (Psa. 94:15).
- "Light is sown for the righteous, and gladness for the upright in heart" (Psa. 97:11).

---

[87] Excerpt copied from this book.

- "Praise the Lord! I will praise the Lord with my whole heart, in the assembly of the upright and in the congregation" (Psa. 111:1)
- "I will praise You with uprightness of heart, when I learn Your righteous judgments" (Psa. 119:7)

Now is the time to return again… to worship the Lord in the beauty of His majesty… warts, scars and all …

> "To console those who mourn in Zion, to give them beauty for ashes, the oil of joy for mourning, the garment of praise for the spirit of heaviness; that they may be called trees of righteousness, the planting of the Lord, that He may be glorified." (Isa. 61:3).

… in this, God is glorified! In this, God is exalted in our weakness!

It's all about Jesus… and God gets the glory! Amen.

Man's soul is what remains before and after good or evil spirits are inhabited within him.

> "But you have come to Mount Zion and to the city of the living God, the heavenly Jerusalem, to an innumerable company of angels, [23] to the general assembly and church of the firstborn who are registered in heaven, to God the Judge of all, **_to the spirits of just men made perfect_**, [24] to Jesus the Mediator of the new covenant, and to the blood of sprinkling that speaks better things than that of Abel" (Heb. 12:22-24)

Make Me Thy Instrument

During the first 28 years of my life on earth, I was a Roman

Catholic. Very early in my faith journey, this prayer by Saint Francis had an enormous impact on me and was hung by me in every bedroom I slept in (and there were a great many). I hope it influences you as much as it did me – and continues to do so even now.

"Lord, make me an instrument of thy peace.
Where there is hatred, let me sow love;
Where there is injury, pardon;
Where there is doubt, faith;
Where there is despair, hope;
Where there is darkness, light;
Where there is sadness, joy.

"O Divine Master, grant that I may not so much seek
To be consoled as to console,
To be understood as to understand,
To be loved as to love;
For it is in giving that we receive;
It is in pardoning that we are pardoned;
It is in dying to self that we are born to eternal life." (Prayer of Saint Francis)

To paraphrase what Jesus taught: it is easy to do good to those who are good to you, and likewise, it is easy to do evil (or goodlessness) toward others who do evil to you; "And if you do good to those who do good to you, what credit is that to you? For even sinners do the same" (Luke 6:33)… **But I say to you, do good to those that do evil toward you:** "Love your enemies, bless those who curse you, do good to those who hate you, and pray for those who spitefully use you and persecute you" (Matt. 5:44)… "love your enemies, do good, and lend, hoping for nothing in return; and your reward will be great (Luke 6:35) … that you may be sons of your Father in heaven" (i.e. your true spiritual Father who is in Heaven; Matt. 5:45).

You 'were' sons of God in Heaven that were sent to do a job on earth as sons of man whereby you are being tested and proofed during your probation to determine whether you shall return home "again" as sons of God – or not.

> "Blessed be the God and Father of our Lord Jesus Christ, who according to His abundant mercy **has begotten us again** [*anagennao*-313-literally: birthed again a second time] to a living hope through the resurrection of Jesus Christ from the dead" (1 Pet. 1:3).

> It's all about Jesus – and God gets the glory! Amen,

Chapter 2: The Spirit Within Us

Now that we understand how we were constructed by the Lord as soul with a spirit within a body, we need to perceive our spirit as an instrument the Lord gave to us to assist the instrumentality of our soul (mind and heart) for these reasons:

- Through which the Lord saves our soul
- Through which we serve the Lord
- Through which the Lord saves other souls alive

The spirit within us is "the light of the world" which was given to us as a lamp from the Lord to disperse the darkness upon the earth – and to turn the reins of man (our mind) toward Him. "This little light of mine" as the children's Sunday school song goes is perhaps the most formidable weapon upon this planet. The spirit within us "receives" the things of God as we host God's presence in us, and then "releases" the atmosphere of heaven through us wherever we go, and thus... we are effecting a regime change upon this world from darkness to light.

"You are not your own!" Everyone on this planet has a purpose according to God's plan to transition this planet from darkness to light, from evil to good, and from error to truth. "Thy kingdom come, Thy will be done, on earth as it is in heaven" is an open invitation by Jesus to become a participant of the Lord's salvation for other men – and the earth itself. We were created for the earth... and the earth was created for us... and we were created in oneness with oneness in the Spirit to love one another. This is the gift of God. Jesus is the Love of God who revealed Himself and visited this earth to redeem all men – and redeem the earth (John 1:29).

Your spirit – that is partnered with the Holy Spirit – is the best friend your soul has on this planet! Your flesh – that is partnered with the things of this world – is your worst enemy (James 4:4; Rom. 8:7).

Apart from Christ, we are nothing. Apart from the Spirit, we are dead (John 6:63).

Everyone on earth is strengthened through their spirit by the Spirit of God… regardless whether they understand this point or not. The power to animate the life of the body comes to us by the Spirit through our spirit. "The Spirit is life" (Rom. 8:10). Any strength we have comes by being strengthened from above – by the Spirit.

> "The Lord is my strength and my shield; my heart trusted in Him, and I am helped; therefore my heart greatly rejoices, and with my song I will praise Him" (Psa. 28:7).

We get life from the Spirit, we get power from the Spirit, we get strength from the Spirit, and we get these things through our spirit by the Spirit. The spirit is the Lord's instrument for man – through which power and life are given to us; and in the resurrection – it is by the Spirit that our soul is raised to newness of life.

The significance of the Spirit's initial and sustained impact upon our life to help us and keep us in "life" apart from death – is substantial, indeed. The Helper is our helper in our time of need, He is our Intercessor when we do not have words enough to pray, He is our Guide to direct our steps, He is our Tutor to teach us how to live like children of God, He is our Encourager when times get tough, and He is our Strengthener in our weakness. He is our Strong Tower when we are under attack, He is our Vanguard when we are being pursued, He is the Light that illuminates our path when we go through periods of darkness, He is our Shield to protect us from the weapons of the enemy. Literally, all that we need to endure, continue and persevere in faith is given to us by the Lord through His Holy Spirit. All things – are from the Lord above – by His Spirit – through our spirit.

You are not alone! The Paraclete of/from God is alongside you every moment of every day.

The problem, it seems, is that some of us continue to think of God's presence as residing in the outer cosmos, and when we cannot feel His presence, we assume (erringly) that God has left us or abandoned us. Even as I write these words, I know and deeply understand the truth that has been revealed to me, and I know that Jesus and the Father abide in me, but the nearness of God to me at times (even now in this moment) is not tangible enough to help me process the constraints of the dire situation that I am in. I am broke, homeless, placeless, writing these missives with a ten year old laptop held together by screws in public libraries and parking lots while living in a 19 year old minivan with a bad transmission and faulty brake system. Consider the reasons why you have a bathroom... and what homeless persons do without one. However, during some weeks, I help anywhere from 6-20 people with food, transportation, meals, small amounts of cash and plenty of hugs with the love of Christ to people I meet along this journey, as well as volunteering at a local Florida church on Thursday morning with a team of 20-30 people to help distribute 5-6,000 pounds of food weekly to needy families in the community, but... no one in the past 20 months has asked me, "What can I do to help you?" They have heard some of my testimony and seen my life in action and they know I live in a minivan and that I am writing under a commission given by Jesus as "His writer" and yet... only one person has asked me if I need help. My answer to him was: "I just want to sleep flat." If you have ever felt alone, then know this ... that I also feel as alone as you in this moment... and Jesus also felt this way and He understands your (our) pain and despair. Consider this: Jesus is Lord, Jesus is God of the Israelites and He came to His own people to save them and show them the way of escape, but they not only treated Him as a social outcast, they also treated Him with scorn and contempt, heaping dishonor and false accusations against Him, and every time He opened His mouth, the religious elite were searching for something and plotting against Him to find some "legal" way to murder Him. Jesus said of Himself, "The Son of Man has nowhere to lay His head," because He was living within a place amongst His people that offered no place or sanctuary for Him to dwell. Jesus created the heavens, the worlds, the nations, the governments, the places with boundaries, the people dwelling in those places, the resources those people needed to dwell and survive, and created even time itself, and yet... no place was found for Him to dwell. Selah. And yet, it is very hard for me (personally) to reconcile this matter: the Lord commissioned me to write and the Spirit speaks to me every day and yet no one has been nudged by the Spirit to ask me if I need assistance. It is easier for me to assume I am in error than to contemplate an accusation against hundreds of people I've encountered in 23 months while living on the road that have turned a deaf ear to the Spirit's nudging to help me – or – to bring an accusation against the Lord for not even getting crumbs that fall from the Master's table. The Lord is my Provider and my Sustainer! My provision *and* my hope come from the Lord of Heaven and Earth. The only thing that I can say in this moment, from the depth of my spirit is:

I WILL NOT FEAR!!!

Nor will I be dismayed! Nor deterred! Nor terrorized! Nor victimized! Nor sidetracked! Nor intimidated by rejection! Nor alienated by family! Not even death itself has any power to prevent me from doing what the Lord has called me to do... neither principalities, powers, demons, unclean spirits, wicked people, fallen angels, nor Slewfoot himself can prevent me from accomplishing the commission given to me. My strength and power come from the Lord – by His Spirit – through my spirit – to accomplish in me everything He has purposed for me.

You are not alone! You are part of His plan; He is not part of yours.

His purposes for every one of us are wonderful, and if there comes a day when it seems you lack the strength and power to take one more step, let me assure you... you are the Lord's beloved... and your next step and breath have already been ordered by the Lord. Take another step! Even when you get to the end of your journey or you've hit the wall and cannot get up, the Lord is abiding within you and His Spirit is dwelling within you. My private journaling the past 23 months is a testimony of the spirit that was given to me by the Lord (i.e. not humanly manufactured determination or engineered will) to keep going in the face of all adversity, heat, cold, rain, wild animals, many needs, most especially... the deep desire to be able to share this truth and revelation _with anyone_ with spiritual ears and grace to hear. Sympathy (born of mercy) is a rare and precious jewel in this world.

"Whatsoever you do" can only be accomplished when we ask one another – whatsoever do you need?

Perhaps this season will get better... or maybe not. Perhaps I am going through this valley to experience what most ministers are insulated from in order that I may write about it and encourage a multitude of others by it. If you somehow misconstrued this message to be self-pity, then perhaps the previous chapter about mercy failed to hit the intended spot in your heart. Not to worry, though, a deeper lesson on mercy appears in a future chapter.

Perhaps this season is not a season at all. This journey may be a designated path the Lord has put me upon that keeps going and going doing odd jobs surviving on about $4,000 a year (equal to one middle-class tithe). Let me ask you: do I have a right to receive provision from the church? Do I have a right to request assistance? Is my commission from the Lord Jesus any less vital to the revival or reformation of the church than a pastor, priest, evangelist or a missionary? Do not muzzle the non-traditional ox as it treads out non-institutional grain. In many respects, it seems, my walk is no less significant or different than the Apostle Paul's message of grace within the legalistic worlds of Judaism and Roman occupation. Therefore, I gladly rejoice in my sufferings so that Jesus gets the glory and the preeminence! I am not a victim! I am His disciple... He is my Lord and Master... and His victory resides in me. I desire never to write on this matter again.

To all, I say: PERSEVERE! Continue with patient endurance. Live according to the Spirit. Little or much are relative terms. Always remember...

The Lord is with you!

Strengthened In Our Spirit

> "But those who wait on the Lord Shall renew their strength; they shall mount up with wings like eagles, they shall run and not be weary, they shall walk and not faint" (Isa. 40:31).

We are strengthened in our spirit – by the Spirit – and then our spirit strengthens our soul and body. 'Digging deep to get more' is how some athletic trainers describe tapping into reserve power, stamina, energy, fortitude, and determination[88] beyond the physical properties of the human body; they are tapping into a reservoir of strength within their spirit. The same is true with believers being trained in righteousness; we must continue to persevere with patient endurance to strive toward the narrow gate. There are days when I simply do not have it in me to take one more step, and then the spirit within me helps me in my weakness to strengthen me which compels me to press onward to my high calling of God in Christ Jesus. Stopping is not an option! Disobedience is not an option. If you truly understand the prize that waits for you at the end of your sojourn, then don't stop! These light and momentary tribulations that endlessly come against you every waking moment – are perfecting the work of God to build His character within you – so that you may receive your reward. Don't lose sight of the big picture!

> Jesus told Paul… "My strength is made perfect in weakness" (2 Cor. 12:9).

Literally: My *dunamis* (miraculous power) in *astheneia* weakness (i.e. within the body of flesh) is *perfected* (divine character consummated and completely accomplished in us according to grace wherein Christ's character has been fully and perfectly formed in us).

---

[88] Determination is also being faithful in doing small things numerous times until something big happens.

"The joy of the Lord is your strength" (Neh. 8:10).

The Spirit of the Lord started the process of salvation, sanctification and transformation in you and He will continue to strengthen you through your spirit so that you may be fully prepared, equipped and mature to accomplish every good work the Lord predestined for you. Throughout this process of renewal and newness, it is God doing it – in you, with you, to you, through you and for you. I've stated this many times: stop striving to do it – just be – and let the Lord accomplish it. It is for His glory, not ours, that we have surrendered our lives and our will in service to Him. Let go – and let Jesus be God through you.

>It's all about Jesus – and God gets the glory!

What are the elements which the Spirit supplants within our spirit that not only strengthens us but also provides the miraculous power we need to do the will of God and save other souls?

> "For God has not given us a spirit of fear, but of power and of love and of a sound mind" (2 Tim. 1:7).

This scripture is magnificent once we fully comprehend the message of faith and life that liberates us by the Spirit of Truth. Fear is faith in reverse. Fear is one of the primary weapons used by all enemies of truth. Fear is the weapon our enemy continually uses against us to thwart our mission and commission – whereby faith in Christ is intended to conquer all fear – and this, then, is how the Spirit of God is able to change us (and this world) by three things:

> Power!!!   Love!!!   Sound mind!!!

The Sound Mind!!!

The Spirit does not start with power and then love to produce a sound mind. Developing a sound mind is the Spirit's starting point for us in the transformation process as the single-most important element we need in order to thoroughly understand and comprehend truth in order for us to become believers, converts and then disciples of Jesus.[89] We live in a crazy world and the war between God and Satan is quite literally being waged within the mind of man for allegiance to one kingdom or the other. Truth is under attack! When we believe the lies of the enemy, the truth of God is compromised within our mind by irrational thoughts which we rationalize as truth which results in stinking-thinking. Within my own family, there are members that have justified abortion as a "choice" using amoral relativistic ideas that are inherently demonic in origin. They go to church on Sunday, but the god of this world has corrupted their thought process to embrace liberal views of "this world" that are unbiblical lies… and no one can convince them otherwise. Abortion is evil. Our life belongs to God. Our body belongs to God (1 Cor. 6:20). The unborn child belongs to God! Abortion is murder. These facts are truths from God.

A sound mind will diligently seek truth, it will not believe lies, neither will it allow fear or worry to take root and become manifest in their life. A sound mind requires truth to be built upon truth which is found in the Bible in order to come against and discredit lies. The Spirit is our Tutor who instructs us in truth, trains us in righteousness and proofs us to confirm the truth is operational within us. Truth is what this world needs more than anything, but "this world" of deception, lies and deceit will attack truth and corrupt many minds with depravity and even mental illness so that these persons never come to faith with a sound mind. Today, many pharmaceuticals and illegal drugs often (not always) become tools by the enemy to negatively alter the mind's ability to hear and receive truth. Apart from sound truth believed within a sound mind under the tutoring of the Spirit, not even love will be honored and respected.

> "And because lawlessness will abound, the love of many will grow cold" (Matt. 24:12).

---

[89] An entire book "Understand" was commissioned by the Lord to this topic: hear, <u>understand</u> – and obey.

Love is being corrupted by this world – which allows fear to take over which then robs the Lord's beloved of joy and peace.

> "There is no fear in love; but **_perfect love casts out fear_**, because fear involves torment. But he who fears has not been made perfect in love" (1 John 4:18).

Establishing a "sound mind" in believers is an enormous undertaking by the Spirit of Truth because many lies and deceptive doctrines have been promulgated by the "spirit of religion" to keep us "under control" in bondage to lies within the kingdom of darkness. The Spirit must sanctify us and renew our mind so that we know the truth before we are trained to think like Jesus and have "the mind of Christ."

The 'sound' mind '*sophronismos*' (4995) means "discipline; literally, this word means saving (*sozo*) the mind (*phren*) through admonishing and calling to soundness of mind and to <u>self-control</u>."[90] Knowing the truth is not enough; being trained in righteousness to live according to the truth as a disciple will result in a sound mind that is obedient to God – and therefore this mind will exercise self control.

Discipline for the mind (sophronismos) will produce (mathetes-3101) disciples for the Lord.

Self-control wherein the mind (soul) subordinates the body in conformity to the truth – will never compromise the truth in order to continue in sexual perversion. A body that remains in bondage to perversion and sexual sin by believing lies of the enemy happens when a person – deceived by lies – converts a sound mind into a reprobate '*adokimos*-96' mind. The NIV translates '*adokimos*' as depraved (morally corrupt, wicked, perverted), but is literally: "unapproved, rejected; by implication worthless"[91] as

---

[90] Strong's Concordance.
[91] IBID.

something *not passing* the test especially in regard to faith (Titus 1:16).

The sound mind sent on probation must not become reprobate: disqualified by sexual perversion!

The long list of reprobate actions produced by immoral character flaws is enumerated in Rom. 1:29-31 which renders reprobate persons "undiscerning, untrustworthy, unloving, unforgiving, unmerciful." These persons are regarded by the Lord *as disqualified*, as being hostile to grace because they 'failed the test' to subordinate their body, wherein their salt has become insidiously worthless… as something to be cast out (castaway) and trampled underfoot. Can the Lord still redeem and deliver them? Absolutely – yet only by a radical work of grace and repentance to bring them into alignment with the truth when they yield their sovereignty to Jesus That is, after all, what the test is all about! We are on probation in a classroom called earth to test us and proof us as disciplined, qualified ones operating according to the truth – in alignment with the sovereignty of King Jesus – and are worthy of salvation! Our body must become subordinate to our soul and spirit… *and* the will of the Lord… or else we disqualify ourselves as unworthy of life eternal.

> "But I discipline my body and bring it into subjection, lest, when I have preached to others, I myself should become disqualified" (1 Cor. 9:27).

Quite literally, this text reads beginning with verse 26b:

"So I box (4438) as not beating air; but I subordinate (*hupopiazo*-5299- treat severely; keep under control) my body and lead it as a slave (*doulagogeo*-1396-'to bring into bondage")[92] lest to others having preached – I may become disqualified (*adokimos*).

How is Paul preventing himself from being disqualified? He will "keep under" (subordinate) his body – under the subjection of the

---

[92] IBID.

sound mind to keep from becoming reprobate. Paul is metaphorically boxing himself '*hupopaizo*' (*hupo*-under and *ops*-eye) which literally means "to strike under the eye" (i.e. to give a black eye) in order to subordinate his body under the control of his soul (mind) and spirit. The Apostle Paul is not aimlessly boxing air ... he is buffeting his body by metaphorically giving himself a black eye and hitting his intended mark (to prevent him from looking at and focusing on morally offensive things) in order to keep his body from trespassing into sin. Using today's vernacular: watch yourself like a hawk! By bringing our body into bondage (submission to our soul and the spirit), we are able to lead (govern) this body of death as a slave... by God's grace with truth...so our soul may continue to live eternally.

The gift of the Spirit includes self control – and for good reason! The fruit (singular) produced by the Spirit... is love. Love is the fruit whereby all the other grace attributes of God are being manifested in us, by us and through us.

> "But the fruit of the Spirit is love, joy, peace, longsuffering, kindness, goodness, faithfulness, [23] gentleness, <u>self-control</u>. Against such there is no law" (Gal. 5:22, 23).

Beloved saints of the Most High God, we must neither engage in sexual immorality nor practice sexual perversion. Period! Any person that cannot control their carnal passions has yet to understand the message of truth, the gospel of Jesus, what is at stake (the salvation of your soul), and the torment of hell for failure, and thus... these reprobate ones judge themselves unworthy and their names will erased from the Book of Life – unless they repent (Rev. 3:5).

How can the reprobate mind weakened by the flesh be overcome by the *energeia* power and *iscus* strength of your sound mind? You are able! Ask the Spirit to guide you into victory!

Do you perceive a consistent theme between the Lord's message

"If your eye is the problem, gouge it out" and Paul's personal solution "give yourself a black eye" to subordinate your body into submission? Let me remind you, the Lord's statement was sarcastic and Paul's statement is metaphoric because I don't want anyone reading these words to go around physically punching themselves in the face. The solution is "to spiritually discipline" your mind by allowing the Holy Spirit to flood your mind with truth and thus… live according to righteousness. The eye isn't the problem! The focus of our attention (mind) and object of our affection (heart) – is the problem – if it is not directed toward Jesus.

We are on probation and the reprobate mind will always be in conflict with a sound mind because it rejects God's truth and refuses to live according to the truth. Our body is an instrument the Lord gave us to either sanctify us – or disqualify us – from life eternal.

Truth is under attack! Truth is not intimidated by fear – because perfect love casts out fear.

Love!!!

Love is the answer. A sound mind will always live according to love. Love is one of the main elements which prove the truth of God is resident and operational within a sound mind which also authenticates you are a follower of Jesus Christ. If you have not love, then you have not the knowledge of God in you. If you claim this knowledge but have not love, then you are a liar.

> "And though I have the gift of prophecy, and understand all mysteries and all knowledge, and though I have all faith, so that I could remove mountains, but *have not love, I am nothing*" (1 Cor. 13:2).

> "Let all that you do be done with love" (1 Cor. 16:14).

> "We know that we have passed from death to life, because we love the brethren. He who does not love his brother abides in death" (1 John 3:14).

Love is a power (a spiritual force) that when fully implemented and operational within our soul, is able to overcome the weakness of our flesh, withstand the temptations of the devil and negate the victory of death itself.

Love is the name of the power within us that enables us to live on earth, as spirit directed men and women, in the similitude of Christ. Love produces joy and peace; loveless people produce anger, hatred, strife and envy.

Love is not good, per se… love is the source of all goodness and is the source through which all Godly attributes, characters, attitudes and grace gifts are manifested within us so they can flow through us.

Love to our spirit is like oxygen to our body. Inhale… then release it. Loving is like breathing; when we cease to love, we begin to die.

Love is the power that enables us to live according to humility and meekness that exalts God as preeminent in our life and considers the needs of others ahead of self.

Love is the fullness of God's grace manifested by men toward one another.

Jesus is the Love of God manifested unto us – as our heavenly example – to save us from this loveless and merciless world and the condemnation of our soul.

God is Love – and we beheld His person. Thank you, Jesus.

> "Since you have purified your souls in obeying the truth through the Spirit in sincere love of the

> brethren, love one another fervently with a pure heart" (1 Pet. 1:22).
>
> "But above all these things put on love, which is the bond of perfection" (Col. 3:14).
>
> "And now abide faith, hope, love, these three; but the greatest of these is love" (1 Cor. 13:13).

Love prevails. Love conquers all. Jesus said:

> "As the Father loved Me, I also have loved you; **abide in My love**" (John 15:9).

And there are six types of power, yet the greatest of these is love

Power!!!

Once love is operational within our sound mind, we are now, by God's grace, able to do exceedingly and abundantly more than we might think, perceive or imagine… according to the power of the Spirit that works in us.

> "Now to Him who is able to do exceedingly abundantly above all that we ask or think, according to the power [*dunamis*] that works [operates] in us" (Eph. 3:20).

God will not make His '*dunamis*' (1411) power operational within us until the other two elements (sound mind and love) have been perfected in us… because we will use this power selfishly to satisfy our personal agenda. All power belongs to God Almighty. God does not have all power, per se… God *is* all power! God is Almighty! Jesus is Lord God Almighty! Any power we have comes to us from God by His Spirit.

The power of God manifested through us (our spirit) is the main element the Apostle Paul mentioned repeatedly as a sign against unbelief in this world.

> "And my speech and my preaching were not with persuasive words of human wisdom, but in demonstration of the Spirit and of power [1411]" (1 Cor. 2:4).

> "For our gospel did not come to you *in word only*, but also in power, and in the Holy Spirit and in much assurance, as you know what kind of men we were among you for your sake" (1 Thess. 1:5).

> "For the kingdom of God is not *in word* [only] but in power [1411]" (1 Cor. 4:20).

The power of God manifested through men must not to be confused with manufactured or engineered power from out of the human spirit (which all men are able to do), which uses God's power given to all of us yet for worldly reasons. The power of God being manifested by the Spirit of God <u>*will give all glory unto God*</u> who releases this power through men. When God's '*dunamis*' miraculous power is manifested, people are amazed and oftentimes filled with wonder as miracles happen despite their belief in a worldly system that is contrary to the ways of God, and yet... this is still not enough for some hard-hearted people to believe in Jesus as Lord of all.

> "This is the word of the Lord to Zerubbabel: 'Not by [human] might nor by [human] power, but by My Spirit,' Says the Lord of hosts" (Zech. 4:6).

God wants us to understand the nature by which we were created in order to implement His destiny (His predestined purpose and commission) for every one of us. The spirit within us is the divine nature that Peter talked about (2 Peter 1:4) that God strengthens with His power (v.1:3) by His Spirit to accomplish His purposes on earth, yet the flesh was also placed upon us for another reason we mentioned previously: to sanctify us. Our enemy, Satan, the devil, is constantly bombarding us and waging war against us through our members (our flesh where sin resides) in order to thwart the revelation of Christ becoming manifest through us. Christ is already "in you all" and waits patiently for every one of us to surrender our total allegiance to Him whereby "we" get off the throne of our heart and exalt Him upon it... as Lord God Almighty.

It is the spirit within us that enables our soul to be who we were originally created to be: mighty warriors, sons, daughters, and fellow heirs of the kingdom. The spirit within us is one key to comprehending our reason for being on earth to begin with – and for this reason we need to remember... and get back... to being about our Father's business.

"While Jesus resided in the flesh, He did everything as "soul with spirit" abiding in human flesh. The miracles that Jesus performed were not done in the (*kratos*) power of His Divinity, but through the (*dunamis*) empowering of the Holy Spirit partnered with the spirit within Him."[93]

And from that time, Jesus walked in the "power [*dunamis*] of the Spirit" (Luke 4:1, 14).

"This is one of the most important points of this book: Jesus operated and performed all His miracles through His spirit (small 's') within Him to show us that we, also, can do the same things He did – and even more so. How can this be possible? Jesus came to show us "the way" as spiritual beings living with the power of God flowing through us – as gateways and conduits for divine power flowing through our divine nature (spirit). This is who, what and why we were created, but we tripped over the threshold of sin and then we forgot about the image made manifest in us."

> "Grace and peace be multiplied to you in the knowledge of God and of Jesus our Lord, ³ **as His divine power** [1411] **has given to us all things** that pertain to life and godliness, through the knowledge of Him who called us by glory and virtue, ⁴ by

---

[93] Excerpt copied from "Image" section titled: "In The Spirit, Jesus Lived."

which have been given to us exceedingly great and precious promises, that ***through these you may be partakers of the divine nature***, having escaped the corruption that is in the world through lust" (2 Peter 1:2-4).

God's divine 'dunamis' power was given to us so we may be partakers of the divine nature and operate in 'exousia' authority to have dominion and thereby establish His kingdom on earth.

That message needs to reverberate over and over until our mind has been transformed by the Spirit's truth and we thoroughly comprehend it whereby we adopt it as our divine authorization to act with delegated authority (*exousia*) as New Earth ambassadors in the name of Christ Jesus.

There are several Greek words translated 'power' that we must examine:[94]

- *Dunamis* (1411) "expresses power, natural ability, general and inherent"
- *Energeia* (1753) "denotes working power in exercise, operational power"
- *Exousia* (1849) "is primarily liberty in action, then authority – either as delegated power or as unrestrained, arbitrary power"
- *Iscus* (2479) "expresses strength, power, (especially physical) as an endowment"
- *Kratos* (2904) "means might, relative and manifested power – chiefly of God"

"*Kratos* "force, strength, might," more specifically "manifested power" is derived from a root word which means "to perfect, to complete" and signifies ***dominion***."[95] '*Kratos*' is the power of dominion: it is the term used of God's dominion in doxologies and

---

[94] Terms and definitions from Strong's Concordance on kratos-2904.
[95] IBID.

implies mighty power belonging chiefly to God – and those to whom He delegates this power.

'*Exousia*' is delegated authority with power to act and:

A) Is oftentimes used about Jesus and by Jesus:

- "But that you may know that the Son of Man has power [*exousia*] on earth to forgive sins"—then He said to the paralytic, "Arise, take up your bed, and go to your house" (Matt. 9:6)
- "And Jesus came and spoke to them, saying, "All authority [*exousia*] has been given to Me in heaven and on earth" (Matt. 28:18)

B) Is used of disciples by Jesus:

- "Then He appointed twelve, that they might be with Him and that He might send them out to preach, [15] and to have power [*exousia*] to heal sicknesses and to cast out demons" (Mark 3:14, 15)
- "And He called the twelve to Himself, and began to send them out two by two, and gave them power [*exousia*] over unclean spirits" (Mark 6:7)

C) And more significantly, is used by Jesus to describe those who operate as His disciples:

- "But as many as received Him, to them He gave the right [*exousia*; power-KJV] to become children of God, to those who believe in His name" (John 1:12)

D) And finally, the transfer of Satan's power and dominion by Jesus to the Lord's disciples – whereby they should have delegated '*exousia*' authority with delegated '*dunamis*' power to exercise dominion over nations – and Satan's kingdom. Adam and Eve delivered this authority to Satan in the Garden, then Jesus got it back and then He returned it to His disciples. Follow carefully these scriptures in sequence:

- "And the devil said to Him [Jesus], "All this authority [*exousia*] I will give You, and their glory; *for this has been delivered to me*, and I give it to whomever I wish" (Luke 4:6)
- "Behold, I give you the authority [*exousia*] to trample on serpents and scorpions, and over all the power of the enemy, and nothing shall by any means hurt you" (Luke 10:19)
- "And he who overcomes, and keeps My works until the end, to him I will give power [*exousia*] over the nations" (Rev. 2:26)

The operation of God's delegated authority with power was always purposed for the sons of men (host of earth) as His original plan for man: "Let them have dominion over the earth" (Gen. 1:26), but Satan deceived Adam and Eve to "deliver" this authority and their glory to him in the Garden. Jesus came to reset the spiritual timeline and restore the kingdom of heaven and earth by recovering all delegated *exousia* authority and dominion from Satan and returning this authority back to the host of earth (sons of men who are being sanctified by faith in Jesus to become disciples and sons of God – again).

This transfer of power into the hands of His disciples originated before Christ's resurrection (Mark 3:15) whereby this point is highly significant: Jesus did not need to die in order to recover it. Jesus died on the cross in order to fulfill "all" Old Covenant obligations and render the sacrificial system obsolete! (Hebrews 8) [96] Jesus is Lord of Heaven and Earth and He (being God always

---

[96] Jesus is the Son of God who came to earth as the Perfect Man to offer Himself as the Lamb of God to satisfy fully all the requirements of the sacrificial system and, thus therefore, rendered the sacrificial system – obsolete. So, if you have heard these words during the Catholic Mass: "May the Lord accept this <u>sacrifice</u> from your hands, to the praise and glory of His name, for our good, and the good

and eternal) had all authority, power *and* dominion the entire time He was on earth, yet He never operated from this position in order to teach us how to become like Him as New Covenant sons and daughters of righteousness, according to grace and truth, that operate under His delegated authority and power (dominion) to govern the nations. This is the New Earth Doctrine that was instituted by Christ Himself so as to authorize His disciples with *exousia* authority and with *dunamis* power – to have *kratos* dominion on earth – against whom not even death itself has any power over.

Why this has yet to occur is a question for which the institutional church must give an account.

The power of God was made manifest through our Lord and Savior, Jesus Christ, so that we who are called according to His purpose should have power and authority over the works of the enemy and, likewise, the sons of lawlessness. Jesus intentionally purposed that we imitate His example:

> "Then they were all amazed and spoke among themselves, saying, "What a word this is! For with authority [*exousia*-1849] and power [*dunamis*-1411] He [Jesus] commands the unclean spirits, and they come out" (Luke 4:36).

> "Behold, I give you the authority [*exousia*] to trample on serpents and scorpions, and over all the [*dunamis*] power of the enemy, and nothing shall by any means hurt you" (Luke 10:19).

We are often amazed when *dunamis* miraculous power is manifested through men, yet when *kratos* divine power in the

---

of all His church" then I suggest you leave the place that continues to offer sacrifices to a religious sacrificial system that A) Jesus rendered obsolete by His sacrificial death as the consummate Lamb of God on the cross, and B) has been declared hostile to the grace and truth of Jesus Christ. Don't walk… run to the truth!

similitude of Christ (that is aligned with the manifold mission of Christ and His dominion) is manifested through the spirit of ordinary men by the Spirit of God, this will cause the world to wonder... whereby two things will happen: either they will glorify God and praise Him – or they will become more violent and hostile to the sovereignty and supremacy of King Jesus – KING OF KINGS AND LORD OF LORDS. (Rev. 19:16)

> "Inasmuch then as the children have partaken of flesh and blood, He Himself likewise shared in the same, that through death He might destroy him who had the power [*kratos*-dominion] of death, that is, the devil, [15] and release those who through fear of death were all their lifetime subject to bondage" (Heb. 2:14, 15).

Jesus recovered *exousia* authority and the power (dominion) of death[97] from Satan and then He granted His authority to His disciples with supernatural power at Pentecost; and this same *exousia* authority with *dunamis* power by the Holy Spirit is available to everyone today – unto all who are called according to His name through faith in Christ Jesus, may exercise dominion in the earth... even to your children's children, but to Satan... only *dunamis* power remains.

> "... and you shall receive the gift of the Holy Spirit. [39] For the promise is to you and to your children, and to all who are afar off, as many as the Lord our God will call" (Acts 2:38, 39).

This study on power brings up an interesting point: what would you do if you had unlimited power and authority to do whatever

---

[97] The dominion of death is the penalty we earn when we voluntarily entered into sin. "In the day that you eat of it you shall surely die" (Gen. 2:17) and thus we became captives of death, but according to grace through faith in Christ, we were delivered from the consequence of our actions (spiritual death) and the place called "Death" (Rev. 1:18), having passed "from death to life" to become new spiritual creatures according to faith.

you wanted? Many dictators, tyrants and despots throughout human history have used this power against other human beings with impunity, but I ask you: what would you do? Would you follow their worldly example to satisfy selfish ambitions or would you attempt a moral and noble means of using your authority? WWJD!

Jesus restored this authority to us so that we should use it to have dominion and establish His dominion in the earth, and this was the message Jesus spoke to the Apostle Paul:

> "So I said, 'Who are You, Lord?' And He said, 'I am Jesus, whom you are persecuting. [16] But rise and stand on your feet; for I have appeared to you for this purpose, to make you a minister and a witness both of the things which you have seen and of the things which I will yet reveal to you. [17] I will deliver you from the Jewish people, as well as from the Gentiles, to whom I now send you, [18] to open their eyes, ***in order to turn them from darkness to light, and from the power [exousia-1849] of Satan to God***, that they may receive forgiveness of sins and an inheritance among those who are sanctified by faith in Me'" (Acts 26:15-18).

Now, consider the fact that Jesus is God Almighty and He had all authority and power in heaven *and* on earth to do whatever He purposed to do – and yet – He offered His life as a ransom for many! Jesus is God Almighty, but Jesus did not operate out of His Own authority and Divine Nature to exercise His power and authority and dominion during His time on earth... which becomes an extraordinary and unparalleled example regarding how we were intended to use the authority and power that Jesus delegates to us in order to exercise His dominion (not ours) over the earth. WWJD! Jesus came to reveal the truth – and set captives free. Go and do likewise!

All authority, power, strength, majesty, glory and dominion belong to Jesus. He didn't earn these things as a reward for living a sinless life and dying on the cross for our sins, as some of our doctrines teach: these have always belonged to Jesus. And yet, Jesus is willing to partner and "go shares" with us regarding His things.

We were given a spirit in order to be partakers of the divine nature and we have been granted (not given) delegated '*exousia*' authority and '*dunamis*' power so we can operate as His representatives; however, Jesus' desire is for us to operate as disciples under His authority to establish His '*kratos*' "dominion of life" as His delegates, ambassadors, magistrates, and mighty warriors against the kingdom of darkness and dominion of death that exalts itself against God's kingdom – and thus we become more than just partners with Christ, we become partakers of the divine nature – here and now! The covenant that we entered into, through faith in Christ to become His disciples, establishes us as rightful heirs of the kingdom – here and now. Wow!

Your nature is more incredible than our doctrines indicate.

Why do you suppose this has not happened yet? The simplest answer is this: the spirit of religion has hoodwinked the church into accepting a less-than understanding of Jesus and a less-than gospel that minimizes the message of grace, truth, freedom, liberty and power – that Christ initiated and established through His disciples – by His Spirit. The spirit of religion seeks to control men – period! The Lord's delegated authority with *dunamis* power made available to disciples is being held hostage by a fear-based institution. The control of men begins by negating the teachings by Jesus, hearing the voice of the Holy Spirit, then they negate the training of disciples, then men begin to trust the words and doctrines of men – then men trust other men rather than trusting Jesus. An entire "alternate reality" in the church was created by the enemy in order to keep sons and daughters of the King enslaved in darkness and captives in the dominion of sin and death by one simple trick: doubt the truth. Then create fear and uncertainty. Then be tempted to act independently of God. Thus, the power of God has been taken hostage by institutional fear.

For this reason the Spirit continues the restoration of the kingdom by the sanctification and renewal of our mind to establish a new base point called: the sound mind. Our mind must be transformed to think a certain way (according to the truth) so we act a certain way (according to righteousness) that is consistent with the kingdom of God which is why we need "the mind of Christ." Jesus wants to partner the governance of the earth with us by using His power and authority that initially He delegated to disciples – as His delegates, representatives, ambassadors, magistrates and rulers that operate under His authority as KING OF KINGS AND LORD OF LORDS. We are disciples of the Most High God, Jesus Christ!

Jesus wants us to act – but act and govern <u>only</u> under His authority and under His command.

Governance is the authority to act with delegated power. The authority to rule and govern the earth has already been delegated to men which God intended be used for good according to His purposes, but men deceived by Satan have used this authority for evil intent.

> "Let every soul be subject to the governing authorities. For there is no authority except from God, and the authorities that exist are appointed by God" (Rom. 13:1).

It's important to note: God not only wants you to partner with Him, He needs your partnership to accomplish His purposes on the earth. You were created *intentionally* for this purpose!

Power In Operation

There are several types of power recorded in the scriptures (already mentioned above). Sleeping lions and hand grenades both have power within them, but this power is not in operation. Static means "power at rest" (it will always draw power no matter what you do), yet dynamic means "power in operation" which varies, for instance, depending upon what you are doing and how much power you need. An electrical outlet has dynamic power (ready for use when activated by a plug attached to an electric device) yet remains static (at rest) until acted upon by some energetic (*energeia*-1753) force or power for it to become dynamic (power in operation).

Our spirit operates along these same lines and within this context – everyone has '*dunamis*' static power within them as the general life-force that sustains the human organism upon us… but the *dunamis* power within us is for much more than just the operational needs of the body. The spirit within us acts like a plug that, when properly connected (in subordination) to the Lord's authority and His will, having been already connected to the Divine Power Outlet (Holy Spirit), enables us with power when we are activated for a particular function, service or commission.

Our commission accomplishes nothing unless the power of the Spirit becomes operational in us.

By faith, we initiate '*energeia*' power by an act of our will which converts "static *dunamis*" into "dynamic *dunamis*" whereby we are empowered in our spirit "by the Spirit" to do the Lord's will. It is the Lord's will *for everyone* that His dynamic power be transmitted through your conduit (i.e. the spirit within you) to perform divine service in His name. The interesting thing is: miraculous '*dunamis*' power resides within everyone. '*Dunamis*' is not restricted to designated miracle workers with special gifts or prophetic ordinations; '*dunamis*' power resides in everyone!

The static resting within you is waiting to be energetically activated into dynamic through you!

This is the working (energeia) of the Holy Spirit in you according to grace! All we need do is surrender our will to Jesus and yield operational control of our spirit so that the Divine Spark[98] can

---

[98] The Lord began my sojourn in 2012 by planting one thought in my mind: "Divine Spark." Five years later, this understanding about the power of God was given to me, and now I know Who the Divine Spark is.

transmit power through us – to the praise and glory of God. It is not we who are doing it; we are merely conduits and gateways for the power of God to become manifest in us and through us.

How does this happen? It begins by believing the truth, then meditating on it (deep thoughts that produce '*dianoia*' understanding – which is a thorough thinking through), and then…

…We must act upon it!
Declare it!

> "Now to Him who is able to do exceedingly abundantly above all that we ask or think, according to the power [*dunamis*] that works [*energeo*-1754] in us" (Eph. 3:20).

Just as faith is the energizer (*energeo*) of love (Gal. 5:9) and is the energizer that strengthens us with patience in suffering (2 Cor. 1:6), likewise, faith is the energizer (1754) of *dunamis* power that works in us to produce operational works through us – to the praise of God's glory.

Faith demands a verdict! Faith is not merely the simple, half-hearted belief in the truth, but rather, faith will manifest *dunamis* power that works operationally in you and through you! *Energeia* is the power that works "in us" that enables *dunamis* power to flow through us. Faith requires action! When we act upon God's truth, through faith, we are plugging our spirit into union with the Holy Spirit for the release of *dunamis* power in us and even perhaps *kratos* power through us.

> "But he who is joined [glued] to the Lord is one spirit with Him" (1 Cor. 6:17).

Stop for a moment and meditate on that scripture… until an epiphany happens in your mind.

Oneness with the Lord in oneness of the Spirit with our spirit is what the victorious life in newness is all about. The Lord Jesus is doing this in us and through us; we are His body, we are His hands and feet, and by grace we are joined to Him – and one Spirit with Him.

> "... and the peace of God, which surpasses all understanding, will guard your hearts and minds through Christ Jesus" (Phil. 4:7).

Again I say, faith is not what you believe, but acting according to what you believe. The energetic power that we need in order to activate *dunamis* power at rest within us – remains at rest until we apply '*energeia*' power by directing our will to focus entirely on Jesus and plugging into the Holy Spirit whereby '*energeia*' activates *dunamis* through our spirit by the Holy Spirit to energize our divine commission on earth with power.

The '*energeia*' power that we initiate by our soul through our spirit, as an act of our will, will perform a service or function, yet it must first be connected to whatever power source we select... either Divine or demonic. This aspect of who we are (as spiritual beings having a human experience) enables us to connect to the power supply of our choice according to free will. The scriptures indicate this "effectual working" can be accomplished – by God, by men and women aligned with Jesus, and by persons under the operational control of Satan in the kingdom of darkness. Let's examine the effectual working "by God" first...

> "... that the God of our Lord Jesus Christ, the Father of glory, may give to you the spirit of wisdom and revelation in the knowledge of Him, [18] the eyes of your understanding [*dianoia*-1271] being enlightened [5461]; that you may know what is the hope of His calling, what are the riches of the glory of His inheritance in the saints, [19] and what is the exceeding greatness of His power [*dunamis*-1411] toward us who believe, ***according to the***

> ***working*** [*energeia*-1753; operation, KJV] ***of His mighty power*** [*kratos*-2904] [20] which He worked [*energeo*-1754] in Christ when He raised Him from the dead and seated Him at His right hand in the heavenly places, [21] far above all principality and power [*exousia*-1849] and might and dominion [2963], and every name that is named, not only in this age but also in that which is to come" (Eph. 1:17-21).

This scripture by Paul is, in my opinion, the most Divinely inspired manifold text ever written to help us comprehend what we are to do, how we are to do it, why we are to do it – and what happens to us when we do it. The same *dunamis* power that God worked *energeia (operated, performed)* in Christ when He was raised from the dead – is already in us and available to us – whereby this power becomes operational (*energeia* – activated through faith) being energized by the indwelling Spirit "toward us who believe." Wow!!! But it gets better… God wants *kratos* "His mighty power" made operational (*energeo*) within us "which He worked in Christ when He raised Him from the dead," but regrettably, fear (rather than faith in the power of God) and unbelief has prevented this from happening. By grace, the resurrection ***and*** the *kratos* power of the resurrection is already in us (at rest) because Christ abides in us… which is waiting to be activated by the Holy Spirit. The days are already very close at hand when this truth shall become operational in New Earth disciples having been commissioned by greater grace for greater works, greater glory – and greater *kratos* power through them by the Divine Spark. Saints… God is waiting on us, so what on earth are we waiting for?

Paul goes on to elaborate on those concepts mentioned above:

- "To this end I also labor, striving according to His working [1753] which works [*energeo*-1754; to be active, operational] in me *mightily* [1722, 1411]" (Col. 1:29)[99]

---

[99] *En* (1722) "in; denotes a fixed position and (by implication) instrumentality, i.e. a relation of rest." Strong's.

- "of which I became a minister according to the gift of the grace of God given to me by the effective working [1753] of His power [*dunamis*-1411]" (Eph. 3:7)
- "from whom the whole body, joined and knit together by what every joint supplies, according to the effective working [1753] by which every part does its share, causes growth of the body for the edifying of itself in love" (Eph. 4:16)
- "who will transform [*metamorphoo*-3345] our lowly body that it may be conformed to His glorious body, according to the working [1753] by which He is able even to subdue all things to Himself" (Phil. 3:21)

Energeia is oftentimes initiated by the Holy Spirit to transform us into effective-working men and women into operational service to God, but *energeia* (or *energeo*-1754) can also be initiated by Satan to deceive many by sinful passions (Rom. 7:5), to produce works of lawlessness in us (2 Thess. 2:7), and by strong delusion to produce a working of error (v.2:11). Satan will also energize the "man of sin" (2 Thess. 2:3, 9; i.e. the man of lawlessness):

> "The coming of the lawless one is according to the working [*energeia*] of Satan, with all power [*dunamis*], signs, and lying wonders, [10] and with all unrighteous deception among those who perish, because they did not receive the love of the truth, that they might be saved. [11] And for this reason God will send them strong delusion, that they should believe the lie, [12] that they all may be condemned who did not believe the truth but had pleasure in unrighteousness" (2 Thess. 3:9-12).

> "And you He made alive, who were dead in trespasses and sins, [2] in which you once walked according to the course of this world, according to the prince of the power of the air, the spirit who now works [*energeo*] in the sons of disobedience,

> ³ among whom also we all once conducted ourselves in the lusts of our flesh, fulfilling the desires of the flesh and of the mind, and were by nature children of wrath, just as the others" (Eph. 2:1-3).

Saints of God, if we are not actively allowing the working of the Spirit to become operational within us (not just as faith abiding in us but as *dunamis* power becoming operational through us), we take a great risk in potential rejection of the truth to produce a working of error. God wants the effective working of His *dunamis* power to become operational in us – period!!! God wants His power that is at rest in us to become operational through us in order to establish His kingdom in the earth! If we are not willing to accept this truth, then perhaps the effective working of Satan to deceive us with his lies – is already operational in you by rejecting this truth whereby (unwitting to many) he has already placed some into effectual service to Satan behind the pulpit of man by saying the Spirit's gifts are no longer operational and no longer necessary since the written word was codified. Pure hogwash from the pit of hell!

> "And my speech and my preaching were not with persuasive words of human wisdom, but in demonstration of the Spirit and of power [*dunamis*]" (1 Cor. 2:4).

Something truly remarkable is contained within these scriptures, especially in Ephesians 1:17-21: when we operate in yielded submission to the Lord as His disciples; sometimes the power activated through us by the Spirit is not miraculous *dunamis* power, but rather… is Divine *kratos* authority with power!!! I don't know about you, but I want to live like that!

More boldly I declare this time: if you are not allowing the power of God to become operational within you, then you have already been deceived to accept a compromised position through a compromised gospel that is inconsistent with the kingdom of God that He placed within you.

> "And with great [*megas*-3173] power [*dunamis*] the apostles gave witness to the resurrection of the Lord Jesus. And great grace was upon them all" (Acts 4:33).

MEGA POWER enabled the apostles to give great witness to the resurrection – and MEGA GRACE was upon then all... yet not on just a cherry-picked few, but rather, on ALL of them!!!

God placed His life, His *dunamis* power, and His spirit [sic] within your body (that also belongs to Him), yet the operation (*energeia*) and administration (working) of these things is initiated and directed by the thoughts of our mind (intellect, soul). Whoever you are plugged into (either God's Spirit or Satan's power) will dictate how you manifest either presence on this planet.

Please keep in mind: God's kratos power is supremely greater than the dunamis power that remains available to Satan in the kingdom of darkness, so when the enemy comes against us, beloved – it is we who have the upper hand! Kratos triumphs over dunamis!

Suffice to say, the *dunamis* power of God is static (at rest) within us, yet when the manifestation of this power becomes activated by the Holy Spirit, the works must <u>never</u> be attributed (credited) to humans because it was never our power to begin with. People with the spiritual gift of healing understand their hands and words are merely the conduit through which the Lord transmits His power (the *energeia* working of miracles; 1 Cor. 12:10) to accomplish His purposes on earth... which is entirely "by grace." It is God doing it – in us, with us, to us, through us, and for us – to the praise of His glory.

Five-fold ministers are not required to be in attendance to initiate this spiritual transaction. The grace of God was manifested to gentiles through faith in Jesus Christ before any hands were laid upon them, which included the gift of the Spirit. Peter went to investigate this phenomenon whereby he concluded:

> "If therefore God gave them the same gift as He gave us when we believed on the Lord Jesus Christ, who was I that I could withstand God?" (Acts 11:17)

Bingo! And yet the Spirit came upon them simply by the hearing of the word through Peter's voice (antithetically "i.e. words not action") without laying hands on them. And yet, the church created hierarchical structures within Christianity that erringly promote mechanisms of exclusion by restricting grace, power and ordination through the laying on of hands. Did Jesus ever lay hands on anyone in order to receive ordination or gifts or power? Search the scriptures carefully before you answer this question. Most of the time, He merely spoke these things into existence.

> "When evening had come, they brought to Him many who were demon-possessed. ***And He cast out the spirits with a word***, and healed all who were sick" (Matt. 8:16).

Don't misconstrue what I am saying as scriptural evidence not to anoint with oil or prohibit the laying of hands on the sick or on anyone for any purpose. These activities help the weak in faith to believe in the power of God, but continuing to reinforce this makes the Lord's sheep dependent upon some ministers and faith merchants rather than relying on the Shepherd to manifest His grace and power. True sheep need dialogue with the Shepherd, not shadows of a former operational pattern found in Judaism.

Consider this: the spontaneous remission of diseases and miracles has occurred without the presence of special gimmicks, oils or religious persons; it seems the child-like *energeia* power initiated through faith (which in this case is faith in wellness or in God's goodness) makes this happen. Miracles continue to happen within every culture, religion and time period because God desires to manifest His love, grace and miraculous power upon the just and the unjust alike. God loves everyone... even our enemies. God loves all of us and He wants to manifest the power of His love through *all of us*.

So I ask you, are you going to use God's *dunamis* power entrusted to you to manipulate and control people in order to have *domination* over them, or are you going to use His *dunamis* power to establish the kingdom of God and have *dominion* on this earth as originally intended by the Lord – in love.

"We live in two states of mind: we live in survival or creation. When we live in those states of anger or aggression or hatred or judgment or fear, anxiety or insecurity or pain or suffering or depression, it's those chemicals that are created from the chemicals of stress or survival that activate those states of mind. It's the redundancy of those chemicals or the chemicals that push the genetic buttons that begin to cause disease.

'You see, every time we have a thought we make a chemical. So if we have a great thought or, if we have an unlimited thought, we make chemicals that make us feel great or feel unlimited. If we have negative thoughts or self-deprecating thoughts, we make chemicals that make us feel negative or unworthy. So this immaterial thing called *thought* fires a set of circuits in the brain that produces a chemical to signal the body for us to feel exactly the way we're just thinking.'"[100]

Again, I say, the "sound mind" that operates according to the heavenly paradigm exemplified by Christ is the starting point for victorious living. It's not enough to just believe the truth… we must understand the truth – having been enlightened in truth by the Spirit of truth – and then act upon the truth; otherwise, truth observed yet never acted upon remains static and will never produce anything worthwhile until it becomes dynamic. *'Energeia'* makes this happen! Our soul initiates the *energeia* process wherein the Spirit releases power through our spirit which is able to transform the mind of ordinary believers into disciples – as truth in action! If we claim to believe yet take no action, we

---

[100] Excerpt by Douglas Wick about spontaneous remission. Http://strategicdiscipline.positioningsystems.com/blog-0/spontaneous-remission-four-common-things-of-miraculous-recoveries.

remain in unbelief. If we pray for wisdom for this truth to be revealed yet have already made a predetermination in our mind 'not' to believe, then we remain doubters being thoroughly double-minded and unstable in all our ways (James 1:8).

The sound mind will produce creative thoughts that are consistent with the kingdom of God because the Father, who is the Source of everything good and noble and loving and true, established all things by the thought of His intellect. The *'ratio'* of the Father – as thought conceived – precedes the *'oratio'* of the Spirit – as thought manifested in word (*logos*).

"The creative thoughts of God and the creative power of His word always precede creation. In this manner, "word is two-fold: λόγος ἐνοιάθετος – word conceived; and λόγος προφόρικος – word uttered. The λόγος ὁ ἔσω and ὁ ἔξω, ratio and oratio – intelligence and utterance."[101] And this explains why Jesus is called Logos – λόγος – "The Word of God" (John 1:1; Rev. 19:13).

> "Finally, brethren, whatever things are true, whatever things are noble, whatever things are just, whatever things are pure, whatever things are lovely, whatever things are of good report, if there is any virtue and if there is anything praiseworthy— meditate [*logizomai*-3049] on these things" (Phil. 4:8)

This is not to be confused with the power of positive thinking; this is the power of truth.

> "But seek first the kingdom of God and His righteousness, and all these things shall be added to you" (Matt. 6:33).

The sound mind must seek first the kingdom of God and then

---

[101] Excerpt copied from Chapter 1, p. 31. Excerpt taken from Matthew Henry's Commentary on the Whole Bible, an exposition on John 1:1; Volume VI, p. 848; MacDonald Publishing Company, McLean, Virginia.

COMMISSION

meditate on how it operates... and then all these things [blessed thoughts, happy thoughts, and persecution] will be added unto you. We need to turn away (from error) and turn toward God's truth (which is called: conversion).

This is a giant circular thought process that we must comprehend: our soul (mind), which is who we are, is able to think things into being, but the spirit that was given to us by God needs *energeia* in order for truth to become operational... whereby the '*energeia*' process our soul initiates makes this connection between thought and "*manifestation through the spirit*" happen!

> "... God, who gives life to the dead and calls those things which do not exist as though they ~~did~~ were" (Rom. 4:17; ~~did~~-NKJV; were-KJV)

Think things not as though they are not, *but as though they are.* God's grace makes this happen.

What is a thought anyway? Can you describe or characterize the immaterial in such a way as to prove its existence? And yet perhaps, the thoughts of man are the best proof that God does exist, since our thoughts originated somewhere and somehow.

> "I think, therefore I am" (Descartes)
> You think, therefore – I AM (Jesus)

How could evolution have produced the impetus whereby a living organism evolves with intellect to produce thoughts in order to produce more thoughts and then higher thoughts? Where did evolution get this idea that thoughts were necessary anyway – or better yet, get the idea that evolutionary organisms needed to evolve into something better yet never knowing what better is or which path of evolution is better or... what "beneficial reason" might mean to primordial slime? Evolution as a "predetermined" push or plan for an organism to desire any change whatsoever is perhaps the best argument in support of "intelligent design" and proof of God!

Not being able to make a case for Christ yet believing in evolution is perhaps the silliest think I've ever thought!

Where could evolution even get the idea that thoughts were necessary for man… if it were not part of the Divine plan for man to converse with His Creator.

> "And he thought within himself, saying, 'What shall I do, since I have no room to store my crops? ^{19} And I will say to my soul, "Soul, you have many goods laid up for many years" (Luke 12:17, 19).

The word "thought" is '*dialogizomai*-1260' (*dialogos*: i.e. through words; English-dialogue) and means: "to reckon thoroughly, to deliberate (by reflection or discussion)" and is translated "reason, think, dispute, consider"[102] oftentimes to calculate the purpose or reason before taking action. Thoughts enable us to deliberate our purpose and actions, but with whom are we deliberating? With "whom" are we reasoning within our mind?

This verse is significant: "he thought within himself." Jesus is teaching us something quite extraordinary and profound, and I want you to grasp it; "he" – is thinking within – "himself." In essence there are two elements of this person "in oneness of heart, soul, mind and spirit" that are dialoging with one another – and likewise, so are you. Our soul dialogues with the heart (the physical man) and spirit (the spiritual man) within this place that I call "the table of our mind."

> "Lest they should understand [4920] *with* their hearts and turn, so that I should *heal* [*iaomai*-2390- spiritually heal] them" (Matt. 13:15)

Jesus wants us to understand in our mind (4920 – *suniemi*, to put together mentally, understand, comprehend) and "deliberate/reason/dialogue" this thought <u>with</u> our heart (*kardia*) and turn.

---

[102] Strong's Concordance.

> "Come now, and let us reason together," Says the
> Lord, "Though your sins are like scarlet, they shall
> be as white as snow; though they are red like
> crimson, they shall be as wool" (Isa. 1:18).

This manner of reasoning with the Lord in the table of our mind is not about getting into a debate with Him so God changes His mind, but rather... coming to our senses (with a disciplined mind, i.e. a *sozo-healed* mind) that concludes rightly: God is right and I will live according to His plans, not mine.

The table of our mind has many participants, yet our soul governs the dialogue; the participants are many: our soul, our soul's other members (spirit and body), our Lord, our adversary Satan... and any others.

The Lord created us with this ability to have "dialogue" with Him in our mind, so that we may reckon thoroughly and deliberate a matter in the table of our mind before taking action – and also that we should have a divine conversation with God as the Maker, the Source of creative thought, and the Origin of all things in creation, so we may inquire of the Lord and dialogue with Him regarding what He thinks about our thoughts and ideas. God loves it when we do that! This is the type of relationship that God desires to have with us! But let me ask evolutionists this: how did dialogue even get started? Dialogue how or why and with whom or what? Where did some rogue single-cell organism get the (imaginative) idea to divide itself in order to become another unique organism it reckoned as "better" than itself? How preposterous, indeed!

The Lord created mankind in "His Own" image according to His likeness with creative thought coupled with *energeia* to make effectual those thoughts and imaginations we conceive – through the soul; we are reasoning into being the substance conceived of/from-out-of creative thought. This is how our heavenly Father framed the existence of everything: from-out-of His creative thoughts. Then Jesus, "the Manifested One" of/from God, created all things through Himself. Likewise, this is how we were created by the Lord Jesus – with the ability (and dominion) to propose good... and do it through our spirit – or propose evil and do it... to our own peril.

> "But the LORD came down to see the city [Babel] and the tower which the sons of men had built. ⁶ And the LORD said, "Indeed the people are one and they all have one language, and this is what they begin to do; now **nothing that they propose to do will be withheld from them**" (Gen. 11:5, 6).

The Lord created us with an enormous capability to do whatever we propose, which includes living in outer space without oxygen or killing unborn babies. The Lord also created us with the ability to converse with Him... which is done by thoughts within our mind. The divine discourse between God and anyone on planet earth occurs in the mind (soul) through dialogue, i.e. conversations using '*logos*' words. Everyone was created with the ability to hear God's voice[103] via the Holy Spirit, and God wants to have a conversation with anyone who wants to seek Him and listen up, which is why book #2: Listen –how to hear the Voice of God better... is the most important topic any person on earth needs to thoroughly comprehend.

> "My sheep hear My voice, and I know them, and they follow Me" (John 10:27).

The Holy Spirit who makes this happen (according to grace) is the same One who transforms our mind to think like Jesus in order that we may become His likeness – as true image bearers!

> "And He said to them [the disciples], "It is not for you to know times or seasons which the Father has put in His own authority [*exousia*-1849]. ⁸ But you shall receive power [*dunamis*] when the Holy Spirit has come upon you; and you shall be witnesses to

---

[103] God's voice is not a sound, but rather, a spontaneous thought in our mind. Read: "Listen" to learn more.

Me in Jerusalem, and in all Judea and Samaria, and to the end of the earth" (Acts 1:8).

Believers may desire this same power that was given to the Lord's disciples, but if we do not want to become disciples and go through what they went through in order to hear and understand what was essential for them to hear and understand, then *dianoia* hasn't happened; a paradigm shift is needed in terms of how our mind thinks – from that reality which was contrary and hostile to the things of God to that which is complementary to the example personified by Jesus Christ. Living in that reality as personified by disciples, apostles and Christ – is impossible – when we continue to remain entrenched in our own reality. Our reality must become changed by the way we think and by the truth we think about to create a paradigm shift in the way we live.

We Need The Mind Of Christ!

"Let this mind be in you which was also in Christ Jesus" (Phil. 2:5).

Beloved, we must operate from a position of victory, not surrender! We are victors, not victims! We are thinking like old covenant believers when we refuse to listen to His voice or disobey what Jesus tells us to do. We must put aside any '*asunetos*' (801) "unintelligent, stupid, without understanding" thoughts (Matt. 15:16; Mk 7:18) that are raised up against the knowledge of God and we must put aside any bad attitudes as well. One of my personal favorite quotes is:

"I will not partner with an attitude that is inconsistent with Christ's character."

Bad attitudes, *asunetos* thoughts and destructive emotions have been crippling the church for centuries – and this must stop now! Either you are a new creation by grace – or you aren't. Either you have been birthed by the Spirit as a new creature to think and operate like Jesus in truth and in power – or you haven't. To what benefit is water baptism if we refuse the Spirit's baptism through sanctification? To what benefit is claiming to know the truth but refusing to act according to faith? Abraham was not justified by what he believed – he was justified by what he did according to faith because – he heard and obeyed. We are hypocrites in our mind when we believe the truth yet refuse to operate according to the truth administered by the Spirit of Truth. Failing to yield the operational control of our members to live under the operating power of the Spirit – is unbelief – "For rebellion is as the sin of witchcraft, and stubbornness is as iniquity and idolatry" (1 Sam. 15:23). Faith demands a verdict of "yes." Unbelief uses "no" as an excuse.

> "Not that I have already attained, or am already perfected; but I press on, that I may lay hold of that for which Christ Jesus has also laid hold of me. [13] Brethren, I do not count myself to have apprehended; but one thing I do, forgetting those things which are behind and reaching forward to those things which are ahead, [14] I press toward the goal for the prize of the upward call of God in Christ Jesus. [15] Therefore let us, as many as are mature, have this mind; and if in anything you think otherwise, God will reveal even this to you" (Phil. 3:12-15).

Static truth will not set you free; dynamic truth according to the '*energeia*' power at work in you will!

Apart from our willingness to be guided by the Holy Spirit into all truth and to walk according to the power of God that is at work in us, we are literally fish out of water. Life without the Spirit is a downward spiral into Death itself. We must embrace truth if we want to walk in the truth.

God is in you!
God is with you!
God placed eternity in your heart!
The kingdom of God is in you!

COMMISSION

> *Dunamis* power is resident within you!
> You are the offspring of God!
> You are the image of God!
> You have a divine nature!
> You were created a little lower than angels,
> Crowned with glory and honor!
> You are more than conquerors!
> You are *elohims*!!!
> And you were never alone!

When are we going to believe God's truth and start living according to it?

> "Jesus answered, "You say rightly that I am a king. For this cause I was born, and for this cause I have come into the world, that I should bear witness to the truth. ***Everyone who is of the truth hears My voice***" (John 18:37).

> The fullness of the Godhead dwells within you.
> The dominion of the earth has been placed under your feet, and yet…
> The choice is yours.

After sharing this message with another believer, his next comment to me was typical: "I can't wait for Jesus to come back in the clouds so I can see Him." Really? So I told Him that Jesus is already in Him and that he is waiting to experience something that has already happened – according to faith. His mindset was stuck (and handicapped) within institutional faith that teaches institutional truth and does not yet comprehend the mystery of Christ abiding in us – which has already happened – through faith.

> "To them God willed to make known what are the riches of the glory of this mystery among the Gentiles: which is ***Christ in you, the hope of glory***" (Col. 1:27)

Beloved in Christ, we are not waiting on God, but rather, God is waiting on us – to believe!

> "From that time Jesus began to preach and to say, "Repent, for the kingdom of heaven is at hand" (Matt. 4:17).

The kingdom of heaven… is (still) at hand… heaven here now is! It has been here since Jesus brought heaven to earth, and He commanded His disciples: "And as you go, preach, saying, 'The kingdom of heaven is at hand,'" but our religious institutions continue to teach doctrines that are contrary to the current paradigm of heaven on earth – here now is!

What more could I possibly say in order for the church to comprehend this truth and arise into her manifest destiny? Meditate on that paradox before you read another word.

Death Is A Not-Laughing Matter

Beloved, when was the last time you had a really good laugh? Laughter has been credited for numerous spontaneous remissions and (has been theorized) laughter triggers positive thoughts within the fun and creative realm of our mind which produces healthy chemicals within our brain. Creative play (akin to joy) with imaginative glee may yet be another fruit of the Spirit.

Just as all men have been granted authority by the Lord to have dominion over the earth, likewise, the Lord has given all men '*dunamis*' power to manifest operational power to effect a regime change in this world – but "who" they plug their spirit into determines whether it is used for good or evil. Our history books are full of men that used this power for evil purposes, but new pages are being inserted into history books today that will focus not on human endeavors but rather divine power manifested through devout disciples. The upcoming millennium will certainly cast radiant joy upon 6,000 years of doom and gloom existence dominated by men with disregard for the Holy Spirit of God.

Are you plugged into the Holy Spirit, or are you plugged into doctrines that say you are plugged into the Holy Spirit? That – is a huge difference. Whatever you choose to do with the *'dunamis'* power residing within you is entirely up to you.

The choice is yours!

The church age is over – the kingdom age has begun. Do you want to be connected to the head or the tail? If you want to be part of the New Earth reality that is happening even now, then plug your *'dunamis'* power into the Holy Spirit's *'kratos'* power outlet and let's get the New Earth revival started!

Allow me to express some additional thoughts regarding power in operation:

- Power in authority (*exusia*)
- Power in glory (*doxa*)
- Power in dynamic operation (*dunamis*)
- Power in thought (*energeia*)
- Power in grace ("My grace is sufficient for you, for My strength is made perfect in weakness" 2 Cor. 12:9)
- Power in truth ("by the word of truth, by the power of God" 2 Cor. 6:7)
- Power in strength ("Not by might nor by power, but by My Spirit" Zech. 4:6)
- Power in understanding (*dianoia* – a thorough thinking through)
- Power in testimony ("with great power He gave the apostles witness"; Acts 4:33)
- Power in purpose ("Let them have dominion" with "authority and power")
- Power in subordination ("Blessed are the meek, for they shall inherit the earth")
- Power in humility (power under restraint vs. manifested power)

- Power in prayer ("effective, fervent prayer of a righteous man avails much; James 5:16)
- Power of a sound mind
- Power in love

All power is static until it is energetically acted upon. All divine power is governed according to the operational power found in love. Love is patient, kind, longsuffering, kind, generous, meek, humble, and full of manifested grace. Love is the divine, dynamic *dunamis* power that governs the paradigm of heaven against which no law is superior nor can any law overpower. Love that proceeds from a sound mind enables God's *'dunamis'* power residing (resting) within us to become activated for service… according to grace. Love is the power that must be plugged into the Spirit of grace and glory with a sound mind if we are ever going to govern this earth in the manner originally intended by the Lord Jesus.

> "For by Him all things were created that are in heaven and that are on earth, visible and invisible, whether thrones or dominions or principalities or powers. All things were created through Him and for Him" (Col. 1:16).

> "To God our Savior, Who alone is wise,
> Be glory and majesty, dominion and power,
> Both now and forever. Amen." (Jude 1:25).

It's all about Jesus – and God gets the glory! Amen!

The Hands of Governance

> "I will commit your responsibility [4475] into his hand [3027]" (Isa. 22:21).

'*Memshalah*-4475' means "dominion (10x), rule (4x), government, power; the realm of a ruler" and is also used of the sun as ruling over the day (and stars ruling over the night; Gen. 1:16; Psa. 136:8,

9). When '*memshalah*' occurs with '*yad*-3027' meaning "hand; the open one (indicating power, means, direction)" it implies "dominion" with authority and power to rule.

> "And David defeated Hadadezer king of Zobah as far as Hamath, as he went to establish his power [yad-3027; dominion-KJV] by the River Euphrates" (1 Chron. 18:3).

The directional use of the hand as a gesture signifying authority has been used throughout history to indicate devotion, allegiance, subordination, preference, power, protection, and kindred affection. How the hand is used and what it represents differ greatly between cultures. For example, when the hand is outstretched, the gesture implies either friendship or mutual understanding, and when the hand is upraised, it often implies allegiance, power or dedication to a calling or responsibility. When officers or elected officials raise their hand in an oath, they are signifying by this gesture any action undertaken by them obligates them to the duty or task to which they have dedicated themselves. This undertaking is not frivolous; the undertaking requires all the strength and understanding (*iscus and dianoia*) rising up from within them to faithfully perform that to which they have taken an oath to uphold and perform.

When the Lord was teaching Moses and Aaron to do His will by hearing His voice, He began by teaching them to carefully observe every detail they heard. When the Lord told them to speak or to raise an outstretched hand, they were not to raise the rod or do anything other than the command given to them.

"The Lord told Moses and Aaron to "stretch out their hand" several times – with mixed results:

- Ex. 8:6 – The Lord told Moses to tell Aaron to stretch out his hand "with the rod" to initiate the second plague, but Aaron only stretched out his hand (without the rod), which

the Egyptian magicians also copied – with outstretched hands – and they also brought forth frogs like Aaron
- Ex. 8:17 – Then Aaron stretched out the rod to strike the dust so that is became lice (#3), exactly as the Lord commanded, but when the magicians tried it, they could not bring forth lice (by now, most people see a trend whereby power is being manifested by the rod, but this is not the lesson the Lord is teaching us; rather, we are to follow His word obediently – and precisely – down to the very letter)
- Ex. 9:22 – Then the Lord said to Moses, "stretch out your hand toward heaven that there may be hail (#7) in the land," but Moses stretched out the rod instead (v.23)
- Ex. 10:12 - Then the Lord said to Moses, "stretch out your hand toward the land for locusts to come upon the land" (#8), but Moses stretched out his rod instead (v.13)
- Ex. 10:21 - Then the Lord said to Moses, "stretch out your hand toward heaven that there may be darkness which may be felt" (#9) ***and so it happened!***

"During the ninth plague against Egypt, the Lord told Moses to "stretch out his hand toward heaven" and thus, great darkness came over the land. No words, no rod, just stretch out the hand. Moses was faithful and he witnessed the power of God manifested in the obedient outstretching of his hand… which will come in 'handy' when they get to the Red Sea.

"The Lord is teaching Moses and Aaron to obey the word of the Lord and do exactly as He commands. Period! We can observe several things happening here, but the seemingly "overlooked" disobedience of Moses in the first plague will cause the Lord to put him to the test – and at great expense to the Egyptians.'"[104]

"When the Lord brought the Israelites to the Red Sea, it is important to see the command given by the Lord to Moses whereby the waters parted: "But lift up your rod, and stretch out your hand over the sea and divide it" (Ex. 14:16).

---

[104] Excerpt copied from "Listen," section titled: "Listening For Spiritual Leaders."

- Ex. 14:15-26 – The Lord told Moses to divide the Red Sea by stretching out his hand (v.21, 26), which he did faithfully, but it is very important that people see this – the Lord never told Moses to stretch out the rod... but only "lift up the rod" (v.16) with his other hand. The Hollywood version teaches a contradictory message that many scripture commentators have erringly endorsed as well, that the rod parted the water when it didn't.

"After the Red Sea (Sea of Reeds) was parted, the Israelites escaped and the Egyptian army was vanquished "by an outstretched hand" once again, whereby the Song of Moses was very forthright in giving this glory to God according to "His" outstretched hand:"[105]

> "Your right hand, O LORD, has become glorious in power; Your right hand, O LORD, has dashed the enemy in pieces" (Ex. 15:6).

Why is this important? Why are these details necessary for us to understand? Every word the Lord utters must be carefully observed and obeyed. The Lord commanded the Israelites to march around Jericho once a day for six days, but on the seventh day, they were told to do it differently... and then... the walls came tumbling down.

Humanity was created by God for a specific reason: have dominion (Gen. 1:26-28). Humanity was placed on earth to fulfill this specific purpose: have dominion, but this must be done under His command. In order for us to accomplish this, we need to be able to hear His thoughts (in our mind). The means whereby we accomplish the Lord's agenda through our yielded, surrendered lives is simple: hear His voice, understand, and obey... as we have dominion in His name for the glory of His name. Consider, now, what the Lord says about us:

---

[105] IBID.

> "You have made him to have dominion over the works of Your hands; You have put all things under his feet" (Psa. 8:6).

The Lord God (Jesus Christ) created the heavens and the earth – and then He created man in "His Own image" to have dominion over His works done by His hands– and then the Lord put all things under our feet as partners in His kingdom by giving us authority and power to successfully accomplish our dominion mandate. Does this resonate with you... or is this high-minded wishfulness too exceeding impossible for you to imagine? Well, the Apostle Paul knew there was much more going on than he was able to experience; he was given logic and reason with divine understanding to unravel many mysteries of the kingdom, as well as power to perform many miracles and experience encounters with the Lord in heaven, but he was not able to walk on water like Peter. Paul wanted the total package. Perhaps this was going on in his mind, to which the Lord said, "My grace is sufficient for you."

Do you want to experience all those things the first century church experienced, even perhaps walking on water like the Apostle Peter or being translated like Phillip? If we say this is impossible, then the fatalistic thoughts of our mind to remain captives in the realm of survival have also taken captive the victory given to us by Jesus in the creation realm of kingdom living.

Man's biggest problem... is his small-minded thinking! You are more than you can imagine.

Unworldly Experiences

Some people have had out-of-body spiritual experiences whereby they traveled to (and encountered) very real places that are impossible within the earthly body.

- The Apostle Paul was taken up into the third heaven (2 Cor. 12:2)
- Isaiah saw the roundness of the earth 200 years before Plato theorized it (Isa. 40:22)

- Philip was able to outrun a chariot and then moments later was instantly translated to a city many miles away – in his physical body, no less (Acts 8:26-40)
- Elijah on multiple occasions was often translated by the Spirit of the Lord so that people 'expected' him to be translated to other places (1 Kings 18:7, 12)
- Ezekiel was lifted up between earth and heaven (Ezek. 8:3; also 3:14; 11:1)
- After Jesus invited Peter to walk on water, He calmed the storm and then climbed into the boat and they were instantly translated to the other side of the lake… boat and all (John 6:19-21)
- Jesus took Peter, James and John on a walk when they transcended this reality "up <u>into</u> a mountain" to observe Moses and Elijah conversing with Jesus within a heavenly reality (Mark 9:2-9)
- A great many modern persons have had spiritual journeys into heaven and written stories of their encounters with Jesus, as well as with angels
- On March 29, 1999, I experienced a spiritual journey to the other side of the world and saw Papua New Guinea in great detail from above the earth

Do not minimize who and what you think you are, as if "I am only human" is a valid excuse from God's perspective. You are no different than Elijah who also served the Lord.

"Elijah was a man with a nature like ours" (James 5:17).

Yet Elijah was translated bodily on multiple occasions. As for the rest of us… how could anyone experience these events as an inhabitant of earth within the human body where the soul resides? The only answer that makes sense to me is: we experience them with our spirit. When our spirit rises up within us and the empowering of the Spirit is upon us, there is no limit to what God can accomplish in us and through us. I even heard a reliable second-hand report of someone walking through a wall into a bathroom where their roommate was taking a shower – behind a locked door. I refer to these spiritual experiences as "spirit-normal" which have been recorded so that we may remember the testimony... because... if God did it once before, then God can do it again!

Our spirit can operate independently of our soul and body. A personal friend of mine shared a "spirit-normal" story with me that may astound you. He was interceding in prayer for a lady going through a very difficult situation, and days later she called to tell him she saw his spirit standing in the door of her bedroom – and while this might alarm most women – she told him it brought immediate peace to her and she was able to fall asleep instantly. Spirit normal!

We Are Spiritual Beings

Suffice to say, there are a great many things we are presently unable to comprehend regarding the spiritual person within us. We were created a little lower than angels, crowned with glory and honor (Psa. 8:5), called *elohim* by God (i.e. lacking little of God; John 10:34-36) and have been given a divine nature (2 Pet. 1:4). We **_existed_** (*thought by God into a state of existence*) in God's presence before we were inserted into the fabric of time (by the Holy Spirit), we were in Christ before the foundation of the world (Eph. 1:4), God knew us before we were born (Psa. 139:13; Jer. 1:5) and we are on earth to accomplish His will for the earth, by grace through faith. I have no idea what we were like before we came to earth, but I do know the soul is eternal, God placed eternity in our heart (Eccl. 3:11), and we (our souls) are currently being tested and sanctified so that we may "continue to live eternally" (Psa. 49:9; John 3:15). This means you (your soul) is eternal (both pre and post humanity): we existed in God's presence before we were inserted into the fabric of time (Gen. 1:26 - 2:1), then we were formed of the earth (Gen. 2:7) and we will continue to live eternally in one of several places after the judgment based upon what we did (or didn't do) on earth.

One thing has been made known to me: we do not remember the

former days and, for whatever reason again, we will not remember our many days upon this world in the New Earth's regeneration (Eccl. 1:11; Isa. 43:18; Rev. 21:4). For nearly all of us, this alone is very wonderful news... which is perhaps why this place is called Paradise.

We are in the place that the Lord God created for us – *and created us for*, and this is where we are supposed to remain: on the earth... as the host of earth (Gen. 2:1). Our proper domain [106] – is earth! Our purpose and reason for being – is to have dominion on this domain!

Do you want to know what you will be doing in the New Earth? Our doctrines about Heaven cannot teach us what we will be doing in heaven, yet there are numerous examples of entering the Promised Land to occupy homes and cities that are vacant.

At the end of the age, when the trumpet sounds, angels will be sent to gather the tares and remove all things that offend (wicked and rebellious people), and a dragnet will divide the unclean and worthless from among the good. We have been taught the righteous will be taken from the earth, but that is just not so; the unrighteous are removed! In the regeneration, saints will inherit the New Earth to rule and reign with Christ to dwell in uninhabited cities and houses for which they did not labor and tend vineyards they did not plant. So I ask you: how big do you want your inheritance to be? Expand your current reality mindset and enlarge the tent-pegs of your heart to start living extraordinarily... even perhaps to govern nations!

> "Thus says the Lord of hosts: 'In this place which is desolate, without man and without beast, and in all its cities, there shall again be a dwelling place of shepherds causing their flocks to lie down" (Jer. 33:12).

---

[106] *Oiketerion* (3613) – habitation; proper domain; Jude 6.

Do a word search to read the other 24 occurrences in the bible for "desolate cities" (including Isa. 6:11-13).

> "For you shall expand to the right and to the left,
> And your descendants will inherit the nations, And
> make the desolate cities inhabited" (Isa. 54:3).

"You are a spiritual being that is eternal that is having a human experience for one season of eternity upon the earth. The reality of heaven and hell is already upon the earth, such that you determine which reality you are going to live in for all eternity according to the way and manner of life you lived. Just like the angels that were in heaven, they had a choice… but one-third were swept away by believing in a false promise by Satan and they lost their rightful place (domain) in heaven; and humans are being given the same choice as well. We will always remain on earth, yet *you* shall determine which kingdom reality you are going to live in (heaven or hell)."[107]

Who you *were* and who you *are*… is not as important as who you are becoming – right now.

Keep in mind… the enemy will continue to attack us, not because of what we've done in our past, but rather… to prevent us from walking into the destiny God purposed for us… which the enemy knows infinitely more than we do because our manifest destiny is to their peril, not ours!

Don't let your history get in the way of your destiny! So, don't look back, keep your eyes upon Jesus, move forward and by faith… endure and persevere. You are taking back enemy territory as you continue to move forward and advance – in the name of Christ Jesus our King.

When we consider the evidence within the scriptures that most certainly confirms our soul is eternal and that we existed in God's

---

[107] Excerpt from "Understand" section titled "Alternate Reality – Oldness Again."

presence before we were given a body (pre-humanity) along with a great multitude of other souls called "the host of earth" (Gen. 2:1), similar evidence confirms we shall also exist eternally (post-humanity), so now then I ask you: what were we without the body? Do we even have need a body except during this season of eternity on earth?

Thoughts – are the ultimate weapon… and ideology is the battlefield of the mind.

> Demons engage us yet we are unaware,
> Perhaps we can do the same by prayer.

Energeia Thoughts

Perhaps the smallest trail of minute breadcrumbs I have yet encountered were diligently pursued in order to bring this word to you. Words have meaning. Words have power. Words are thoughts in operational effect. Words have the power of life and death (Prov. 18:21). Jesus said, "My words are spirit and life" (John 6:63). And likewise, so are yours!

Words matter, yet even more so… words represent manifested thoughts originating from an immaterial source (your soul). Words are begotten of creative thoughts produced by our soul and brought into existence that beforehand were not – as calling those things which were not as though they are – into existence. This is not a simple message, yet with this concept firmly in mind – let's begin by remembering the Lord's greatest commandment:

> "And you shall love the Lord your God with all your heart, with all your soul, with all your mind [*dianoia* understanding – deep meditative thoughts of the mind] and with all your strength [*iscus* – all strength and power that is spiritually within you].' This is the first commandment" (Mark 12:30).

The Lord called this command into existence as something

originating in the mind of the Father, as thoughts conceived "of God" whereby these Divine thoughts became manifested into existence through the Spirit as thoughts expressed by Jesus – "The Word of God." This truth is the baseline for understanding scripture: ***thoughts (conceived) precede words (expressed).***

The "heart and mind" of our soul (the spiritual man) influences the actions of the material man (the body) and our spirit. The immaterial thoughts we produce by our immaterial soul are manifested in our material mind by this immaterial power within us called *energeia*. <u>Do not</u> read these words quickly: the immaterial effects material reality!

> "By faith we understand that the worlds were framed by the word of God, so that the things which are seen were not made of things which are visible" (Heb. 11:3).
>
> "While we do not look at the things which are seen, but at the things which are not seen. For the things which are seen are temporary, but the things which are not seen are eternal" (2 Cor. 4:18).

We produce immaterial thoughts by our immaterial soul all the time; however, there are two other sources of thought that enter our mind as originating from either the *energeia* power of God or the *energeia* power of Satan.[108] Three thoughts (by our soul, by God and by demons) can be manifested in our mind at any time by these three sources, so if we want to hear the pure, precious Voice of the Lord, then we need to learn how to silence the other two voices.[109]

Within this context, here is the only difference that I've discerned

---

[108] For example, the two previous sentences were not constructed by the intellect of my mind; these words were given to me by the Lord to help explain the message He wants to share with us: tap into His energeia.

[109] Read: Listen – how to hear God's voice… better, to learn more about silencing the other voices.

from the Holy Spirit between the soul and mind: the soul, which is who you are, only produces thoughts by the owner of that soul – who entertains them to ponder a matter in their mind, but the mind entertains all thoughts "And I will say to my soul" (Luke 12:19), and can "dialogue" with all three sources in many ways to deliberate, wrestle, reason and debate these thoughts (or voices) – to engage in God's goodness or Satan's lawlessness.

> "For this reason we also thank God without ceasing, because when you received the word [*logos*] of God which you heard from us, you welcomed it not as the word [*logos*] of men, but as it is in truth, the word [*logos*] of God, which also *effectively works* [*energeo*-1754] in you who believe" (1 Thess. 2:13).

"From this point forward, we must not think simplistically about *logos* as the written word. It implies so much more (which we will discuss in depth a little later), but before we go any further, let us try to understand the meaning of *logos* as "the many ways God chooses to express Himself," not just as words written or spoken, but as ***expressions revealed to us as thoughts and utterances***. And the fullest expression of God was revealed to us as *Logos*, Jesus Christ Himself (John 1:1)."[110] "The scriptures are not the *logos* or *rhema* words of men; they are the *logos* of God having been communicated to them through *rhema* (utterances) words of/from Christ."[111] "We get *logos* (the message) by *rhema* (the hearing of utterances spoken by men or as spontaneous thoughts from God), but this is not as logos coming from men, but as ***all*** logos coming from God!"[112]

> ***"For I know the thoughts that I think toward you, says the LORD***, thoughts of peace and not of evil, to give you a future and a hope. ¹² Then you will call

---

[110] Excerpt from "Listen."
[111] IBID, p. 86.
[112] IBID, p. 56.

> upon Me and go and pray to Me, and I will listen to you. ¹³ And you will seek Me and find Me, when you search for Me with all your heart" (Jer. 29:11-13).

"The LORD said: "I know the thoughts (plans; NIV) that I have for you" and if He has thoughts and plans '*machashabah*-4284' "purpose, plan, thought, intention, plot,"[113] then He wants to tell you about those plans. If you want to hear "your" message, then you must go to the Source!"[114]

The thoughts that the Lord has for you are revealed to you within the realm of spiritual thought, and thus, it is mission critical to be able to hear His thoughts (voice) – and understand the message – in order to walk according to His ways, as disciples of Jesus Christ.

The Power of Thought

> "(for when Gentiles, who do not have the law, by nature do the things in the law, these, although not having the law, are a law to themselves, ¹⁵ who show the work of the law written in their hearts, their conscience also bearing witness, and between themselves ***their thoughts accusing or else excusing them***)" (Rom. 2:14, 15; thoughts sometimes accusing and at other times even defending them -NIV).

Thoughts are immaterial to the material mind, yet we produce them by the millions. The only material proof we have of them is when '*rhema*' utterances are produced (being manifested as written, spoken or other forms of expression). Modern science has proven the existence of electrical impulses, the activation of neurons and the release of chemicals in the brain as material proof of immaterial energy when creative thought happens, and I want to focus on this concept: immaterial thoughts becoming material by

---

[113] Strong's Concordance.
[114] Excerpt copied from "Listen."

this thing called: thought-*energeia*-word-faith.

Immaterial *energeia* power (let's just call it energy) is activated by the soul to become power in operation in which creative thought happens. Whether we act upon a thought (or not) will have an effect upon the way and manner in which our mind operates – either for positive or negative, or for constructive or destructive purposes. Our thoughts do more than just produce positive or negative forms of energy, they are the building blocks which we use to build one kingdom or another (heaven of hell) in our heart... and likewise, by our actions, build on earth.

For good or for evil, our thoughts either give glory to God or we sinfully take this glory unto ourselves for our own glory.

For this reason, in this manner, we were made in the likeness of God so as to operate in goodness and righteousness according to the paradigm of heaven as exemplified by Jesus – to think creative thoughts and then manifest goodness in the earth; however, let me remind you... we were taken captive to sin behind enemy lines. The good that we know to do (that is resident within our soul) is being alternately influenced and confronted by an adversary hell-bent on keeping us dead in trespasses and sin... "by corrupt thoughts in our mind." The soul that remains resolute to the truth of God is able to withstand this power of deceptive (*energeia*) thoughts by the enemy.

Saints, it is imperative that we know the truth and meditate upon the truth in order for us to manifest God's *logos* (His message of truth) in our heart, whereby the enemy is vanquished by our sanctified (*hagios*), sound (*sophronismos*), disciplined mind that operates with – truth!

Selah. Meditate on these things.

Our willingness to think goodly and act goodly begins with Godly thought-*energeia*-word-faith. We often congratulate ourselves when we have a good thought and more-so when we produce a goodly word or deed, but when was the last time you congratulated yourself on Godly faith? There are some aspects of the word-faith movement that cause me to bristle, especially when people attempt to "call into being those things which are not" in order to satisfy worldly passions which are contradictory to the Father's plan for the earth, but the impetus behind this movement is on target! Their thoughts and ideas are oftentimes incompatible with the kingdom of God, yet they have tapped into the spiritual process of creative thought which brings into being (existence) things produced by thought-*energeia*-faith. Positive immaterial thoughts produced by the mind will produce positive material results; likewise, negative thoughts, feelings and emotions will produce negative materials results.

> Truth in – righteousness out
> Garbage in – lawlessness out.

Three *energeia* powers are working in your mind (yours, God's, Satan's) to produce works in this earth, and for this reason we need the sanctification of the Holy Spirit to work His *energeia* and *dunamis* power in us in order to produce a "sound mind." We can think it and believe it, but until our soul has activated *energeia rhema (energetic utterances)*, then our faith remains static, silent and avails nothing.

At this point, I need to caution you in the manner which thoughts produce things into being:

1. One of my sons was a very impulsive child, to which I counseled him often: "Think twice. Don't do every thought that comes into your head." We would all do well to heed this advice... myself included.
2. The enemy can hear all our words and they can see our actions, so if you have a private personal matter that you are lifting up in prayer, then keep your prayers silent. God hears all our thoughts because He dwells in everyone, so it is not necessary to pray audibly; the divine conversation (dialogue – with words) between me and the Lord is always by silent thought language, so I encourage you to do

likewise – in your mind. In this manner, the enemy cannot influence my prayers with evil ideas because they have no clue what I am praying about – yet when the Lord responds to my specific prayer request, it is with great confidence that I have heard the delightful *logos* of my Lord. If your prayers have grown cold or the Lord has stopped talking with you, perhaps He knows something you don't, so change it up a little. Purpose in your heart to pray in a new place (without a lot of noise) or pray in a new way without verbalizing it to anyone... and see if the Lord visits you in your secret place (i.e. your heart) and dialogues with you in your mind. The enemy is very predictable; they want to prevent your intimacy with Jesus, and when our pre-packaged prayer life becomes unpredictable, this drives the enemy crazy. There is no right or wrong way to pray when intimacy with Jesus is the goal, so change it up... and see what happens. [Let me tell you a personal story: One day, I was joyfully sharing with another saint the manner in which the Holy Spirit speaks to me in the morning, so can you guess what happened several days later? Yup, the enemy counterfeited it.]

3. If you are working to establish the kingdom of God, either in your life as His disciple or in your life's work under His commission, then you are an agent of change that is tearing down principalities and powers in the kingdom of darkness – and you WILL come under attack! If you have constant headaches, anxiety, or worry... which lead to fear, then check with the Holy Spirit first to see what the source of the problem may be, and then, barring none... come against the enemy with *audible* words of prayer. You have the upper hand because the Lord Jesus gave you His authority over the enemy and you CAN come against them – and indeed, you must! Beloved, you can confuse the enemy with audible prayer directed against them, and scatter them just by mentioning His name, and even cause demons to tremble in fear with praise and thanksgiving. Saints of God, you can do this by audible prayer. So do it!!! Under

His authority and with His power, DO IT!!! Declare it and have dominion over the enemy!

4. Pray a protective covering over yourself. I begin prayer this way: "Jesus, you are my Lord and protector, hide me under the shadow of your wing, and protect me under the shield of faith." This simple prayer is two-fold: 1) once you are hidden in Christ, the enemy is unaware of your location and you can proceed with spiritual warfare without them knowing who you are or (more importantly) where you are. You will come under enemy attack, to be certain, so don't leave yourself vulnerable to attack by making yourself an open target, and 2) the shield of faith will protect you from the arrows of the enemy. Many people suffering from headaches and physical anomalies during periods of intense prayer and ministry are literally being attacked by weapons from the enemy.

5. Saints, if you pray to Jesus the same way every day, then understand this: the enemy knows what you are going to do even before you start. And if you have verbalized your thoughts or prayers, then they have a good idea what you will be praying for (even in silence – days or weeks from now) whereby they may influence your mind with preemptive thoughts which you may interpret as words from the Lord. This has happened to me a couple times, so I caution you to keep private spiritual matters between you and the Lord – silent. If you are going to pray about a matter with another saint, which I strongly encourage you do, then begin any and every prayer session (small or large) with this simple prayer: "In the authority the Lord Jesus has given to me, I take authority over (name them) – powers, principalities, demons and every unclean wicked thing that is raised up against the knowledge of God and Jesus Christ, and command them all to go back to the pit where they belong – in the name of Jesus." And then I pray: "Lord, I pray a hedge of protection around me and this place to prevent the enemy from entering in. In the authority you have given me, I cast them from this place and I bind them in silence in their place, and I place a hedge of protection around me to keep them (and others)

from entering." Once you have bound the enemy, as that which we were taught by the Lord, "Whatever you bind or loose on earth is bound or loosed in heaven," the second part of this authority is the fun part: start loosing things from heaven onto earth. Worship and praise are audible forms of prayer that demons and wicked spirit cannot tolerate (it drives them crazy). Stop praying for new houses and new cars and worldly things; seek first the kingdom of God and pray for the New Earth where you will be able to enjoy (truly enjoy) true riches where thieves cannot steal (because they will all be in hell) and where moths and rust cannot destroy.

The weapons of our warfare are not carnal (fleshly), but they are mighty in word and in power. The weapons of our warfare are words of truth... with effectual fervent *energeo* power.

> "For the weapons of our warfare are not carnal but mighty in God for pulling down strongholds" (2 Cor. 10:4).

An effective soldier in spiritual warfare will weaponize their prayers effectively – yet remain hidden from attack. For many years, I was "a hidden one" for such a time as this, as I prayed often, "Hide me under the shelter of Your wing" whereby the enemy had no idea where I was or where these prayers were coming from. Furthermore, they cannot attack what they have been veiled from seeing. Thus, I enjoyed warring against the enemy in relative obscurity as someone considered a low value target. Please understand what I mean by this: I am not like a pastor or evangelist that has a spiritual target on their back (which is why we must clothe our pastors in prayer), yet I constantly encounter attacks from the enemy against me within my mind – all the time. We are admonished to put on the helmet of salvation... for good reason!

The Battlefield Is The Mind!

Why did the Lord create us in this manner? This may sound repugnant to some yet revelatory to most: God created us to be like Him in every regard except one… we are not Divine. We are His image bearers created on purpose according to this purpose: to operate like Him, think like Him, live like Him, love like Him, talk like Him, work like Him and have dominion like Him.

Our soul operates in the same manner as the Father: with creative thought. Our spirit operates in the same manner as Jesus: we manifest the thoughts we create through our spirit.

> "For My thoughts are not your thoughts, nor are your ways My ways," says the LORD" (ISA. 55:7, 8).

The interesting thing about this scripture which is often overlooked: it does not tell us to stop thinking, but rather, it admonishes us to think like our Lord. God wants us to think like Him, yet some of our doctrines regard this as heresy. We think – because we were made like our heavenly Father (Gen; 1:26) – to think and originate everything by creative thought. Just as the Father is the Origin and Source of everything, so too our creative thoughts are the origin and source of everything we think – and say – and do! This is how we were designed to function before we were manifestly created by our Creator, Jesus Christ (John 1:3; Col. 1:16).

This is not such a great mystery to actually think we were made and created to function according to the heavenly pattern of our Maker and Creator, yet the big mystery in my mind is: why modern man isn't able to think this way? Since God made and created us to be like Him, in His image according to His Own likeness, then isn't it elementary to draw this elementary conclusion: we operate in the same manner as the One who created us? We teach our own children to operate in this manner and then discipline them when they get out of line, so why, then, is this concept construed as heretical and antithetical to faith? Even managers and corporate execs hire like-minded people, yet banish the thought of this ever being embraced within the institutional church because… we are more valuable as sheep than as disciples with the mind of Christ.

The main point of this book is to teach us how we were created so that we understand how we are supposed to function in order to accomplish greater works with the commission that we were predestined to accomplish. Now you know!

Your soul operates like your heavenly Father to originate (make) creative thoughts – and then your spirit operates like Jesus to manifestly create these thoughts into words, utterances, architectural designs, mathematical equations, chemical formulas, musical songs, theatrical plays, forward passes, triple plays, and a host of other actions and effectual workings initiated 'from-out-of' one thing: creative thoughts by *energeia* power.

Thoughts and ways
Thinking and doing
Expression and manifestation
Soul and spirit
Expression and manifestation
Spiritual and physical
Expression and manifestation
Immaterial and material
Expression and manifestation
Invisible and visible
Expression and manifestation
Faith by hearing and obedience

"I have given you the keys of the kingdom of heaven" (Matt. 16:19)

Our visible manifest reality was initiated from-out-of an invisible spiritual paradigm

Oneness of the Spirit
Trust in the Lord Jesus!

>...expression and manifestation...

The spiritual precedes the physical, and thus... everything is spiritual... before it is physical.

> Jesus is the Manifested One of/from God
> And likewise, you are a manifested one of/from God

Hold onto your bootstraps buttercup because this next revelation will expound your mind into the outer cosmos: your mind entertains the thoughts of three (and sometimes four) individuals all the time. When you ponder a matter, three "persons" are at this table all the time and they all speak messages to you regarding the matter you are deliberating, if (that is) you let them. The three people are: your soul, the Lord, and the devil. This is not the news flash you were expecting since you already know this, but this thought is paramount in your walk with grace: your soul (you) controls the dialogue (discussion). If you want to talk with the Lord, the channel is open for you to talk with Him. If you want to talk with the devil, that channel is open for you to talk also. And if you want to talk to the fourth person (family members, teachers or friends that planted messages into your mind... which I suggest you *not* do), then you may be able to talk to them as well. In the spiritual dimension, thoughts are exchanged without boundaries or borders.

For example, the Lord calls everyone to assemble before Him, which includes all sons of God (spirits, angels) and Satan himself (Job 1:6; 2:1), but Satan isn't allowed to speak unless he is given permission to speak. This point is important: if you want to speak with Satan with your thought-life, then I suppose you can (but I strenuously discourage this!). The Lord is always able to speak with you – unless you consider Him persona non grata (a not welcome person).

You (i.e. your soul) control the dialogue that you have with God or Satan, which I call: co-manifest realities. You can manifest the reality of God or the reality of Satan in near split-second time, as we can see by our Lord's response to Peter, who was able to hear the Father's message (as a *logos* thought in his mind) and declare Jesus the Christ, yet moments later Peter rebuked Jesus (who is God) whereby Jesus turned and rebuked Satan (who was co-manifested with Peter at the table of his mind). You may be asking yourself in your mind right now... how can anyone know this is happening or are these words just the fanciful bantering of someone who thinks they know something revelatory? Well, I was given this message by the Holy Spirit over two years ago yet the Spirit did not confirm these words until this moment. You may not yet believe me, so let me ask this: did God create us in His Own image? (A: yes). Did God intend for us to think like Him and act like Him according to the example demonstrated to us by Jesus? (A: yes). Did God send us to earth as a soul with a spirit to inhabit a body to see what might happen, or did God intend all along that we should align our allegiance to Him and manifest His presence that has been dwelling in us the entire time to accomplish one thing: become like Him. (A: the correct answer is yes!) Beloved: we were sent to earth as His mighty ambassadors to be governed by faith under the guidance of the Holy Spirit – to host His presence – and be His image bearers – to think like Him in the table of our mind – and operate like Him upon the earth!

You are the light of the world and His Spirit is guiding your spirit to usher in a regime change!

You were predestined since the moment the Father thought you into existence (Gen. 1:26; 2:1) and Jesus created you through Himself to (get this) become a representative image of Jesus Himself upon the earth. We host His presence and then we manifest His image! We are elohims, created in goodness, crowned with glory and honor, a little lower than angels as the host (army) of earth to accomplish the Lord's plan for the earth. This is who you are: *elohims* – lacking little of God. This is what you do: manifest the Father in everything you think, say and do – just like Jesus. The Father's kingdom is in you (Luke 17:21)... and yet... you are an independent soul that can decide to live under His authority – or any other. God created us to manifest His Divine goodness, grace, glory and greater works in the earth though our surrendered yielded life, but it seems our doctrines teach we are waiting on God to manifest Himself, when in truth – God is waiting on us to manifest "Christ in us." If you don't want to believe this... then that is your choice. You (i.e. your soul) can think whatever it wants and likewise direct your spirit and body to act however you want, but if you are not manifesting the Father of heaven in the similitude of Christ... then know this: by default, you are manifesting the father of darkness.

> "Now John answered and said, "Master, we saw someone casting out demons in Your name, and we forbade him because he does not follow with us." ^{50} But Jesus said to him, "Do not forbid him, for he who is not against us is on our side" (Luke 9:49, 50).

What spiritual family do you belong to – or stated a little differently – whose family do you think you belong to? Whose family do you think like? If Jesus is the one you behold, then Jesus is the one you must worship and serve... so start thinking like Him!

What does light have in common with darkness? Nothing at all! They are kingdoms in conflict!

> "Do not be unequally yoked together with unbelievers. For what fellowship has righteousness with lawlessness? And what communion has light with darkness?" (2 Cor. 6:14).

Beloved, you have never been alone while on this journey; the Father has been dwelling within you and His Spirit has been guiding you the entire time... but that does not mean you are going to be saved just because of this! You are saved through conversion as someone being transformed by the Spirit of God through the renewing of your mind – to have a sound mind – so as to think as Jesus would think and act as Jesus would act... and thus, become like Jesus – who manifested the Father by appearing for Him and as Him.[115] Jesus is our example. Learn to live like Jesus... and forsake all other imposters and counterfeit doctrines.

The renewed mind will manifest the Father – by appearing for Him and as Him – just like Jesus.

Jesus wants us to become transformed (*metamorphoo*) by the renewing of our mind to become radiant and brilliant... like Him... resembling lightning as when it flashes across the sky! Think brilliant thoughts, speak brilliant words and perform brilliant deeds – and become like Jesus!

Since God created us as soul with spirit, just like Him, according to His likeness, and since we are able to conduct spiritual business by creative thought (our intellect) exactly according to the manner as our heavenly Father who made us to think like Him, and operate like Jesus according to our spirit, then why not take a leap of faith and consider the scriptures on the merit of this truth: we were made like Him to become like Him and operate like Him.

Still skeptical of this, I imagine? What did God reveal to us in the message of Job?

> "Now there was a day when the sons of God came to present themselves before the LORD, and Satan also came among them. ⁷ And the LORD said to Satan, "From where do you come?" So Satan answered the LORD and said, "From going to and fro on the earth, and from walking back and forth on it." ⁸ Then the LORD said to Satan, "Have you considered My servant Job, that there *is* none like him on the earth, a blameless and upright man, one who fears God and shuns evil?" (Job 1:6-8)
>
> "*Again* there was a day when the sons of God came to present themselves before the LORD, and Satan

---

[115] Read: "Image" to learn more about the Jesus: the revelation of God Himself.

came also among them to present himself before the LORD. ² And the LORD said to Satan, "From where do you come?" Satan answered the LORD and said, "From going to and fro on the earth, and from walking back and forth on it." ³ Then the LORD said to Satan, "Have you considered My servant Job, that there is none like him on the earth, a blameless and upright man, one who fears God and shuns evil? And still he holds fast to his integrity, although you incited Me against him, to destroy him without cause." ⁴ So Satan answered the LORD and said, "Skin for skin! Yes, all that a man has he will give for his life. ⁵ But stretch out Your hand now, and touch his bone and his flesh, and he will surely curse You to Your face!" ⁶ And the LORD said to Satan, "Behold, he *is* in your hand, but spare his life" (Job 2:1-6).

If you think what happened to Job only happened to Job, then you misunderstand the message. You are someone like Job, having been sent to earth and Satan is hell-bent on "skin for skin." Satan cannot kill you, but he can (and certainly does) deceive other evil-minded "Jobs" to kill and destroy other Job's like you. He deceived the Sabeans and the Chaldeans to kill both livestock and servants, and it also seems he has authority (albeit limited) to direct fire and wind as well. Man often blames God when bad things happen, but truth be known… there is an enemy's hand in it! Who are you listening to? In Whom are you putting your trust?

The co-manifest reality is all around you… but you determine who you want to listen to!

> "Shall the throne of iniquity, which devises evil by law, have fellowship with You?" (Psa. 94:20).

You can manifest the Father and operate according to His kingdom within you (Luke 17:21) – or you can manifest the devil, the god of iniquity and lawlessness, to operate according to the kingdom of darkness around you… but you cannot to both!!!

Two Kingdoms In Conflict

There are two kingdoms: one within you (Luke 17:21) and one around you.

The kingdom of God within you operates according to the spirit to become manifest through you, but the kingdom of darkness that is around you operates according to sin to invade you and take you captive. I hope you can see this: two kingdoms are at work – one within you as an inner working to become manifest through your spirit, and the other around you that is trying to invade and control you through your flesh. Saints – we are being pulled apart in two directions!

Inside out – or outside in – represent two spiritual kingdoms that are working life or death through you. You are a member of an invading army sent by God to usher in a regime change in this world, and our adversary is invading us through our flesh with sin to prevent us from accomplishing our mission to have dominion over him. We are at war... and the mind is the battlefield. The body is either an instrument or peace or lawlessness, yet this choice is yours!

God gave you your body to be used as an instrument of righteousness for His glory, but Satan is using your body as an instrument against you. He is using your own body as a weapon against you! How does he do this? He is speaking into your mind by tempting you with corrupt thoughts to act according to lawlessness. Literally, he is bombarding us with corrupt thoughts, songs, images, doctrines, attitudes, perceptions, feelings, and emotions – with things that are not aligned with the truth of God so that we might act upon any of them and free-fall into bondage to lawlessness, sin, depression, despair and ultimately... disobedience leading to death. Please comprehend this one truth: your "temporary" body is being used by God to sanctify you **_and_** it is also being used by Satan to keep you captive to sin and death. How you allow God or Satan to influence your mind to use your body (your earthen vessel) is the mystery of man upon the earth.

And yet, the spirit within us is the key to comprehending this mystery of Christ dwelling in us.

You are in the world, but not of it!

> "I have given them Your word; and the world has hated them because they are not of the world, just as I am not of the world. ¹⁵ ***I do not pray that You should take them out of the world, but that You should keep them from the evil one***. ¹⁶ They are not of the world, just as I am not of the world.
> ¹⁷ Sanctify them by Your truth. Your word is truth.
> ¹⁸ As You sent Me into the world, I also have sent them into the world" (John 17:14-18).

You are the light of the world (Matt. 5:14). Jesus placed His light within our spirit, but woe unto us when we allow the darkness of this evil and corrupt world to infiltrate our flesh and invade our spirit and thus… compromise our soul through the temporary flesh superimposed upon us.

> "But if your eye [focus] is bad, your whole body will be full of darkness. If therefore the light that is in you is darkness, how great is that darkness!" (Matt. 6:23).

> "Therefore take heed that the light which is in you is not darkness" (Luke 11:35).

We may find ourselves trapped in sin without any known way of escape because our adversary has taught us many lies to doubt the truth; these you must reject – and truth you must embrace:

1. You are not a human being having a spiritual experience; you are a spiritual being having a human experience on earth
2. God loves you – unconditionally
3. God is Sovereign over the hearts and minds of men

4. God is dwelling in you and He is waiting for you to surrender your will to the Lord Jesus
5. God wants your full allegiance in order to be restored to Him
6. There is no invitation! You must get off the throne of your heart and exalt Jesus upon it
7. God is in control – and sovereign in His kingdom… if that is where you want to dwell
8. Through repentance, by grace and newness, you are a new person through faith in Christ
9. God wants you to act under His authority through your spirit – but not according to your authority or any other authority through your flesh, but "by My Spirit" through your spirit
10. God owns everything in this world and everything belongs to Him, so acknowledge this: you are merely a steward of everything that belongs to Him; so let go and let God
11. Live by grace according to the Spirit – in a spirit of love, meekness, goodness and truth
12. Imitate Jesus – you were created to bear His image and likeness – but "no other"

> Jesus said: "I have come as a light into the world, that whoever believes in Me should not abide in darkness" (John 12:46).

You can listen to whoever you want and you can do whatever you want and you can build whatever kingdom you want in your heart… ***but you need glory to do it***! Satan stole God's glory in order to build his own kingdom in this world… and so can you. You can use the glory God entrusted to you in order to build whatever kingdom you want; however, if you do not build like a faithful builder as a servant of righteousness, then everything you build will be consumed in the judgment fire. Build, build, build the enemy says, but the Lord says:

> "Unless the Lord builds the house, they labor in vain who build it; unless the Lord guards the city,

the watchman stays awake in vain" (Psa. 127:1).

What is the house the Lord wants you to build? And where does He want you to build it?

The Lord wants to establish His permanent presence in the heart-house of your soul, which vacates your body when you die while your soul waits for the judgment of the living and the dead (2 Tim. 4:1; 1 Pet. 4:5).

Saints… who are you listening to? Are you listening to the Lord, or are you listening to you, or worse even – are you listening to Satan. All the sons of God are being gathered in assembly before the presence of God according the purpose of God – to give an account! This has been going on since the beginning and it will continue until the last day: what will you say when the Lord calls you, as one of His stewards, to give an account for what you did with His things? Did you use your soul to think like Him or did you use your soul to think like you – or worse – like the enemy? Did your spirit produce goodness and righteousness in the earth or did it fail to produce any goodness at all? Do you have any idea "who" you are and "what" you are supposed to be doing on this planet??? Do you glorify the Lord or do you give glory to yourself or any other (i.e. the devil)?

Some are still pondering these words yet refuse to understand, so let me ask this: do earthly fathers teach their sons to become just like them? Absolutely! And how do they do this? They spend time with them and tutor them to teach them what they want their sons to know. Our heavenly Father is no different in this regard… and Jesus told us so. Whose son you are depends upon which father you spend time with.

> "Then Jesus answered and said to them, "Most assuredly, I say to you, the Son can do nothing of Himself, but what He sees the Father do; for whatever He does, the Son also does in like manner" (John 5:19).

God is our Father when we devote our time, attention and affection toward Him. Beloved, we are more than servants of the Most High God, and we are more than friends because the wall of hostility has been removed; beloved... we are the brethren of Jesus Christ, and He is not ashamed to call us brethren.

> "No longer do I call you servants, for a servant does not know what his master is doing; but I have called you friends, for all things that I heard from My Father I have made known to you" (John 15:15).

> "For both He who sanctifies and those who are being sanctified are all of one, for which reason He is not ashamed to call them brethren" (Heb. 2:11).

The Father is in you, yet I ask again... who are you listening to? When you are called into God's presence, are you worthy to be called a son of God and a brethren of Christ?

The devil always wants to speak to us because he wants to destroy us and keep us dead in death, but we must not set a place for him in the table of our mind or give him the authority to speak. Who your soul chooses to talk to in your mind is governed by a '*sophronismos*/disciplined' sound mind. Do not give the enemy a comfortable place at the table, and furthermore... command him to shut up and remain silent!

> "And the Lord said, "Simon, Simon! Indeed, Satan has asked for you, that he may sift you as wheat" (Luke 22:31).

When we give Satan the right to speak into our lives, he can sift us up to a point the Lord allows as a means of drawing us into repentance and sanctifying us, and for this reason Jesus is also Lord of "the spoiler to destroy."

> "Behold, I have created the blacksmith, who blows the coals in the fire, who brings forth an instrument

for his work; *and I have created the spoiler to destroy.* ¹⁷ No weapon formed against you shall prosper, and every tongue which rises against you in judgment you shall condemn. This is the heritage of the servants of the LORD, and their righteousness is from Me," Says the LORD" (Isa. 54:16, 17).

Beloved, we need a sound mind! When Jesus encountered the demon-possessed man, He asked "what is your name" and the man said his name is Legion[116] because thousands demons had taken control of his mind and body. Jesus cast the demons out of him into a herd of swine nearby… and this man was restored in his right mind. The word "right" (*sophroneo*-4993) is nearly identical to "sound" (*sophronismos*-4995) as they share the same root words: (*sozo*-to save) and (*phren*-the mind). The mind is being saved and set free (from the influence of sin and the path of destruction) by the tutoring and discipline of the Holy Spirit *with* the word of God so that we may become disciples of Jesus.

Jesus saved this man's mind – and He wants to save your mind also.

If you are restricting the Holy Spirit from speaking to you about anything – anywhere and anytime He chooses – then you are, by default, listening to your thoughts and the thoughts of the enemy "above whatever" He might want to dialogue with you about. Every morning, I look forward to hearing His voice and then I continue to keep an open ~~ear~~ mind throughout the day.

Beloved, we need a sound mind! We are living in a time period when thousands of voices and messages are competing against the small, still voice of the Lord. The constant bombardment of lies and noisy distractions fill our disillusioned lives with fear and anxiety which successfully prevents us from seeking and maintaining intimacy with Jesus. There was an earlier point in time when I asked the Lord to speak louder so I could hear Him better, but that's not how it works… we must seek quiet places and

---

[116] A Roman legion is 6,000 soldiers.

quiet our thoughts to hear Him better. "Be still...and know that I am God" (Psa. 46:10). When you get still.... then you will know!

What are thoughts anyway? Thoughts are as-of-yet unspoken words and utterances that are as strong as any from the tongue. Who is sitting at the table of your mind? Who are you listening to? Who are you plugged in to? What are you going to do when the destroyer speaks a word, a message, a charge, an accusation or a tongue against you? The Apostle Paul understood our dilemma and wrote powerfully under the Anointing in order to help us understand the spiritual paradigm surrounding us by asking four rhetorical questions: "Who" is against us?

> "What then shall we say to these things? If God is for us, [1] who can be against us? [32] He who did not spare His own Son, but delivered Him up for us all, how shall He not with Him also freely give us all things? [33] [2] Who shall bring a charge against God's elect? It is God who justifies. [34] [3] Who is he who condemns? It is Christ who died, and furthermore is also risen, who is even at the right hand of God, who also makes intercession for us. [35] [4] Who shall separate us from the love of Christ? Shall tribulation, or distress, or persecution, or famine, or nakedness, or peril, or sword? [36] As it is written:
>
> "For Your sake we are killed all day long;
> We are accounted as sheep for the slaughter."
> (Romans 8:31-36)

It may surprise you to know that all spiritual language is within the realm of thought. Both kingdoms – of light and darkness – are able to speak into your mind and influence you either for good or for evil. Sitting at "the table of your mind" are three entities: your soul, the Spirit of Christ, and the spirit of antichrist i.e. darkness (1 John 4:3; Eph. 6:12). Your heart, spirit and body are also in attendance, as they are under the governance of your soul[117], but I want to key in on those three entities at this table. Dialogue – through words – is happening all the time because all three have a right to be there, but your soul determines who speaks and communicates at the table of your mind.

Beloved, stop communicating with the enemy; give him no quarter in your mind. We are at war, and we are being led to slaughter, and anyone who thinks the enemy can quarter (be given a free place to stay) in your mind without taking over your house… is utter foolishness.

We will manifest the thoughts of our soul in our mind to entertain them and ponder them (in our heart). That is the power of thought because it originates from (is born of) *energeia* power. We can manifest Jesus, the Father, the devil, yourself… or any other[118]; however, the Father wants us to manifest Him and operate like Him to become His adopted children – by creative thoughts produced by the intellect of our soul… and by manifesting creative goodness through our heart and spirit according to our Divine example: Jesus Christ our Lord and Savior.

> "Now *the Lord is the Spirit*; and where the Spirit of the Lord is, there is liberty" (2 Cor. 3:17).

Allow that scripture to wash over your soul. Jesus is God. Jesus is the Holy One. Jesus is the Lord… and the Lord is the Spirit. Jesus is our Creator and Jesus is the Spirit who created us with a spirit according to His Own likeness so that we should become like Him in everything we think, say and do. (Ponder that!) Jesus came to set us free from the bondage of lies, doubt and deception to live in liberty, truth and righteousness! If these thoughts do not align with your doctrines or your understanding of who Jesus is, then the

---

[117] The term "nature" in 1 Cor. 15:44 is '*psuchikos*-5591' (from '*psuche*-5591-soul') "constitutes a person who yields everything to the human reasonings of the soul, not thinking there is need of help from above." Strong's.

[118] Have you ever noticed the conversations you have with other people in your dreams are by thought? Their lips don't move, which means we communicate in our dreams by "thought."

enemy has successfully deceived you to think something that is contrary to the truth. If the enemy can minimize your understanding to adopt a less-than understanding of "Who" Jesus is, then he has also successfully minimized your understanding of who you are because... we get our identity from Christ! Please keep in mind: this understanding was given to me 33 years 'after' the baptism of the Spirit wherein I knew some of the truth, but my doctrines prevented me from walking in liberty, grace and power. If you embrace this truth, then revelation light with power shall be made available to you so that you may live a victorious life – in Christ.

Weaponized Thoughts

> "For the weapons of our warfare are not carnal but mighty in God for pulling down strongholds" (2 Cor. 10:4).

Thoughts are the weapons of spiritual warfare! We are tapping into the *energeia* power of/from God when we produce thoughts in our soul and mind, yet we have been given free will to use this power of thought to produce good or evil to influence this world. You have the right to think and say whatever you want, but doing so does not mean you are right; it merely means God gave you this right... so use it according to His righteousness and not for unrighteous means that you control for your benefit. He gave you this right (authority) to create thoughts, so use them rightly... according to grace.

> "Death and life are in the power of the tongue, and those who love it will eat its fruit" (Prov. 18:21).

Every thought we entertain is *energeia* power manifested in us, and every word we speak is *energeia* power released through us. *Logos* thoughts or *rhema* utterances are words born of *energeia* power intended to accomplish a purpose – either to produce life or promote death.

> "But Jesus knew their thoughts [1761], and said to them: "Every kingdom divided against itself is brought to desolation, and every city or house divided against itself will not stand" (Matt. 12:25).

The word "thoughts" is '*enthumesis*-1761' meaning "deliberation; thoughts; cogitation; an inward reasoning and intentions; of man's production of images."[119] Jesus created us according to His Own image with the ability to produce "images" in the mind, yet Jesus knew their imaginations were evil toward Him because He is Lord God… and He is a discerner of the thoughts and intents of men (Heb. 4:12). Our thoughts will be judged by Jesus… as well as our actions and our ideologies.

> "… casting down arguments and every high thing that exalts itself against the knowledge of God, **bringing every thought into captivity to the obedience of Christ**" (2 Cor. 10:5).

Ideology Of Thought

> Jesus said: "Do you suppose that I came to give peace on earth? I tell you, not at all, but rather division" (Luke 12:51).

Jesus did not come to create peace in this world… but division. Two kingdoms are in conflict – the kingdom of light and truth versus the kingdom of darkness and lies – and Jesus is dividing and separating those things that belong to Him from those things that are of "this world."

Much divisiveness has occurred in America during (and following) the election of Donald Trump in 2016 (and for many years leading up to this as well) for mainly this reason: the nation became divided into two camps resembling forms of religion. The political Left supports and functions as 'the one world religion' with climate control, population control and abortion (among many

---

[119] Strong's Concordance.

other controls) as unequivocal positions that, unless everyone agrees with these positions, will culminate in the cataclysmic destruction of this world. The Left wants "control" (authority and power = dominion) and uses weaponized fear called global Armageddon to either pull you or push you into world-loving or world-hating camps... and America is being torn asunder as a result. Study the political movement of the Left's ideology during the past 60 years and you will see a trend: the worship of nature, praise for Gaia, dehumanization of persons, redefining words to imply opposite values, and then abounding confusion in everything from gender to marriage to law and truth and religion in order create an alternate reality that contradicts and attacks that which is lawful and orderly (i.e. the conservative values of the political Right). They can't control their lawless passions, but they think they can control the temperature of the earth. Go figure.

The ideological positions of the political left are often-times unsubstantiated irreverent lies from the prince of this world (Satan) who governs the dominion of "this world" unbeknownst to clueless goats that are diametrically opposed to Jesus Christ and His dominion over the earth. It pretends to preach a world religion of love and tolerance, not hate ... unless you disagree with their ideological position... and now you've become a target of their hateful vengeance, violence and vitriol.

Conservatism, as an ideology, represents one way of living as closely to Christian-biblical values without corrupting one or the other by attempting to blend the two, and this is why progressives see conservatives as a threat against their liberal-lifestyle agenda. Vigilance from the Right will encounter violence from the Left; this is to be expected, so do not be shaken or worried, but remain courageous and stand strong... the end of this age is approaching.

America as a nation is now embroiled within an irrevocable and irreconcilable political and spiritual civil war whose political ideologies, once a moderate handshake away, are now miles apart. To put it mildly, America is in transition; to put it bluntly, America is having a spiritual revolution. The spiritual came first, then the material; all things material originated from-out-of one spiritual reality or the other, and Jesus created us in this manner: to love the one and hate the other. Yet the church has no understanding why this is happening, nor is it able to discern good apart from evil; absolute truth was the first victim in order to promote the Left's radical ideology. Ideology represents thoughts made manifest... and yet...

Thoughts are greater than actions. Think about it for a moment... regardless if you act upon a thought or not, your thoughts exist. ***Actions cannot occur unless preceded by thoughts.*** In the above scripture, we know Jesus is able to perceive '*enthumesis*' thoughts and imaginations as being evil. If you've thought about doing evil – or good, Jesus knows your thoughts regardless if you have acted upon them or not. The battle between good and evil is being waged in the mind of man, and even though I took a foray into the political arena to explain why many things are happening in America, we must return to the manner in which each of us – by thought – make individual choices to operate according to the belief system we embrace. The thoughts we think produces the reality we desire to live in.

> "But I say to you that whoever looks at a woman to lust for her has already committed adultery with her in his heart" (Matt. 5:28).

Let's examine this scripture carefully. Before adultery happens, adultery is committed in the heart by focusing the eyes to look and see in a lustful manner. What action causes (precipitates) the eyes to focus in this sinful manner? These actions originate as thoughts contemplated in the mind of the soul to focus the attention so as to gratify the lust of the heart.

Our thoughts become the originating factor resulting in our deliberate actions – either according to grace or according to sin. We operate according to thought! We think... and then we act.

Herein is a critical message: thoughts are greater than actions, which supports Jesus' statement, "My Father... is greater than all"

(John 10:29). The creative thoughts of the Father are greater than the manifested words or actions of the Son, and yet, the Father and Son are One. Thoughts and manifestations (words, utterances, actions) – are one!

> "My sheep hear My voice, and I know them, and they follow Me. [28] And I give them eternal life, and they shall never perish; neither shall anyone snatch them out of My hand. [29] ***My Father***, who has given them to Me, ***is greater than all***; and no one is able to snatch them out of My Father's hand. [30] I and My Father are one" (John 10:27-30).

The Lord's voice is a creative thought the Spirit speaks into our mind... and our willingness to listen, hear, understand and obey is the benchmark for claiming our salvation as a follower of Jesus Christ. Our doctrines teach us we are followers of Jesus, but if you cannot hear His voice, then you cannot prove you have a personal relationship with Jesus.

This is why it is very important for us to say what we mean – and mean what we say. Your words, utterances and actions represent the creative thought life of your soul... yet sometimes we speak spontaneously and "without thinking" (i.e. without filtering it through the table of our mind and pondering it "with" our heart; Matt. 13:15). Whatever proceeds "from out of" the heart (i.e. thoughts energized by our soul and manifested through our spirit of the inner man) will become manifested as words and actions through the outer man (the body of flesh). In you – then through you – is how the immaterial spiritual paradigm is materially made manifest by you.

The thought-life of your soul is greater than the manifested word-life through your spirit.

What you think – and believe – determines what you say as well as the actions you take. This is why the sound mind that listens to the Voice of the Spirit is so vitally important... because this is the cornerstone of your salvation in Christ! Hear and follow – Shema – hear and obey! The thoughts we think are influenced by what we hear, so if you want to guard your heart and protect the good seed of God's glory placed within your soul, then it is imperative to guard the ears of your spirit-man… and keep your ears and eyes attentively focused on Jesus and listen to Him.

"My sheep hear My voice, and I know them, ***and they follow Me!!!!!!***" Who are you listening to? What are you looking for and who are you seeking? Better yet – what are you thinking?

> "…so that they should seek the Lord, in the hope that they might grope for Him and find Him, though He is not far from each one of us; [28] for in Him we live and move and have our being, as also some of your own poets have said, 'For we are also His offspring.' [29] Therefore, since we are the offspring of God, we ought not to *think* [*enthumesis*-1761; imagine] that the Divine Nature is like gold or silver or stone, something shaped by art and man's devising" (Acts 17:27-29).

Our thoughts regarding who (and what) God is… has been getting us into trouble since the beginning! The Father and Son – are One! And if you are in Christ, then so are you! Through faith in Christ, you are united in oneness of the Spirit into the Oneness of the Godhead who dwells mightily in you. ***Beloved… you are a manifested one***, having been predestined and predetermined by the creative thought and purposes of the Father, to live according to the spirit within you – in the similitude and likeness of the Son who abides in oneness with the Father. Meditate on this for a moment… or millennia… or as long as it takes until, by grace, you believe it, own it and live according to it!

The kingdom of heaven is already – HERE!

> "And I will give you the keys of the kingdom of heaven, and whatever you bind on earth will be bound in heaven, and whatever you loose on earth

will be loosed in heaven" (Matt. 16:19). "And the gates of Hades shall not prevail against it" (Matt. 16:18).

Jesus is the Manifested One, the Image of the Holy One who manifests the Father with His Spirit. His kingdom is an everlasting kingdom and His dominion is without end – yet He is giving all men the option of partnering the dominion of this earth in oneness with Him in unity of the Spirit in His kingdom… or choosing to remain a child of rebellion against Him. Jesus is Victorious and He is dividing and conquering and separating and shaking and sifting everything from itself in order to gather together all things aligned with His sovereignty as Lord of Heaven and Earth. Jesus is Lord! Either you are with Him – or you are against Him. "Somewhere in between" is an illusion created by the enemy to keep you captive to sin and abiding in death.

> "The *effective fervent* [*energeo*-1754] prayer of a righteous man avails much" (James 5:16).

Energetic righteous prayers produce much effect! Words originate as thoughts produced by *energeia* power. Prayer is the means whereby *energeia* power is released through thoughts to produce paradigm shifts in spiritual atmospheres (heavens). You may not understand this completely, but even if you do not see any evidence that your prayers have had any effect, let me counsel you: energy is being released into heavenly places. Shifts are happening! Beginning in 1727, the Moravian community prayed for revival and then it happened four months later, and then they prayed around the clock every day for 100 years– and within the first 65 years over 300 missionaries had been sent out. Prayer is powerful. Prayer is effectual and never returns void. Intercessory prayer is able to pull down strongholds and shift atmospheres!

> "Pray without ceasing" (1 Thess. 5:17).

Prayer employs words (both spoken and unspoken) to initiate dialogue with the Lord, but dialogue hasn't happened until we stop and wait long enough to hear His response. The reason many of our prayers in church end abruptly by the three-word punctuation "In Jesus' name" and move quickly into the next item on the church service agenda is because… we are terrified by the slightest chance God will actually respond to our spoken words. A mature church will allow ample time (in silence or soft music) to wait for the Lord to respond, and when He does respond, this church will continue to wait for the Holy Spirit to continue His work of sanctification in the hearts and minds of those persons that desire to hear His Voice… and hear it!!! Show me a church that is bold enough to pause when the Spirit becomes manifest in worship – even for long periods of time – and I will show you a mature church that is manifesting heaven on earth for the tearing down of powers, principalities and strongholds!!! This church wants to hear Words from the Lord and be directed by the Spirit – against which the power of the enemy hasn't got a chance! Amen!

Sadly, it seems, we believe what we want to believe – and then have the audacity to call it faith, and then we sing the messages we want to hear – and then have the audacity to call it worship.

> "For the kingdom of God is not in *word* [*logos* only] but in *power* [*dunamis*]" (1 Cor. 4:20).

> "…through whom also He made the worlds; ³ who being the brightness of His glory and the express image [*charakter*] of His person, and upholding all things by the *word* [*rhema*-utterance] of His *power* [*dunamis*], when He had by Himself purged our sins, sat down at the right hand of the Majesty on high" (Heb. 1:2, 3).

Energeia power is instrumental in making thought- *energeia*-word- faith effectual and fervent with dunamis power (which represents authority or the release power) because they originate in power.

In conclusion:

- All power belongs to God Almighty. God does not have all power; God *IS* all power.
- *Energeia* power in our soul originates creative thoughts… in the similitude of our Father
- *Dunamis* power resides within our spirit and body (the instruments of our soul)
- Static *dunamis* energy becomes operational (dynamic *dunamis*) by every thought which, when energetically acted upon by our soul, becomes an act of our will that we commission through our spirit… in the similitude of the Spirit of Christ
- *Kratos* power will become the manifested means whereby God "perfects and completes" His glorious plan of dominion on earth through His sons and daughters now – and in glory in the New Earth
- All power and authority (i.e. the fullness of God's glory) belongs to God Almighty

If you still think your thoughts never amount to anything or your prayers never result in anything effectual, then you misunderstand the power of prayer; just because you cannot see the result does not mean the result has not shaken the very foundations of worlds and kingdoms.

> "Be anxious for nothing, but in everything by prayer and supplication, with thanksgiving, let your requests be made known to God; [7] and the peace of God, which surpasses all understanding, will guard your hearts and minds through Christ Jesus" (Phil. 4:6, 7).

Man's biggest problem… is his small-minded thinking!

Eternity Exists

This next point might be the truth that stimulates an epiphany to perceive your spiritual nature.

There is no past or future in eternity; those are elements of time. Energy is never lost; it becomes (transitions into) something else. Since you existed in the past, you may have some remembrance of those former times (though the scriptures indicate we cannot), but our soul is eternal... and since our spirit is able to move about within the heavenly realm as it did pre-humanity and post-humanity (forward and backward in time), this then may explain the odd notion of reincarnation (wherein some claim to have existed in a prior dimension) and also the odd manifestation of déjà vu (when you have a real-time event that you feel you've experienced before). These ideas have been rejected outright by the church (and myself included) as merely hyperactive neurons sending and receiving data in the mind slightly out of sequence, or perhaps highly imaginative science-fiction born out of creative speculation, but let me challenge you with this biblical fact: prophets are able to receive truth about future events that have not happened yet. Moses received truth about the origin of creation and prophets received messages about previous events, such as the cataclysm in heaven, even before a word was spoken. The bible is full of such individuals on both sides of the good-evil spectrum. Now... process this biblical fact: the Apostle John was shown end times events by the Lord and His angel whereby he recorded those future events in the book: Revelation. Those events have not happened yet... but they will! In truth, John was brought (in the spirit) into a heavenly dimension to experience future events while his soul and body were still imprisoned on the island of Patmos.

Spirit normal!

Are these events possible? The Bible documents many such instances in which God in His infinite goodness has influenced and continues to influence human activities on earth by telling prophets about future (and past) events, yet the same can also be said of demonic influences that are able to tell (foretell) future events (such as the girl with the spirit of divination; Acts 16:16). The more I know about supernatural spiritual events, the more convinced I become... the other side is able to influence this side of reality... _and_ they are fully aware of past and future events.

Demons (unclean spirits) knew exactly who Jesus was, yet Jesus silenced them... which seems counterintuitive to me if you are leading an army of humans to initiate a regime change against those very same demons. The Holy Spirit is our Tutor and Source for truth... so seek Him and not demons or unclean spirits.

The main distinction being: demons and unclean spirits *cannot* create, recreate or procreate anything, but they can copy and counterfeit everything that God inspires yet with an evil twist to support their evil intent (agenda). Some people claim to have experienced the past life of former persons and explained that life with such accuracy so as to insinuate they are the reincarnated person of a previous life. Reincarnation is another deception from the pit of hell, and yet, even my writings give much evidence to support another life is lived after this one that Jesus called: life eternal. Resurrection is real, reincarnation is the counterfeit. The enemy will always distort the truth to create a counterfeit (alternate) reality with twisted truth in order to deceive as many people as are willing to listen and believe, and for this reason we must listen to the voice of the Spirit (myself included) because He is the Voice of Truth – and the only Truth that matters!

Eternity exists within an infinite dimension without the limitation of time. Now, I would like you to create this word picture in your mind:

There is a thin rope hovering about 4' above the floor of a room that has no sides. As far left or right as you can look, the rope continues into "eternity." The rope is visible in front of you and you can clearly see the woven strands of this rope... as well as six strands of yarn hanging down from the rope. These six strands are spaced about an inch apart to demarcate millennial (1,000 year) periods of time (seasons) on earth. Then you notice another strand of yarn on the ground in front of you that has not been attached yet (a time period yet to occur). Our human bodies are constrained and confined to exist within these six strands of yarn (and then a seventh), but our soul and spirit are not confined in this manner; they are only constrained by – life and death. If the Spirit of the

Lord wants to pick you up and transport you into another dimension, then let the Spirit have His way with you. The Apostles' John, Paul and Philip were translated in this manner, as well as the Prophets' Ezekiel and Isaiah. Therefore… we must be careful to test the spirits, as both the principality of good (God's Spirit) and the principality of evil (demonic angels) are able to invade our reality to do this.

Yet some may argue: is there empirical evidence for this? Did Jesus ever teach about this? It is very rare, yet Jesus gives us the proof we seek in these two examples:

1. Jesus told Nathaniel, "Before Philip called you, when you were under the fig tree, I saw you" (John 1:48). Jesus moved back in time (by His spirit) while residing in the present reality (within His body) to make a real time demonstration of this principle.
2. When a crowd gathered to throw Jesus off a cliff, He passed (like a spirit) through the midst of them (John 8:59).

Understanding the spiritual reality of man in this manner may still be considered "madness" by many religious elite, and yet this is exactly what they said of the Apostle Paul when he described the resurrection to them… "You are beside yourself! Much learning is driving you mad!" (Acts 26:24) In modern terms: "You are out of your mind. Your intellect has made you crazy!" All I can say is: our "Future" holds the key.

Paradigm of Co-Existing Realities

Man was placed "in between." In the midst of two realities, man was placed… to pass through.

The reality of heaven and hell are upon the earth even now. Which one you are able to perceive is relative to the focus of your soul: you will either focus on good or evil. You cannot serve two masters: you will love the one and hate the other.

You are the light of the world. If you profess to be spiritual but have a worldly focus, then the light of truth has not been activated by you. Some of you may be asking: "How much light do I have?" If you have a heavenly focus, then perhaps you should be asking: "How much darkness is being dispersed with the light the Lord is shining through me?" One reality perceives light as a possession to "have" and be used while the other sees light as a tool or instrument given by the Lord to be administered by the Holy Spirit for kingdom purposes. We are gateways of light and glory, not gatekeepers. Can you see the difference?

How much light is being released through you (not by you) to establish the kingdom of heaven?

The worldly focus on "having and possessing things" is to serve self; the kingdom focus is on surrendering all to serve the Lord thereby doing His business to accomplish His will.

You are the salt of the earth. Are you flavoring the earth to glorify God and receive glory for yourself? Do you see yourself as a seed sown upon the earth to yield more glory unto the Lord? Are you promoting and marketing your self-image or are you being conformed into the image of Christ by the Spirit of Christ so as to become His manifest representative on earth?

You are one spirit with the Lord. Do you consider the Holy Spirit dwelling within you as something you have? You may have even asked: "If the Spirit is dwelling in me, then how much of the Holy Spirit do I have?" To quote a dear brother in Christ who told me:

> ***"It's not how much Holy Spirit you have,***
> ***but how much of you the Holy Spirit has?"***

Do you see the difference? Embracing the revelation of that truth is the gospel message. We were all born into the paradigm of darkness and sin, yet the Spirit desires to birth us into the kingdom of God! We are in bondage and need to be set free from the tyranny of self – as well as many human-engineered doctrines that are works-based rather than relationship-based.

The paradigms of heaven and hell are already upon the earth. It is not important to know how much you have of one or the other... however, it is critical to know how much one or the other *has of YOU*!

How much of God do you think you have? Now, doesn't that sound silly, and yet, throughout history, men have congregated into groups and tribes for a variety of reasons, and the worship of God or gods was always part of this gathering together. Nation went to war against nation for supremacy (i.e. dominion) and called upon divine intervention to give them advantage over their (perceived) enemies. The habitual habit of mankind claiming one god as being superior over another god is the trick of the enemy... which continues to this day. There is only <u>One</u> True Living God whereby all other manifestations are false expressions. The One Tue Living God selected one nation from out of many nations to be His chosen people and the Lord instituted a covenant with Israel, but they refused to listen to His voice and obey the messages they received. So, the One True Living God, the Lord Jesus, visited earth to establish another covenant with mankind that desires to follow Him and be guided by the Spirit of God, but they fell into the same pattern of claiming God as the leader of their special "one true" tradition and then they rejected the guidance and counsel of the Holy Spirit. Another group emerged from that form of institutionalized religion wherein a protestant reformation sought to return mankind back to the original pattern established by God, but they, likewise, also created doctrines that implied "our God is the one true God" and you cannot be saved unless you think like we think and believe what we believe.

Our protestant doctrines have become very exclusionary and proprietary to even indicate God does not dwell in anyone until they have made a profession of faith in Christ Jesus. By faith, they say, God will come into us and dwell with us and save us, yet once again... the enemy delights in tricking us to think only certain people or select people groups can have God dwelling in them <u>until after</u> they have jumped through various religious hoops of obedience. Hogwash!

God is everywhere! If God is not in the unsaved, then God is not everywhere. You cannot have it both ways. Got it?

And then – we present covenantal-faith prospects with an altar call to invite Jesus into their heart. Do we even consider the lunacy of this? We (mere humans) are "inviting" God to come into our heart and dwell in us, as if God will do as we command. God did not ask us if we wanted to be saved… He commanded us to be saved! Jesus is already in us, but we kicked God off the throne in our heart and exalted our pathetic sinful life upon it as lord of our life; thus, we are commanded to get off it and exalt Jesus as Lord upon it and establish His Preeminence as Lord in our life. Our altar-call invitation is just another example wherein we "have Jesus" instead of "Jesus governing us."

God is everywhere and God inhabits everyone. God is not the head of any club, select people group or religious institution, as if God belongs to us. How primordial!

***God does not belong to us – we belong to God*!!!** God is everywhere, and God dwells (temporarily) in everyone – *and in you all*!

> "There is one body and one Spirit, just as you were called in one hope of your calling; ⁵ one Lord, one faith, one baptism; ⁶ one God and Father of all, who is above all, and through all, ***and in you all***' (Eph. 4:4-6).

How much God do you have dwelling in you? The spirit of religion wants you to believe He isn't even in you except on certain holy occasions or in certain places or until you perform certain religious rituals or receive certain sacraments. God is already in us! God does not enter into us when we enter into certain places like churches or synagogues – God is already in us, and yet, we do not become His children adopted into His eternal kingdom apart from faith in Jesus Christ and the Spirit's sanctification. Abraham's example of hearing and obeying the voice of the Lord was an example for all of us to follow... through whom (by his example) all the families of man are blessed. You are just as much an offspring of Abraham, as an offspring of God's Spirit, when you follow Abraham's example. Shema! Hear and obey!

> "I will bless those who bless you, and I will curse him who curses you; ***and in you all the families*** of the earth shall be blessed" (Gen. 12:3).

You are no different than Abraham, any prophet or any spiritual leader. Even Elijah was a man with a nature like yours! (James 5:17) The only difference between them and anyone else (such as you) on planet earth is: do you want to listen to God, understand and obey His voice – or not?

> Jesus said: "Therefore bear fruits worthy of repentance, and do not begin to say to yourselves, 'We have Abraham as our father.' For I say to you that God is able to raise up children to Abraham from these stones" (Luke 3:8).

Satan, our enemy, would have us fight one another over the supremacy of God in our culture, doctrines or traditions when, in fact, this is yet another trick by the enemy to deceive us into thinking it is better for God to be in our culture – rather than ***the culture of God being in us***. God is not the head of any religious denomination! God is "in us" and "in you all" – yet we are only "in Christ" by grace through faith... when we declare our allegiance to Jesus Christ who dwells within us whereby we become God's offspring and are then permanently grafted onto the Tree of Life into His everlasting kingdom as sons and daughters of righteousness in the kingdom of Truth. Our allegiance to Jesus sets us free from the tyranny of man-made doctrines and the fear-based lies of works-based traditions... and our adversary, the devil, as well.

No religion has a corner market on God or His truth. How presumptuous!

Jesus said: "The kingdom of God is in you" (Luke 17:21). The kingdom of God is already within you!!! How much of His kingdom – the kingdom of heaven – *are you* allowing to be established within you *and* established on earth through you? And consequently, how much of His kingdom might you be withholding and refusing to release so that others may be saved?

Hosting the Lord's presence within you is the single-most important thing you do as you establish His kingdom, have dominion on earth, and give Him all glory. You aren't doing it for the hope of heaven or rewards in life eternal; you do this because this is "who" you really are and you love Jesus more than anything... including life itself. Love is your motivation.

Intimacy with Jesus – is paramount!!!

The revelation of Jesus in you and the reality of His kingdom being manifested through you is entirely determined by you. Deeply consider this condition: either you are a gateway for heavenly things being released through you – or are you a gatekeeper that is micromanaging and restricting God who dwells in you.

This is such a strange reality, indeed, because your spirit and your body belong to God who dwells within you... and yet you refuse to subordinate yourself to God as the Governor of your soul. Truly, angels look down with dread in their eyes upon our puny fist of indignation raised against God when we refuse to yield our sovereignty to Him. Truly, we know not what we do! By our insubordination, we are judging ourselves unworthy of life eternal – or worse – eternal damnation in fiery torment.

"If the Spirit of Christ dwells in you" then you will manifest the gifts of the Spirit and produce the fruit of the Spirit. ***Love is the reason – not the byproduct.*** The outward manifestation of spiritual gifts from a worldly perspective will oftentimes cause the weak in faith to seek the power gifts rather than the service (humility) gifts because this person's knowledge is immature – wherein self importance and having a positive worldly image remains their focus. In contrast, a mature man or woman of God will obediently do all the Lord requests regardless if they are seen as foolish, irrational or even 'ungodly' because their focus is not on self but rather on serving the Lord and building His kingdom. Their love for the Lord compels them, as disciples, to surrender all they "have" in this life to attain Christ and abide with Him in Paradise.

The most important things in this life... are not things!

New Earth Promises

"Surrender all" is such an interesting term, and yet... it is the most important expression in new covenant living we need to comprehend! Surrender all... in order to know everything, to have everything, to attain everything, and to be everything you ever wanted to be – according to what you originally were. What, you say... in order to become what you already were? Hello... paradigm shift! Our sacrifice in this probationary life is to get us back to what we were once before! Shazam! We are becoming again – what we were already (sons and daughters of God in His presence daily). If you don't feel bamboozled by the spirit of religion in this moment, then you aren't paying attention.

"Surrender all" and "forsaking everything" is to get us back to our original operating position "in" Christ. You aren't surrendering all to get nothing... you surrender all to get everything back (redeemed)! You are on probation and you are being tested to see if you will "sacrifice it all" for the sake of Christ – in order to get it all back – for the sake of Christ. (Even I am belittled by the revelation the Lord is teaching me.) Do you love Jesus enough to surrender it all to Him and give it all away – in order to get back what rightfully belongs to you – through faith?

> "For behold, I create new heavens and a new earth; and the former shall not be remembered or come to mind. [18] But be glad and rejoice forever in what I create......... [21] They shall build houses and inhabit them; they shall plant vineyards and eat their fruit.

²² They shall not build and another inhabit; they shall not plant and another eat; for as the days of a tree, so shall be the days of My people, and My elect shall long enjoy the work of their hands" (Isa. 65:17, 17, 21, 22; read all of Isaiah 65).

This life is a test of our dedication and devotion to Jesus, the Lord of all. When we surrender it all – we get it all back, plus interest – as a prize with an inheritance — for all eternity!!! Hold onto this life and the things of this world – and lose it all! Surrender it all – for the sake of Christ – and you shall redeem much with your Redeemer in life eternal:

- "And everyone who has left houses or brothers or sisters or father or mother or wife or children or lands, *for My name's sake*, shall receive a hundredfold, _and_ inherit eternal life" (Matt. 19:29)
- "So it shall be, when the LORD your God brings you into the land of which He swore to your fathers, to Abraham, Isaac, and Jacob, to give you large and beautiful cities which you did not build, ¹¹ houses full of all good things, which you did not fill, hewn-out wells which you did not dig, vineyards and olive trees which you did not plant— when you have eaten and are full" (Deut. 6:10, 11)
- "Well done, good and faithful servant; you were faithful over a few things, I will make you ruler over many things. Enter into the joy of your lord" (Matt. 25:21)
- "Ask of Me, and I will give You The nations for Your inheritance, and the ends of the earth for Your possession" (Psa. 2:8)
- We shall govern places, towns, cities, regions and nations
- And we shall get possessions forfeited by those who refused to understand – and believe

These promises in the Old Testament deal with the reward saints will receive in the New Earth. It is better to be forsaken in this life to enjoy the blessed inheritance of the saints in life eternal.

Whatever you have surrendered "for His sake" will be recompensed by the Lord of glory, so… what have you got to lose? Even if your life is required of you, those who are martyred for the sake of Christ are coming back in the first resurrection to rule and reign with Christ for a thousand years – never to die again.

We may be beggars in this life, but when we return home in glory – with glory – we will be kings and queens and princes in authority with power to rule as governors and magistrates. Earth is your true and rightful inheritance (domain) in the New Earth – and beloved – you are Christ's inheritance! There is a dramatic drama unfolding before your eyes as you read these words, and yet, unless the Spirit has *'dianoigo'* opened your mind to receive this truth, these words will only be things you hoped for, which remain apart from the promise, for just one reason: because you refused to believe, surrender all – and serve Christ Jesus, your Savior, Redeemer and Deliverer.

The hardest part of believing this message … is believing! We struggle to endure many trials in this life (myself included) and there are some days when it seems… the struggle doesn't seem worth it… especially when we have no tangible proof, nor any assurance beyond what is mentioned in the scriptures. Through patient endurance, in confidence, we hope for these things, yet the absence of any verifiable proof causes the faith of many to grow cold and detached.

You are the redemption and the deliverance who will be returning to your former places in the restoration and regeneration as adopted sons and daughters…through faith and obedience… <u>into</u> Christ's kingdom… to receive your inheritance with true riches that you painstakingly endeavored with great perseverance to produce through deeds of righteousness – in His name.
Believe it! Wait for it! Persevere with patient endurance! Your great reward draws nigh!

> "Strive to enter through the narrow gate, for many, I say to you, will seek to enter and will not be able"
> (Luke 13:24).

"The word "strive" is '*agonizomai*-75' and means, "to struggle, to compete for a prize, to contend with an adversary." [120] This word summarizes our struggle on this earth as we have dominion in His name while our adversary seeks to destroy the message of grace and truth that is being manifested in us and through us. This struggle is not easily won by simply flicking a wrist, or making a verbal profession, or signing a membership roster, or attending the Sunday morning fraternal order of any denomination. Folks, we are in a spiritual battle on this earth and our adversary has been deceiving us with many lies and eating the church's lunch to keep us captive to sin and controlled by sin for one purpose: to deceive us, obliterate us – and maintain possession of "this world.""[121]

Saints of the Living God... do you know what's at stake??? Strive for the narrow gate!!!

Do you want restoration now in this life, or are you willing to endure this life a little while longer... until you get to the other side? The reason we don't live like this is because we really don't believe what we already claim to believe. Faith, however, is doing what we believe is the truth. The institutional church cannot receive this revelation because you are more valuable as timid sheep with basic faith than mighty warriors coming against principalities and powers to destroy strongholds with greater faith through patient endurance. This truth will set you free!

Endurance is an attribute of grace operating within you – to persevere – for the sake of Christ!

The Lord created you for a purpose and He has a commission waiting for you. Disciples thoroughly understand and comprehend what is being asked of them because they comprehend the prize, so I ask you: do you prefer to sit on the sidelines – or – do you want to be all in?

---

[120] Strong's Concordance.
[121] Excerpt from "Understand" section titled "Why Do You Strive?"

On or In

When we believed ON the name of Jesus, this was more than a profession that says, "I believe Jesus is real and Jesus is Lord" which is believing IN Jesus. Believers need to believe ON Jesus.

> "Believe on the Lord Jesus Christ, and you will be saved, you and your household" (Acts 16:31).

> "If therefore God gave them the same gift as He gave us when we believed on the Lord Jesus Christ, who was I that I could withstand God?" (Acts 11:17)

Believing *on* – is much different than believing *in*. What you believe really doesn't matter. Did you receive the gift of the Holy Spirit when you believed – or not? Did the operational power of the Spirit become manifest at the moment of your conversion – or not? Did something manifestly change in your life – or not??? Allow me use an example from my own life: when I accepted Jesus as "my Savior," very little changed in my life and I became even more decadent in sinful behavior. My belief changed nothing. Nine months later, under much conviction by the Holy Spirit, I attended a Jesus revival in an effort to seek forgiveness from Jesus. I was grieved and grieving deeply regarding my sin. I went to an open-air tent and got down on my knees to beg His forgiveness and declare Jesus "my Lord." In that moment, my left arm began to rise up on its' own as if reaching toward heaven. When I saw this, I commanded it to stop, but instead, my right arm began to rise up like the left arm… and then it happened: I entered into worship. What happened to me was done by the Spirit Himself… and I worshipped in this manner for an unknown length of time totally oblivious to anyone or anything happening around me. When I came to my senses, a tent that beforehand was filled with over 100 people listening to various teachings… was now empty. Hours had vanished instantly.

This was my baptism by the Spirit. No shaking, tongues, no bold proclamations or anything remotely exhibiting some gift with power – except – the unmistakable evidence that the Spirit took control of my arms and I entered into worship. A radical supernatural moment of grace released within me a very silent grace gift called: wisdom and understanding. In that moment, I was changed; I was a new creation... I was made white as snow... and the process of the Spirit's sanctification had been initiated, by grace.

The Holy Spirit is always a gentleman yet in this moment (and perhaps yours as well) He took control of two members of my body (which actually belong to the Lord) whereby the Spirit authenticated the Lord's ownership and sovereignty of my life and consummated His covenant agreement with the Spirit's gift to me: upraised hands. The Spirit's gift is often different from one person to the next, just as one tongue is different than another tongue, so it is more important to understand... that a spiritual transaction has occurred in the heavenly realm whereby the Spirit certifies and authenticates your adoption into God's family. Did you receive a gift at your adoption according to the covenant? A deposit to guarantee the transaction happened? Did you receive the seal of the Holy Spirit (Eph. 1:13)? If you did not receive a gift, then go back and ask Jesus... and wait for His response. If you go to pastors or priests for advice rather than the Spirit Himself, then you have initiated the wrong search. Ask the Holy Spirit! Human advice is often conflicted by many "religious" opinions... and agendas.

People may think about sacraments as holy moments in which God comes to dwell in them, so I ask you: when did God come to dwell in you? Saints, He has always dwelled in you ever since He formed His spirit (small 's') in you. He established this temporary place for Him to dwell until such time when you dedicate your life in total allegiance to Him, whereby He gives you a new heart and forms a new spirit within you (Ezek. 36:26) to establish a permanent abode (home) within you where He abides _and_ His Spirit also takes up residence within you as well – as a new creature in His kingdom... according to faith.

As new creatures in His kingdom, every one of us has a commission waiting for us. God doesn't ask us to do what we can't accomplish... He asks us to do things that He knows we can accomplish. He knows you – inside and out!

God is in us and with us every step of the way, and He endures everything with us. We were never alone at any time during this sojourn. From conception until death, God has been in us, His power has been in us, His eternity has been in us, His life has been in us, His kingdom has been in us, and his spirit [sic] has been in us, but sadly we have been completely unaware because our doctrines do not teach this truth. Why do teachers and faith merchants teach us about sacraments and ordinances in order to get things from God that we already have – even apart from faith? It seems counterintuitive, and yet, it seems our doctrines are tempting us to search for things in order to get things that have already been freely given to us by God – which sounds remarkably similar to Satan's temptation in the garden. Saints of God – truth is always under attack! Listen to the Voice of the Spirit – and hear the truth.

Back on point: during that moment when faith happened (the epiphany in your mind according to truth), several activities occurred simultaneously in this moment of faith:

- Your profession (the declaration of faith)
- Your conversion and sustained conversion through sanctification
- Your steadfast allegiance and obedience to Jesus
- Your admission into His family by covenant
- The Spirit's baptism and the impartation of His gift

Most people are clueless regarding the covenant that was established between them and the Lord Jesus. When two people enter into a legal spiritual agreement known as covenant, they openly make proclamations in the presence of their families and declare:

- My family is your family – and your family is now my family
- My things are your things – and your things are now my things
- My lands are your lands – and your dominion is my dominion
- My allegiance is to protect you and your family in case of enemy threat – and likewise you unto me

When Jesus enters into an individual covenant with us, He tells us we must surrender our will in obedience to Him whereby gifts are exchanged unto one another: my old life for His life in newness. Such a deal! Our old, depraved, broken-down, busted and mismanaged life of sin is offered in exchange for the Spirit of life in Christ Jesus (Rom. 8:2) so that we may live life as born anew creatures according to the Spirit who birthed us into His kingdom through faith… wherein we shall also attain life eternal "if" we continue in faithfulness to the covenant and "if" we continue willingly to be sanctified and transformed into the image of Christ. Beloved, Jesus will never break His covenant with us, but we can render this covenant "null and void" when we break our covenant with Him.

The covenant ceremony (antiquity) typically includes the sacrifice (death) of an animal divided lengthwise wherein both parties passed through it proclaiming: "So be it unto me as this animal if I break the conditions of this covenant." This solemn moment is never entered into lightly by flicking a wrist with half-hearted affection. And yet, the church's message of salvation rarely includes mention of any of this, as if being a member of Christ's family is a free gift of grace.

I disagree! Nothing could be farther from the truth!

How we live according to what we believe – is what matters!

The Free Gift

There is a phrase within Christianity that causes me to bristle every time I hear it: receive the free gift of salvation that Jesus Christ gives to all that ask. My issue is the *fusion* of terms free and gift. Let me explain. Recently, my daughter gave me a gift to get my first massage; she called the place and pre-paid the visit so all I had to do was walk in and receive a massage. Afterward, as I was checking out, there was some *confusion* by a new employee in terms of how to process the final paperwork, so the office manager came out to see how the transaction transpired beforehand – and then she said, "Your first visit was free." This confused me, so I asked if all first time massage patients are given a free massage. "No" was the reply, and then she said, "my massage was pre-paid" which she then added "was free."

Herein is the problem generated by this office manager, including well-meaning evangelists, that erringly confuse and combine the terms "free" and "gift."[122] The massage was a gift to me by my daughter, BUT the massage was not free… because it cost my daughter something. Some of you are already jumping ahead to predict what I am going to say next – and that is wonderful. Jesus offers every person on planet earth the gift of salvation – which we ourselves cannot earn – it is the gift of God that was pre-paid by Jesus. This is not a free gift, as many evangelists erringly say, because it cost Jesus more than you or I could conceivably pay: it cost Him His life! Calling the gift of salvation "free" is a cheap and deceptive way of enticing people to come to faith without a full reckoning that thoroughly understands this: Jesus pre-paid your debt that you were unable to pay. A covenant is required with Jesus if you intend to "redeem" this gift of salvation!

"Greater love has no one than this, than to lay down

---

[122] The actual word (not two words) "*charisma*-5486' as found in Romans 5:15, 16 is "a spiritual endowment; a favor which one receives without any merit of his own; a gift of grace; a gift involving grace." It is translated fifteen times as "gift" yet twice as "free gift" (this word is absent in Rom. 5:18, yet erringly added). Strong's Concordance.

one's life for his friends" (John 15:13).

The second thing that causes me to bristle is when people embrace "grace" as a license to continue living according to sinful patterns while referring to Jesus as "friend."

Jesus sacrificed His life for yours, so that "through faith" you sacrifice your life for His. The gift of salvation is born out of a covenant relationship between two people (God and any person) that agree to enter into this covenant willingly whereby both parties bring "gifts" to offer to one another and pledge unto one another: "What's mine is yours, and what's yours is mine. My enemies are your enemies and my family is your family." The bond of covenant between two persons abandons the concept of self-interest and adopts the concepts of fellowship and meekness to look out for one another's common (*koinos, koinonia*) interests.

A lot of people believe they are standing on first base because they said yes to the preacher's invitation and have entered into the Lord's salvation by making a verbal confession, yet they failed to bring their gift (their surrendered life and their body as a living sacrifice; Rom. 12:1) to Jesus in order to consummate the covenant. And for this reason believers do not advance toward second base to be sanctified because it requires more sacrifice than they are willing to offer. The "free" gift of salvation was on their terms, yet not according to covenantal terms of the kingdom governed by Jesus our Lord whereby you must forfeit your life – just like the King of Glory has done for you. Jesus said to His disciples:

> "For I have given you an example, that you should do as I have done to you" (John 13:15).

Jesus sacrificed His life for you. Jesus washed your feet. What, then, is a reasonable service you might offer to Jesus?

> "I beseech you therefore, brethren, by the mercies of God, ***that you present your bodies a living***

> *sacrifice*, holy, acceptable to God, which is your reasonable service. ² And do not be conformed to this world, but be transformed by the renewing of your mind, that you may prove what *is* that good and acceptable and perfect will of God" (Rom. 12:1, 2)

What did you bring to the covenant ceremony in which the Spirit served as Witness? Did you offer some of you (all the problematic, broken-down, sinful parts)… or did you surrender all sovereignty of your soul, spirit and body into the formative hands of the Spirit for sanctification? Did you present your body as a living sacrifice?

May I remind you of the story about a chicken and a pig that decided to have breakfast together. "Bacon and eggs" was proposed by the chicken, to which the pig replied: "That's because you've got no skin involved." Beloved… do you have any skin involved to consummate your covenant agreement with Jesus… or are you offering Him eggs instead?

> "Nothing but leaves for the master,
> Oh how His loving heart grieves,
> When instead of the fruit He is seeking,
> We offer Him nothing but leaves." (Author unknown)

Beloved, we still need to be transitioned from member ideology into discipleship theology.

Water Into Wine

Understanding "who we are" is not the hardest part of being a human on earth; living according to the truth we understand – is! If I were to tell you all the marvelous and wonderful things about your true identity in Christ, you might believe them, yet if I showed them to you in the scriptures, your tendency to believe them will increase; however, this does not mean you will make a conscious decision to operate according to these truths and live by them. It simply means: you believe. Faith without works to authenticate the things you believe by faith – is dead faith produced by unbelief. Faith is: doing what you believe is truth.

You are sons and daughters of God – having been inserted into the fabric of time by the Holy Spirit. Just as Jesus, who is God, was inserted into the fabric of time by the Holy Spirit whereby Mary conceived Christ Jesus, so likewise, your soul was also inserted and supplanted in the union of two people during the miracle of conception. It is God who is given attribution when a woman conceives a child… not the elements of the man and woman (the union of sperm and egg) when they unite during intercourse. This theme is very prevalent within scripture.

You are sons and daughters of God, having been sent to earth as sons and daughters of men, so as to be transitioned back into sons and daughters of God – by the Spirit's sanctification of your soul. Your soul got inserted here by the Spirit, your soul is being transformed into the likeness of Christ Jesus by the Spirit, and "this same Spirit that raised Jesus from the dead" will raise you in resurrection glory and in power (1 Cor. 15:43). Who you are *and* what you do – is all about the Spirit of God transforming you into the image and likeness of Christ Jesus!!! And yet, very little is ever mentioned in church about the Holy Spirit who leads us in all righteousness.

You are the light of the world. Jesus put the light of truth in you for you to illuminate His truth into this world of darkness as His "manifested" agent of change.

You are the salt of the earth. You are the "new earth" seasoning that Jesus is using to flavor the earth with the character attributes of Christ in you. You are spiritual MSG (messenger of saving grace) that was sent to share the good news of Jesus and save other souls from pollution and condemnation.

Your light is for "the world" yet your salt is for "the earth."
Your dominion over the earth that was granted to you by God is a two-fold commission: to take authority over the kingdom of

darkness (with light) and to institute the kingdom of heaven on earth (as salt). Ask Him what He purposed and planned for you (your commission) since before the foundation of this world and I guarantee this: it will change the world! <u>*That is your purpose… because that is His plan*</u>.

> Jesus spoke to them again, saying, "I am the light of the world. He who follows Me shall not walk in darkness, but have the light of life" (John 8:12).

We are *elohims*, having been sent by *Elohim*, to usher in a regime change. We are '*koinos*' the common things of God that are being converted and transformed into '*hagios*' the uncommon sanctified holy things of God. Our ordinary water is being transformed into holy wine so that we become sanctified saints so as to fill the earth with His glory!

This is an interesting point: A) the earth was created for man – and man was created for the earth, and yet B) we are going to live eternally within whatever kingdom we built during this life (either in the kingdom of heaven on earth – or the dominion of hell in torment).

Who you were 'before' you got here and what you did 'before' this very moment is irrelevant – if you have repented and converted! Who you are becoming now *and* how you purpose to continue living according to the truth Jesus taught – will determine your eternal place within one of two realities: heaven on earth – or continue in hell. It is far better to enter life eternal (even without any reward for deeds of righteousness)… than to live in hellish torment.

Do pigs fly? Unless you repent, convert and allow the Spirit to sanctify you wherein you are transformed into the image of Christ, then you will never know.

> "Then comes the end, when He delivers the kingdom to God the Father, when He puts an end to all rule and all authority and power" (1 Cor. 15:24).

It's all about Jesus – and God gets the glory!

Chapter 3: Spirit (small 's')

> "But he who is joined to the Lord is one spirit with Him" (1 Cor. 6:17).

Through our heart – we manifest the kingdom of heaven on earth – through our spirit (small "s"). This is the example whereby Jesus taught us, that even though He was God the entire time He was on earth, He did not operate out of His Divine Nature or out of His Divine authority – He operated out of His spirit (small 's') in order to teach us how to operate like Him – out of the spirit He gave us. It is mission critical to thoroughly comprehend this truth because it is the benchmark for living as New Earth disciples – both now and eternally.

Your spirit united in oneness with the Holy Spirit becomes the operational means whereby supernatural power is being manifested in you and through you – in order to accomplish the purposes and plans of God upon the earth. You are a conduit and gateway for heavenly things to pass through you!

> "But He [Jesus] sighed deeply in His *spirit*, and said, "Why does this generation seek a sign? Assuredly, I say to you, no sign shall be given to this generation." (Mark 8:12).

Truly, generations both past and present have been seeking signs from God to authenticate the works of God, but perhaps "it is God" who is seeking a sign of faith and obedience... from us.

"Jesus had Divine authority all His life – He had full authority to lay down His life and He had the authority to pick it up again (John 10:17, 18). As a child, Jesus became strong in spirit (Luke 2:40), began His Galilean ministry in the power of the Spirit (v.4:14), rejoiced in the Spirit (v.10:21), sighed deeply in His spirit (Mark 8:12), was troubled in His spirit when one of the disciples was going to betray Him (John 13:21), and yielded up His spirit to the

Father in His final moments on the cross (notice when Spirit is capitalized, referring to the Holy Spirit, and when it is not).

'Jesus had Divine authority all His life (Matt. 11:25-27; Luke 10:21, 22; John 3:35; 5:27:17:2), and all authority had been delivered to Him by His Father, so why do you think He consulted the Father and submitted His entire will to the Father?

- Jesus is Holy and God and without sin, and yet He was sanctified (John 10:36; 17:19) and then was sacrificed as a sin offering
- Jesus is the Son of/from God, and He is God Almighty, and yet He participated in ritual cleansing and ceremonial purification according to Jewish law
- Jesus is God, and yet He was baptized by John to fulfill all legalistic righteousness under the very law that He instituted (Matt. 3:15)

'Let me say that another way... Jesus is God – and Jesus and the Father have always been God in Oneness, so...why did Jesus live His life in total yielded submission to the Father? For only one reason: *to teach us by example how to live life* as mere men and women (in the flesh) operating out of (through) our spirit man, partnered with the Spirit in yielded obedience through faith... and to walk "in the way and example and pattern" of our Archetype according to the Spirit. There is no other reason. *Jesus operated from His spirit – to teach us how to do it!!!*

'Jesus came as "the Way" to teach us the way – and to show us how to walk in the way – as a yielded servant operating out of our inner spirit-man, to live in supernatural (spirit normal) victory, in the fullness of the Holy Spirit.'"[123]

This truth, therefore, is the cornerstone of Christ's dominion over the Earth: Jesus created us as *elohims* (small "e") with a spirit (small "s") according to His likeness so that we may imitate His example and have dominion in His name. This is "one of the

---

[123] Excerpt from "Image" section titled: "In the Spirit, Jesus Lived."

keys" to understanding how the kingdom of God operates!

We are being changed and renewed and transformed – from glory to glory – so that we may thoroughly understand and comprehend this great mystery regarding man on earth: we were given a divine nature (a spirit) to become like the Lord our God – and God strengthens us with His power (v.1:3) by His Spirit to accomplish His purposes on earth (2 Pet. 1:3-4). We were made with the ability to think like our Maker and we were created to operate like our Creator – and then we were sent to earth as representatives of His dominion with a commission to transition this planet from darkness to light and usher in a New Earth regime change "on earth as it is in heaven" – in the name of Jesus Christ!

This is "who" you are... and this is "what" you should be doing! You are a regime changer!

Everything we do will either glorify Jesus – or it will rob Jesus of the glory that belongs to Him.

This is His planet, and we were commissioned to love Him, trust Him and serve Him by the hearing of His voice. When we stop listening, we stop loving; and when we stop loving Him, this then is when our spirit begins to fail us... even unto death. We get our life from Jesus (who is the Life), but when we turn away from Jesus... our soul slowly enters into death.

The first place we (our soul) will experience this weakness is in our spirit ... and then it will become manifest in the body of flesh. Not all, but certainly most physical ailments originate first in our spirit and then are manifested in our body, and thus, understanding the importance of our spirit (small "s") is paramount to living as New Earth residents – here and now – and eternally.

Iscus - Spiritual Attribute Called Strength

Your spirit is an instrument from God to strengthen you and assist your soul and body.

> "The Lord is my light and my salvation; whom shall I fear? ***The Lord is the strength of my life***; of whom shall I be afraid?" (Psa. 27:1).

> "The Lord is my strength and song, and He has become my salvation" (Psa. 118:14).

> "Be of good courage, and He shall strengthen your heart, all you who hope in the Lord" (Psa. 31:24).

This next point is vitally important: we will all run out of the power we need to endure. When we run out of juice, this is to be expected because we were created by our Creator to go back to the Vine for our daily juice and back to the Source for our daily bread. Jesus is the Power of God made manifest, and He sent His Spirit to empower us through our spirit to continue His work upon the earth as "disciples."

You are not your own – and you are not alone. Not only has God been in you and with you the entire time – you are surrounded by a great cloud of witness and by a multitude of angelic warriors as well!

> "Therefore we also, since we are surrounded by so great a cloud of witnesses, let us lay aside every weight, and the sin which so easily ensnares us, and let us run with endurance the race that is set before us" (Heb. 12:1).

We were never meant to do this on our own or in our own strength. If you are trying to pastor or preach or do whatever without staying connected to the Vine for continuous flow of power by the Spirit through your spirit, then you will eventually run out of strength. We are strengthened in His presence. There is no substitute for intimacy with Jesus – and this great wisdom I have embraced: His Word (in Presence and Spirit) is life itself to me. When I cannot hear the Lord's wonderful voice, my spirit begins to fail within me.

> "Thus says the Lord: "Cursed is the man who trusts
> in man and makes flesh his strength, whose heart
> departs from the Lord" (Jer. 17:5).

Either we choose to operate according to the worldly pattern and trust in man – or we elect to operate according to the spiritual pattern as exemplified by Jesus. We "can do all things through Christ who strengthens" us (Phil. 4:13) because Jesus wants us to do the same things He did by operating under God's authority, strength and power to have dominion, but with one exception: Jesus want us to do "greater works" than His:

> "Most assuredly, I say to you, he who believes in
> Me, the works that I do he will do also; and *greater
> works* than these he will do, because I go to My
> Father" (John 14:12).

The single greatest trick by the enemy is to deceive us into thinking (erringly) that we can do it on our own and in our own strength; we have this ability, but that is not how we were originally intended to operate. We were created to be partners and co-laborers with Christ as being co-dependent upon the Lord for everything we think, say and do... including life itself. Our spirit and our life were given to us by the Lord – and they belong to Him – and they will return to Him because they belong to Him; however, how we use them during this probationary time period on earth is the test we either pass or fail. We belong to Him; He does not belong to us.

> "It is the Spirit who gives life; the flesh profits
> nothing. The words that I speak to you are spirit,
> and they are life" (John 6:63).

Just like Jesus, your words are spirit, and they are life. (*Energeia* thoughts + *rhema* utterance = produce *dunamis* words) and these words are expressions being manifested within two dimensions (spirit – and – life).

> "But the hour is coming, and now is, when the ***true worshipers will worship the Father in spirit and truth***; for the Father is seeking such to worship Him. God is Spirit, and those who worship Him must worship in spirit and truth" (John 4:23, 24).

Jesus is the Way, the Truth, and the Life (John 14:6). Truth is the connecting element between way and life – for those who desire to live according to the Spirit as New Earth disciples – in spirit and in truth.

The Weakened spirit

> "For you have need of endurance, so that after you have done the will of God, you may receive the promise:" (Heb. 10:36).

So, what happens when we run out of power and strength on this sojourn? When the spirit within us fails, not only do our bodies begin to perish, but our commission which was granted to us begins to fail also. So, what do we do when the spirit within us begins to fail us and we lose strength? Go back to Jesus Christ; go back to the well of Living Water and drink of Him; and go back to the Tree of Life and eat of Him. The written word merely props us up, but the Spirit of God in Christ Jesus will stand us up and strengthen us with *dunamis* power and *iscus* strength.

> "The spirit of a man will sustain him in sickness, but who can bear a broken spirit?" (Prov. 18:14).

Having a broken spirit and being broken-hearted is not something to be ashamed of. If anything, it means your soul is still sensitive to the spiritual reality of God's presence around you and in you... even though you may not discern His nearness in times of trial, testing and tribulation. During these times, our soul and spirit seek comfort, yet oftentimes man in his folly will seek comfort from numerous vices before returning to the One who comforts and heals us.

"The Spirit of the Lord is upon Me, because He has anointed Me to preach the gospel to the poor [*ptochos*]; He has sent Me to heal the brokenhearted, to proclaim liberty to the captives and recovery of sight to the blind, to set at liberty those who are oppressed" (Luke 4:18).

Consider these bible passages regarding this:

- "Answer me speedily, O Lord; My spirit fails! Do not hide Your face [presence] from me, lest I be like those who go down into the pit" (Psa. 143:7)
- "For I will not contend forever, nor will I always be angry; for the spirit would fail before Me, and the souls which I have made" (Isa. 57:16).
- "For thus says the High and Lofty One Who inhabits eternity, whose name is Holy: "I dwell in the high and holy place, with him who has a contrite and humble spirit, **to revive the spirit of the humble, and to revive the heart of the contrite ones**" (Isa. 57:15).
- "So God split the hollow place that is in Lehi, and water came out, and he drank; and his spirit returned, and he revived. Therefore he called its name *En Hakkore*, which is in Lehi to this day" (Judges 15:19; *En Hakkore* literally means: "*Spring of the Caller*").
- "My heart pants, my strength fails me; as for the light of my eyes, it also has gone from me" (Psa. 38:10).

    "Behold, God works all these things, twice, in fact, three times with a man, [30] To bring back his soul from the Pit, that he may be enlightened with the light of life" (Job 33: 29, 30).

There are multitudes of scriptures that reinforce this theme: when our spirit fails, our heart and flesh become weakened, but when our spirit is strengthened by grace, we are enlivened and rejuvenated to live as we were intended to live: as spiritual beings having a human experience.

> "And He said to me, "My grace is sufficient for you, for My strength is made perfect in weakness." Therefore most gladly I will rather boast in my weaknesses, that the power of Christ may rest upon me" (2 Cor. 12:9).

> "Likewise the Spirit also helps in our weaknesses" (Rom. 8:26).

God's Divine exchange with man seeks to trade our old spirit for a new spirit, to trade our weaknesses for His strength, our rags for His riches in glory, and our temporary corruptible life for life eternal according to the Spirit of life in Christ Jesus – in Paradise. This is awesome and magnificent in many respects. It begins as a small seed of faith planted in the garden of your heart by the Spirit, but then it is up to you (your soul) to discipline your mind to ensure the seed grows and continues to mature in faith – so that it produces the fruit of righteousness worthy of harvest. Claiming this seed by faith yet doing nothing about it is the trademark of poor stewardship… and such a servant will not be rewarded (Matt. 25:24-29).

The Strengthened spirit

> "But the Lord stood with me and strengthened me, so that the message might be preached fully through me, and that all the Gentiles might hear. Also I was delivered out of the mouth of the lion" (2 Tim. 4:17).

Pray for more grace and strength and power to get through the difficult times! We are in the world but not of it! So I say to you: pray for more grace and power and strength to endure the difficulties of this life rather than adopting an escape-pod mentality out of the kingdom of darkness. Pray for more *dunamis* power, grace and *iscus* strength to persevere, rather than adopting a victim mentality from a position of surrender.

- Be strong and courageous (Joshua 1:6)
- Be strong and _very_ courageous (Joshua 1:7)
- **"Have I not commanded you? Be strong and of good courage**; do not be afraid, nor be dismayed, for the Lord your God is with you wherever you go" (Joshua 1:9)
- "Be strong and of good courage, do not fear nor be afraid of them; for the Lord your God, He is the One who goes with you. He will not leave you nor forsake you" (Deut. 31:6)
- "Be strong and courageous; do not be afraid nor dismayed before the king of Assyria, nor before all the multitude that is with him; for there are more with us than with him" (2 Chron. 32:7)
- "And David said to his son Solomon, "Be strong and of good courage, and do it; do not fear nor be dismayed, for the Lord God—my God—will be with you. He will not leave you nor forsake you, until you have finished all the work for the service... of the Lord" (1 Chron. 28:20)

Beloved... it's about time we awaken from our slumber and take this fight to the enemy!

The authority Satan had – has been returned to the Lord's disciples – both past and present. The Lord established us as the army of earth with authority and dominion over powers, principalities and the devil, to live by grace, with truth and power, to pierce the darkness with the light of truth, but regrettably...we have been poor stewards of this _exousia_ authority.

Never surrender! The Lord always leads us from a position of victory into victory.

> "Now thanks be to God who always leads us in triumph in Christ" (1 Cor. 2:14).

> "But thanks be to God, who gives us the victory through our Lord Jesus Christ" (1 Cor. 15:57).

> "For whatever is born of God overcomes the world. And this is the victory that has overcome the world—our faith" (1 John 5:4).

Saints and warriors of the Most High God, it's time to awaken and arise – and collect the spoils!

Thoroughly Open Heaven

Are you aware that there is nothing separating heaven from earth? There is no ceiling and there are no walls of separation or hostility between God and man. We have been living under a "thoroughly open" heaven '*dianoigo*-1272' (*dia*-1223-thoroughly, *anoigo*-455-open) for 2,000 years yet praying all the while for the gates of heaven be opened unto us in our times of great human need when heaven has been thoroughly open to us the entire time.

"There are several words used to convey 'open' in the Bible, but the word with endued power is '*dianoigo*,' in the Greek meaning: "thoroughly open, completely open." This is not the kind of 'open' which can also be shut, like a window or a door; it is the kind of open that, once opened, can never be shut, like a womb after childbirth (Luke 2:23). This is the same word used to describe the mind after coming to know the truth about Jesus; it cannot be shut, ever again (Luke 24: 31, 32, 45; Mark 7:32-35; Acts 17:3)!'

> "He who has the key of David, He who opens and no one shuts, and shuts and no one opens" (Rev. 3:7).

"Our mind and our eyes may be only partially opened to the knowledge of this truth, but when the Spirit brings revelation to our understanding, then we can fully comprehend the truth. This is a work of grace that needs to be received through faith. The Holy Spirit opened their eyes (Mark 7:34); opened their hearts (Acts 16:13, 14), opened their minds (Acts 17:3), and opened their understanding (Luke 24:45). It is not enough for us to keep an open mind regarding Christ; the Spirit of God must thoroughly and completely open our mind. This is not something we can accomplish through human effort because this is a working of the Holy Spirit – to draw us to the truth and reveal Christ to us.

"Most importantly, access to the Father and the heavenly realm has been completely opened because of Christ. Stephen saw the heavens opened *'anoigo'* as he was being stoned to death (Acts 7:56). The veil between heaven and earth and the veil between God and man has been torn in two, *from top (anothen) to bottom* – completely and permanently opened – by Christ's redemptive work upon the cross.

"This is a highly significant moment in history that is often glossed over. Jesus left heaven and came to earth to die on a cross so that heaven would be opened to everyone, once and for all, thoroughly and permanently opened (*dianoigo*), perfectly, with love. The opening came from heaven in the only manner possible: *'anothen'* from above, which is also the same word used in "you must be born again (*anothen*)," anew, from above. God has done everything possible in order for man to get right with His Creator, including coming to earth in the form of a man in order to rescue us from the pit of earth. What more must a loving Father do?

"We have been living for 2,000 years with a thoroughly-open gate to heaven (known as open heaven theology). This is the same gate that was opened temporarily in "a certain place" approximately 5,000 years ago so that Jacob would experience a pre-incarnate visitation with the Lord Jesus (Gen. 28:10-17). In a dream, he saw a ladder that reached from earth and "its top reached to heaven," and Jacob saw angels ascending and descending on the ladder." [124]

Even now the resources of heaven are being released in these last days to change human history with a simple choice: do you want spiritual revival or do you prefer tribulation?

---

[124] Excerpt from: "Regenesis" section titled "An Open Mind."

"Jesus came proclaiming, "The kingdom of heaven is at hand," and it is just as true today as it was 2,000 years ago. All it takes is conversion according to divine truth for us to operate in spirit and in truth with a spiritually renewed and transformed mind. Newness is happening all around us!"[125]

"When I first realized (in 2013) that we have been living under an open '*dianoigo*' heaven for the past 2,000 years, I became overwhelmingly excited about knowing God and His truth hidden for us in the scriptures. Under the direction of the Holy Spirit, I looked up obscure words and phrases to capture the essence of God's truth revealed *within* His scriptures, not by consulting any of man's teachings or religious doctrines, but by listening to "His" voice. Not long ago, the Holy Spirit revealed to me the truth about Jesus from an "all in or all out" perspective. It was then that I began to see Jesus for who He really is: God's manifest representative for the earth. And Jesus created us, as His manifest representatives, whereby He sent us to earth as His image bearers according to His likeness to have dominion in His name. Verily, it is all about Jesus – and God gets the glory!."[126]

Saints: wake up!!! We were granted dominion over the earth, we have been given *exousia* authority to fulfill our commission, we have been empowered with miraculous *dunamis* power by the Holy Spirit to accomplish greater works, and the gates of heaven have been *dianoigo* thoroughly open for us, so let me ask you this: what are you waiting for? And let me ask you this: are you a gatekeeper that is restricting God's plan by doubting and refusing to believe – or are allowing your spirit to become a gateway for heavenly things to be released through you – according to faith – and in these last days usher into history the New Earth revival?

We are not waiting on God, but rather… He is waiting on us to awaken and arise!

---

[125] Excerpt from: "Image" Chapter 2.
[126] Excerpt from "Here: The Kingdom of Heaven Is Here" section titled: "Nigh At Hand."

Spirit Strengthened With Power

> "... that He would grant you, according to the riches of His glory, to be strengthened with might through His Spirit in the inner man" (Eph. 3:16).

> "For our gospel did not come to you in word only, but also in power, and in the Holy Spirit and in much assurance, as you know what kind of men we were among you for your sake" (1 Thess. 1:5)

We need God's power, in all its manifold variety, to strengthen our inner man: *energeia* for the soul, *dunamis* for the spirit and body, *exousia* to fulfill our commission by operating under His authority, and *kratos* to perfect the work of God through us by greater grace with greater power unto greater works and dominion resulting in greater glory. Failure is NOT an option!!!

Receiving God's power does not come as a result from doing the right things, as Simon the sorcerer discovered (Acts 8:18); power is released from being in a right relationship with Jesus who is "the power and the glory." **We don't get more from Jesus, but rather – we become more of who He is** – glory and power. We need to maintain our relationship with Jesus and remain in His Presence and Spirit to accomplish God's plan for our life; failure to continue in the way of the Lord is a predetermined recipe for disaster.

> "These shall be punished with everlasting destruction from the presence of the Lord and from the glory of His power" (2 Thess. 1:9).

> Therefore: "Watch and pray, lest you enter into temptation. The spirit indeed is willing, but the flesh is weak" (Mark 14:38).

Refreshed In Our Spirit [127]

The new spirit within man which was given to us in the new birth by the Spirit (Ezek. 36:26, 27) – is expandable. The Lord will continue to add grace attributes to our spirit as He wills in order to accomplish His plan. He desires to enlarge the territory of our soul [tent] through our new spirit, and there are many things that can be added to our spirit in order to strengthen our faith in times of weakness, but He will never give us a spirit of fear or anxiety. Rather, He has given us a sound mind (2 Tim. 1:7; Luke 12:29), as well as His peace, to accomplish all that the Lord has entrusted to you.

> "All things that the Father has are Mine. Therefore I said that He [*the Holy Spirit*] will take of Mine and declare it to you" (John 16:15 *italics* by the author).

Here are just a few of the spiritual attributes He has given us according to the new birth:

- The spirit of love, joy, peace, patience/longsuffering, kindness, goodness, gentleness and self-control (these are the fruit of the Spirit for all believers – Gal. 5:22)
- The spirit of adoption so we can call God 'Father' (Gal. 4:6; Rom. 8:23)
- The spirit of sonship (Rom. 1:15, 16)
- The spirit of life (Rom. 8:11)
- The spirit of love (Rom. 5:5; Col. 1:8)
- The spirit of faith (2 Cor. 4:13)
- The spirit of righteousness (Rom. 8:10; Gal. 5:5)
- The spirit of holiness (2 Cor. 7:1)
- The spirit of endurance (Heb. 10:36; 12:1; James 1:12)
- The spirit of obedience (1 John 3:24)
- The spirit of discernment (1 John 4:1)
- The spirit of unity (Rom. 15:5; Eph. 4:3)

---

[127] Excerpt taken from "Regenesis" chapter titled: "The Spirit Of Man" section titled "The spirit for man"

- The spirit of purpose (Phil. 2:2)
- The spirit of hope (Rom. 15:13)
- The spirit of refreshing (1 Cor. 16:18; 2 Cor. 7:13)
- The spirit of encouragement (Phil. 2:4)
- The spirit of competency (2 Cor. 3:16)
- The spirit of liberty (2 Cor. 3:17)
- The spirit of freedom (2 cor. 3:17)
- The spirit of joy (1 Thess.1:6)
- The spirit of propriety (2 Cor. 12:18)
- The spirit of good report (Gal. 5:25)
- The spirit of witness (Acts 5:32)
- The spirit of compulsion (Acts 20:22)
- The spirit of promise (Eph. 1:13)
- The spirit of vigilance in prayer (Eph. 6:18)
- The spirit of praise and thanksgiving (1 Cor. 14:16)
- The spirit of steadfastness and togetherness (Phil. 1:27)
- The spirit of wisdom and revelation (Eph. 1:17)
- The spirit of comfort and fellowship (Phil. 2:1)
- The spirit of tenderness and compassion (Phil. 2:2)
- The spirit of gentleness and peacefulness (1 Pet. 3:4)
- The spirit of like-mindedness (Phil. 2:2)
- The spirit of oneness (Eph. 4:4-6)
- The spirit of confidence in Christ (Phil. 3:3)
- The spirit with power (Eph. 3:16; 1 Thess. 1:5)
- The spirit of power and of love and of a sound mind (2 Tim. 1:7)

Divinity aside, we also have all the spiritual attributes of Christ, who is the Spirit of grace and truth (John 1:14).

Now do you understand why the Lord created us with one temporary spirit that was *expendable* in order to receive a new spirit that is *expandable* and hosts His presence? **Our soul was created with an original spirit that craves the hope residing within a new spirit.** We have been born of water, yet we must be born anew by the Spirit with a new spirit in order for God to enlarge our tent (the territory of our soul) and to manifest the manifold goodness of God in our members. The old man must be undone (because it continues to increase in sinfulness and will perish) in order that we should desire to become like Christ – in newness of the spirit by the Holy Spirit!

> "For thus says the High and Lofty One Who inhabits eternity, whose name is Holy: "I dwell in the high and holy place, with him who has a contrite and humble spirit, to revive the spirit of the humble, and to revive the heart of the contrite ones. [16] For I will not contend forever, nor will I always be angry; for the spirit would fail before Me, and the souls which I have made" (Isa. 57:15, 16).

> "… rather let it be the hidden person of the heart, with the incorruptible beauty of a gentle and quiet spirit, which is very precious in the sight of God" (1 Pet. 3:4).

Authority To Cast Out Spirits

Jesus has the authority to cast out spirits…

> "When evening had come, they brought to Him [Jesus] many who were demon-possessed. And He cast out the spirits *with a word*, and healed all who were sick" (Matt. 8:16).

> "Then they were all amazed, so that they questioned among themselves, saying, "What is this? What new doctrine *is* this? For with authority He commands even the unclean spirits, and they obey Him." (Mark 1:27).

… and He gave this authority to His disciples.

> "And when He had called His twelve disciples to Him, He gave them power over unclean spirits, to

cast them out, and to heal all kinds of sickness and all kinds of disease" (Matt. 10:1).

This is an interesting scripture! Jesus gave His disciples ~~power~~ (*exousia* authority) over unclean spirits that people had dwelling with them. Let me ask this: how did the unclean spirit get into them? A: they partnered with them and invited them into "their house" (i.e. their physical body). Thus, it is very important to understand several things from this scripture:

- The physical body will manifest all kinds of sickness and disease if our spirit has been or is being compromised by an unclean spirit
- When we pray for the healing of others, our efforts may be unsuccessful if these persons have partnered with spirits and have given them the right (authority) to remain there
- If an unclean spirit dwells in them, then it needs to be cast out before healing can begin
- The first thing we should do for healing to begin – is inquire of the Lord to discern if the sickness or disease has a right to be there (as this person may not remember partnering with anything, or know it as such, especially if done many years earlier in childhood, or as the result of iniquity). Don't jump immediately into words or the laying of hands. Wait upon the Lord and ask Him how you are to proceed in order for healing to begin.

Praying "band-aid healing" on people without understanding the problem is why many have yet to receive healing despite weekly trips to the altar. Even if intercessors and prayer warriors have cast out principalities and powers from the house before a church service begins, some people coming in may have unclean spirits dwelling in them – and these spirits may have a right to be there! It may be painful for these spirits to endure the name of Jesus, but some unclean spirits would rather endure this torment rather than leave the host in whom they have taken residency.

> "When an unclean spirit goes out of a man, he goes through dry places, seeking rest, and finds none. ⁴⁴ Then he says, 'I will return to my house from which I came.' And when he comes, he finds it empty, swept, and put in order. ⁴⁵ Then he goes and takes with him seven other spirits more wicked than himself, and they enter and dwell there; and the last state of that man is worse than the first. So shall it also be with this wicked generation" (Matt. 12:43-45).

Even if we cast spirits or demons out of a person, that person may allow them to return if they are not walking in the truth with a sound mind. Such a person (mentioned by Jesus above) is the spiritual condition of Legion (below) multiplied hundreds of times over:

> "For He [Jesus] said to him, "Come out of the man, unclean spirit!" ⁹ Then He asked him, "What *is* your name?" And he answered, saying, "My name *is* Legion; for we are many." ¹⁰ Also he begged Him earnestly that He would not send them out of the country. ¹¹ Now a large herd of swine was feeding there near the mountains. ¹² So all the demons begged Him, saying, "Send us to the swine, that we may enter them." ¹³ And at once Jesus gave them permission. Then the unclean spirits went out and entered the swine (there were about two thousand); and the herd ran violently down the steep place into the sea, and drowned in the sea" (Mark 5:8-13).

Likewise, this was the condition of Mary Magdalene:

> "… and certain women who had been healed of evil spirits and infirmities—Mary called Magdalene, out of whom had come seven demons" (Luke 8:2).

This book was never intended to teach about demonic oppression, the spiritual gift of healing or demonic deliverance, but rather, to teach us "the spirit within us" is the key to understanding the mystery of man on earth; however, other spirits within us may be preventing us from entering into the promises of God which our soul and new spirit desperately craves! Our spirit craves liberty and freedom – and life, yet oftentimes our soul remains captive unbeknownst to us.

Therefore, it is important that we ask the Lord what (if anything) may be dwelling within us or what lies we have erringly believed that continues to corrupt our sound mind or prevents us from entering into the healing we so desperately desire. A great many people seeking healing come to church (initially) on Sunday because of some physical health crisis. They are willing to go to church and give Jesus a try (which is usually their last resort), but if they are bound in bondage to unclean spirits, they come seeking healing being double-minded... and they leave even more bitterly hostile toward God than before.

All pain and suffering is spiritual in nature, but not all pain and physical suffering is natural. For example, I have been living with chronic pain in my side resulting from a back injury the entire time I've been writing the Image Bearer series. This pain is so intense at times that I must put strong pressure onto three lower ribs to stop the pain. Have I received prayer for healing? Yes. Do I have a spirit or demon within me? Banish the thought! Do I have a right to be healed in Jesus' name? Yes! Did the Apostle Paul have a physical infirmity that reminded him daily of his weakness and total dependence upon the Lord regarding his pain and suffering? Absolutely! Have I repented from the reason whereby I was injured? Wooah – I bet you weren't expecting that! To be honest, I went through a very dark period in 2010 and I resorted to whiskey to help me cope; I drank too much and lost my balance and fell sideways onto a log and landed on three lower ribs. Ten days later, I did it again... but never again after that. From that moment (i.e. the morning after), I told the Lord I would not touch strong alcohol again. I repented, and I have prayed for healing, however... "God's grace is sufficient for any weakness" including the self-inflicted kind.

Not all healing will happen, especially when it helps us remain dependent upon the Lord and walk faithfully according to obedience in righteousness. Miracles are instantaneous healings, but most healings are a process, meaning – the healing takes time – and requires faith.

Intercessory prayer by watchmen and intercessors will help facilitate healing because they are listeners who desire to hear the voice of the Lord in these circumstances. Healing is available – but healing is dependent upon the Healer to heal!

We are not "entitled" to physical healing as something we can claim as an entitlement afforded to us by promises in the scriptures; our healing is not authenticated by the word of God (the bible) until it is authenticated by the Word – Jesus Christ. Furthermore, our spiritual healing and the salvation of our soul is far more precious to Jesus than this body of flesh… that will experience death… regardless of any healing or how much "effort" we spend making it look good or feel good.

Truly – we need to understand what kind (manner, type) of spirit we are of – if we are ever going to help other "hosts of earth" comprehend the forces that are working for them – or against them:

> "But He turned and rebuked them, and said, "You do not know what manner of spirit you are of" (Luke 9:55).

We have been sent here to manifest the truth of God, save souls alive and set captives free – just like Jesus. And we need to understand the manner in which the Spirit enables us to live out of our spirit.

> "For you did not receive the spirit of bondage again to fear, but you received the Spirit of adoption by whom we cry out, "Abba, Father." The Spirit Himself bears witness with our spirit that we are

children of God and if children, then heirs—heirs of God and joint heirs with Christ, if indeed we suffer with Him, that we may also be glorified together" (Rom. 8:15-17).

And if we are heirs of the kingdom, then we are also brethren of Jesus (Psa. 22:22)…

- When we do the Father's will (Matt. 12:48)
- When we profess Jesus as Teacher and Christ (Matt. 23:8)
- When we do what Jesus tells us to do (Matt. 28:10)

"Listen, my beloved brethren: has God *not chosen* the poor of this world to be rich in faith and heirs of the kingdom which He promised to those who love Him?" (James 2:5; *this is a rhetorical question*).

In Closure

In order to walk according to your true nature (your spirit), you must be born anew into the kingdom of God by the Spirit of God and be given a new heart and a new spirit. No other means has been provided whereby men are saved, by grace through faith; you MUST be born anew in order to live and operate according to Christ's heavenly paradigm on earth – for His glory!.

> ***"That which is born of the flesh is flesh, and that which is born of the Spirit is spirit"*** (John 3:6).

"God is Spirit, and those who worship Him must worship ***in spirit and truth***" (John 4:24).

"The Lord Jesus Christ be with your spirit. Grace be with you. Amen" (2 Tim. 4:22).

"Brethren, the grace of our Lord Jesus Christ be

with your spirit. Amen" (Gal. 6:18).

"The grace of our Lord Jesus Christ be with your spirit. Amen" (Philemon 1:25).

"He who is joined to the Lord is one spirit with Him" (1 Cor. 6:17).

It's all about Jesus – and God gets the glory! Amen!

Chapter 4: The Beatitudes - Guidance for New Earth residents

> "Blessed is the man to whom the Lord does not impute iniquity, and in whose spirit there is no deceit" (Psa. 32:2).

The Sermon on the Mount is the most famous sermon in human history which presents us with a spiritual roadmap instructing us how to live on earth 'now' in preparation for life eternal in the New Earth (Paradise). We are being instructed how to live by grace according to goodness – which begins by embracing the divine attributes of grace – and releasing goodness into the earth.

The Spirit had me look at the entire Beatitude message as a sequence of events beginning in Matt. 4:23 (He went up the mountain)… through verse 8:1 (He came down the mountain). The Beatitudes appear at the beginning of this very important message to provide us with the heavenly template we need to live as we manifest God within us (our soul) and express our dependence upon Him (through our spirit).

There are many applications for this wisdom taught by Jesus, yet I am only going to focus on two aspects:

1. Who are we
2. What we are supposed to be doing

Blessed Are The Poor In Spirit

This statement by Jesus had me perplexed for a very long time. Sure, I could have read hundreds of commentaries and consulted Matthew Henry; however, the journey the Lord put me on was to trust Him, consult Him, seek His wisdom… and listen to the Voice of Truth. So, I waited and meditated and researched and waited many months to understand six words.

Understanding the spirit in man was a four month-long lesson the Spirit needed to teach me; our spirit was given so that we may rejoice and be glad in the Lord, and exalt His greatness and goodness through our spirit – and thus we become earthen instruments that are able to worship the Lord in spirit and in truth. Even now, after I read what I just heard – it makes perfect sense. We were designed by God not only as earthen vessels to contain something of value (the pearl of great price) so as to produce more glory by us (in our soul), but we are also earthen instruments operating as instruments of worship (through our spirit).[128] This puts an entirely fresh nuance on the term "spirit filled worship." Our spirit was designed by God and placed *with* our soul whereby we may become heavenly (spiritual) instruments of worship upon the earth. Wow!

> "Sing praise to the Lord, you saints of His, and give thanks at the remembrance of His holy name" (Psa. 30:4).

> "Praise the Lord! Sing to the Lord a new song, and His praise in the assembly of saints" (Psa. 149:1).

And yet, we can be poor stewards of our spirit and deny its intended use to glorify God by choosing to glorify self (the rebellious ego). And thus, we rob God of the glory He deserves.

A measure of God's glory was given to all men and placed as a seed within their soul to produce more glory for the Lord wherein we shall glorify the Lord (return and yield this glory) through our spirit – or be temporarily deposed by God until the issue of pride is resolved (Dan. 5:20). Our divine purpose and high calling in Christ Jesus whereby we yield our glory unto Him – is our reasonable service unto Him (worship-Rom. 12:1), yet some prefer to harden their heart and deny Jesus the glory He deserves.

> "Blessed are the poor in spirit, for theirs is the kingdom of heaven" (Matt. 5:3).

---

[128] In this regard, we need to see Lucifer as the fallen angel that God created as an instrument of worship.

What does this phrase mean? As I waited on the Lord many days to teach me the meaning from His perspective, it became very evident that I needed to understand the purpose of the spirit before I understood the meaning of "poor."

After thirty more days of research and meditation, and much prayer as well, this understanding by the Spirit came to me: the godly attributes of grace mentioned by Jesus are spiritual in nature – and not physical. We often attribute the word "poor" in terms of being physical, as in financially destitute and impoverished according to the standards of this world, but *this is not* what this word means (which will be discussed shortly). Jesus is teaching us about the character attributes of goodness in the kingdom that are honorable, praiseworthy, commendable and worthy of recompense in the New Earth. In contrast, Jesus is also going to point out ungodly mannerisms that are reprehensible to God as exemplified by the religious and wealthy elite who are also listening nearby.

Let's read the Beatitudes as found in the gospel of Matthew:

- Blessed are the poor in spirit – for theirs is the kingdom of heaven (v.3)
- Blessed are those who mourn – for they shall be comforted (v.4)
- Blessed are the meek[129] – for they shall inherit the *earth* (v.5; i.e. New Earth Paradise)
- Blessed are those who hunger and thirst for righteousness – for they shall be filled (v.6)
- Blessed are the merciful – for they shall obtain mercy (v.7)
- Blessed are the pure in heart – for they shall see God (v.8)
- Blessed are the peacemakers – for they shall be called sons of God (v.9)
- Blessed are those who are persecuted for righteousness' sake – for theirs is the kingdom of heaven (v.10)

---

[129] Meekness means: to give God the preeminence in all things (put Him first) *and* put others ahead of self.

- Blessed are you when they revile and persecute you, and say all kinds of evil against you falsely for My sake (v.11)
- Rejoice and be exceedingly glad, for great *is* your reward in heaven, for so they persecuted the prophets who were before you (v.12)

As we can see, these terms apply to our spiritual character – and not our status in this world. All of these attributes are grace attributes given by God to all men (without exception) so that we may operate by goodness 'according to goodness' upon this earth as children of God; yet many choose not to operate in this manner, and some quite defiantly.

Jesus did not say: blessed are the healthy, wealthy, wise, generous, prosperous, safe, influential, benevolent, religious, pious, or whatever. Jesus is focusing on the lowly in this moment for a good reason: the multitude that has gathered before Him is a veritable city that is sitting upon a hill… and the light within them is about to be activated for duty.

To see these terms in greater context, we need to pay close attention to what Jesus says next:

> "You are the salt *of the earth*; but if the salt loses its flavor, how shall it be seasoned? It is then good for nothing but to be thrown out and trampled underfoot by men" (v.13)

> "You are the light *of the world*. A city that is set on a hill cannot be hidden. [15] Nor do they light a lamp and put it under a basket, but on a lampstand, and it gives light to all who are in the house. [16] Let your light so shine before men, that they may see your good works and glorify your Father in heaven" (v.14-16).

Jesus has now begun to tell us "who" we really are: you are the salt of the earth – and you are the light of the world. Jesus is not changing the subject; He is building truth layer upon layer. Your mission is two-fold: flavor the earth – and – illuminate "this world."

"But if salt loses its flavor" – this verse has been translated in such a way that loses much of the crescendo Jesus is getting ready to elaborate on! The term "flavor" (savor-KJV) is '*moraino*-3471' and literally means: "to become insipid; tasteless."[130] In other words, if salt becomes insipid and has lost its saltiness, as having become corrupted or contaminated by some external influence whereby this salt no longer operates like salt according to its original character or mannerism as salt, then it has become insipidly, worthless salt. The implication here is: if children of God become so contaminated by the cares of this world whereby these spiritual attributes mentioned by Jesus have become compromised, then another definition of '*moraino*' becomes applicable: "to become a fool."[131]

With this interpretation, we should expect to see another similar expression by Jesus about the light (aka the lamp of the Lord) that is in us: you cannot hide a city set on a hill (or translated perhaps – a city set on a hill is not intended to be hid). It was never the Lord's intention for us to hide the godly attributes of grace that were given to us, but rather… to exemplify them for all to see; we were created and sent here to manifest God's attributes of grace as an example so the entire world can see "the light" (spirit) that God placed within us. These are not grandiose or braggadocios acts by us to tell the world how good we are (which is the manner of the Pharisees that Jesus will confront soon enough), but rather… we are to live a quiet and peaceful life that typifies the attributes of God's goodness being implemented by us according to faith.

> "… rather let it be the hidden person of the heart, with the incorruptible beauty of a gentle and quiet spirit, which is very precious in the sight of God" (1 Pet. 3:4).

---

[130] Strong's Concordance.
[131] IBID.

Any time we position this light that minimizes the benefits of this godly illumination or we showcase our works to bring glory to us rather than God is contrary to God's intended purpose for the light (spirit) within us.

> "The ***earth*** *is* the Lord's, and all its fullness, the ***world*** and those who dwell therein" (Psa. 24:1)

> "Let all the ***earth*** fear the Lord; Let all the ***inhabitants of the world*** stand in awe of Him" (Psa. 33:8; see also Isa. 26:9).

If you aren't flavoring this earth with spiritual salt and you aren't illuminating this world with the spiritual light that is within you, then the rest of the Lord's sermon is for you. The problem at this moment is the heaviness of people's hearts that have become heavily burdened (waxed gross) by numerous doctrines and teachings... and they are having difficulty understanding the message... so Jesus is about to set them free from much religious baggage and legalistic bondage under the Law.

> "But there is a spirit in man, and the breath of the Almighty gives him understanding" (Job 32:8).

Keep in mind "the kingdom of heaven" (small 'h') is the current spiritual reality upon the earth that Jesus established before He ascended into Heaven. The "Beatitudes" in the respect describe those saints imitating and personifying Christ as their example in this life... as well residents of the New Earth in the life hereafter. So, then, what possible meanings may be derived from "poor in spirit"? Does Jesus give us some indication what "poor in spirit" means? Sadly, He does not.

The Poor Indicative

The word 'poor-*ptochos*-4434' means: "to crouch, cower from fear, distressed, begging" and conveys the image of someone lowly who is begging to obtain some measure of mercy, compassion, deliverance and/or assistance in their "poverty-stricken condition"

[132] (from God or from others). Poor, in this context, does not pertain to being poor in earthly matters of finance, nor is *ptochos* the act of "begging;" *ptochos* is the status, state or condition of a person within the limitations of their lowly circumstance that they are unable to escape or rise above.

The Greek word '*penes*-3993' (also translated poor) is more consistent with our modern understanding of someone being financially poor who gets up day after day "to earn his bread by daily labor;" [133] however, this word with this context only occurs once in the New Testament (2 Cor. 9:9). Thus, it seems, the word "poor" expressed perhaps an entirely different cultural meaning centuries ago as those persons being contrasted to or compared with those who are rich and great in health, wealth, possessions and social standing from a worldly perspective... and this is the conclusion most teachers have settled on... but this would be incorrect.

Ptochos – is a spiritual condition, literally translated: "beggar" denotes persons that live by begging as their only means of acquiring food, money or other forms of assistance; and Jesus used this term to describe Lazarus, the beggar (not His friend raised from the dead).

> "There was a certain rich man who was clothed in purple and fine linen and fared sumptuously every day. [20] But there was a certain beggar [*ptochos*] named Lazarus, full of sores, *who was laid at his gate*, [21] desiring to be fed with the crumbs which fell from the rich man's table" (Luke 16:19-21).

Within this context, it implies someone who is crushed, downcast, brokenhearted, oppressed, distraught, poverty stricken, lowly and full of lamentations who only gets what they need by begging. Their life is seemingly defined by circumstances of woe and

---

[132] Strong's Concordance.
[133] IBID.

despair... which appear inescapable. In effect, this world has diminished them, denigrated them, disregarded them, discarded them and has turned a blind eye to their deep material and or spiritual need for someone or ANYONE to have a care and offer a shred of mercy... with compassion.

When you read this, are you not immediately flooded with hundreds of Old Testament messages about showing mercy and compassion to those in distress, especially your neighbors, kin and members within your spiritual family. How about this one:

> "But go and learn what this means: 'I desire mercy and not sacrifice.' For I did not come to call the righteous, but sinners, to repentance" (Matt. 9:13; Hosea 6:6).

Then Jesus took this scripture one step further:

> "But if you had known what this means, 'I desire mercy and not sacrifice,' you would not have condemned the guiltless" (Matt. 12:7).

Jesus is focusing on mercy (or the withholding of it) throughout His Sermon because mercy toward one another in our relationships and dealings with other people is what God desires. By grace through faith, we are able to receive God's mercy because we have shown mercy.

Grace and mercy shown toward us – is what we must show toward others. And yet, His intense love for His people is about to unleash a volley of attacks against the religious elite that placed heavy burdens on people while disregarding the more important matters that God truly desires us to implement as children of His kingdom. Mercy is what God desires!

> "Woe to you, scribes and Pharisees, hypocrites! For you pay tithe of mint and anise and cummin, and **have neglected the weightier matters of the law: justice and mercy and faith**. These you ought to

have done, without leaving the others undone" (Matt. 23:23).

Yet Jesus is also focusing on another key aspect of this sermon regarding the spiritual reality we are living in: <u>we are all beggars in the presence of a King</u>!

"When Jesus told us He came "to seek and save the lost" (Luke 19:10), we think we were just a little lost when, in actuality, the word "lost" means: "utterly destroyed." We were more than just lost; we were destroyed beyond recognition and we desperately need a Savior, but the alternate reality of Satan within this worldly paradigm tells us we are doing just fine, when in fact – we are already destroyed and destined for destruction. Those unbelieving ones have been blinded from the truth (by sin) and do not sense the need of a Savior… not even when calamity falls upon them. The Parable of the Prodigal Son has much to teach us in this regard."[134]

Jesus is the King of kings and He is the One who is teaching us to show mercy to one another – so that we may receive one thing above all things: God's mercy!

"Grace removes guilt; mercy removes suffering!" [135]

God knows how difficult life on this planet will get because we were sent to earth where our adversary, the devil, seeks to devour us and keep us enslaved in sin. God knows that we are dust and that "the spirit is willing but the flesh is weak" (Matt. 26:41), which is why God put a heart of mercy and compassion within us so we may take care of one another and help meet one another's needs – as we both avoid the fowler's snare. The problem, it seems, is we became selfish, hardhearted and therefore have turned our hearts of flesh into stone… and our refusal to offer mercy has, in effect, condemned us… and the guiltless.

---

[134] Excerpt copied from "Here" section titled "Judgment Happens."
[135] Strong's Concordance; study on 'eleios-1656.'

> "If there is among you a poor man of your brethren, within any of the gates in your land which the LORD your God is giving you, you shall not harden your heart nor shut your hand from your poor brother, [8] but you shall open your hand wide to him and willingly lend him sufficient for his need, whatever he needs. [9] Beware lest there be a wicked thought in your heart, saying, 'The seventh year, the year of release, is at hand,' and your eye be evil against your poor brother and you give him nothing, and he cry out to the LORD against you, and it become sin among you. [10] You shall surely give to him, and your heart should not be grieved when you give to him, **because for this thing the LORD your God will bless you** in all your works and in all to which you put your hand. [11] **For the poor** [a] **will never cease from the land**; therefore I command you, saying, 'You shall open your hand wide to your brother, to your poor [b] and your needy [34], in your land'" (Deut. 15:7-11).

The Hebrew word "poor" used in verses 15:7-11a is '*ebyon*-34' meaning: "the sense of want, destitute, needy, poor in a material sense" as well as poor "in social standing causing a need for protection" (Ex. 23:6, 11).[136]

The word "poor' changes in verse 15b, which occurs three other times in Deut. 24:12, 14, 15 to '*aniy*-6041' meaning: "depressed in mind or circumstances; poor, weak, afflicted, lowly; emphasizing some kind of disability or distress" is oftentimes translated humble (see below), lowly, and is frequently used with '*ebyon*-34' (needy)[137] such as in verse 11 (above).

> "Why do You stand afar off, O LORD? Why do You hide in times of trouble? [2] **The wicked in his pride persecutes the poor** [6041]; let them be caught in

---

[136] Strong's Concordance.
[137] IBID.

the plots which they have devised.³ For the wicked boasts of his heart's desire; he blesses the greedy and renounces the LORD.⁴ The wicked in his proud countenance does not seek God; **God is in none of his thoughts**. ⁵ His ways are always prospering; Your judgments are far above, out of his sight; as for all his enemies, he sneers at them. ⁶ He has said in his heart, "I shall not be moved; I shall never be in adversity." ⁷ His mouth is full of cursing and deceit and oppression; under his tongue is trouble and iniquity. ⁸ He sits in the lurking places of the villages; in the secret places he murders the innocent; his eyes are secretly *fixed on the helpless* [2489; *against the poor*-KJV]. ⁹ He lies in wait secretly, as a lion in his den; he lies in wait to catch the poor [6041]; he catches the poor [6041] when he draws him into his net. ¹⁰ So he crouches, he lies low, that the helpless [2489] may fall by his strength. ¹¹ He has said in his heart, "God has forgotten; He hides His face; He will never see." ¹² Arise, O LORD! O God, lift up Your hand! Do not forget the humble [6041]. ¹³ Why do the wicked renounce God? He has said in his heart, "You will not require an account." ¹⁴ But You have seen, for You observe trouble and grief, to repay it by Your hand. The helpless [2489] commits himself to You; You are the helper of the fatherless. ¹⁵ Break the arm of the wicked and the evil man; seek out his wickedness until You find none. ¹⁶ The LORD is King forever and ever; the nations have perished out of His land. ¹⁷ LORD, You have heard the desire of the humble [6041]; You will prepare their heart; You will cause Your ear to hear, ¹⁸ to do justice to the fatherless and the oppressed, that the man of the earth may oppress no more" (Psalm 10).

This Psalm speaks for itself. The rich oppress the poor simply by refusing to help them... and worse even... by laying traps to ensnare them. They could do anything to help them, yet they prefer to do nothing. Again, I say, Jesus came to reset the spiritual timeline... with truth.

> "The Spirit of the Lord is upon Me, because He has anointed Me to preach the gospel to the poor [*ptochos*]; He has sent Me to heal the brokenhearted, to proclaim liberty to the captives and recovery of sight to the blind, to set at liberty those who are oppressed" (Luke 4:18).

> "The Spirit of the Lord God is upon Me, because the Lord has anointed Me to preach good tidings to the poor [*anav*; meek-KJV]; He has sent Me to heal the brokenhearted, to proclaim liberty to the captives, and the opening of the prison to those who are bound" (Isa. 61:1).

Jesus used a word that was translated in Greek as '*ptochos*' but the word He quotes in Isaiah 61:1 is: '*anav*-6035' meaning: "depressed (fig), in mind or circumstances; meek (13x), humble (5x), poor (5x), lowly (2x), very meek (1x). It appears almost exclusively in poetical passages to describe the intended outcome of affliction by God, namely "humility"[138] and is "closely related to '*aniy*-6041.'

Humility, more appropriately defined means: to be humiliated, to be made humble, which in reference to being poor – implies being humiliated or afflicted by the Lord in a lowly state or by a state of poverty. This is most interesting because God does not think of us as being poor or lowly... because that is not WHO we really are! We are saints of the Most High God, and we have been crowned with glory and honor, yet some of us have been placed (temporarily) in a beggarly status or position for reasons known only to the Father. From the Father's perspective, we are not poor or impoverished or wealthy or successful or black/white/male/female/slaves/free or whatever – we are His

---

[138] Strong's Concordance.

children that He has specifically placed on earth to accomplish His plan in all positions – some placed in positions with wealth, and others without – but all of us are lost and we all stand as beggars in the presence of a King.

This next point is so important to comprehend: we need to see ourselves from God's perspective... because circumstances do not define us; rich or poor "classifications" do not define us; titles and positions and denominations do not define us; rather, they divide us.

Poverty is as much a state of mind as being wealthy, yet wisdom is supreme! If you want to see yourself as poor or disadvantaged, then you have been tricked by the enemy to accept a designation that God never assigned to you. What you have does not determine who you are!

How do you perceive yourself? This goes to the core and substance of "who" you really are! If you perceive yourself to be poor or wealthy, then you will act poor or wealthy. For example, I don't perceive myself as homeless just because I live in a minivan; rather.... I am home-free, and I perceive myself as greatly blessed and highly favored of God. Do you see the distinction? I hope you see it also, because some days (truth be told) I know that I am His favorite! (chuckling) I amuse myself because His grace apportioned to me as His writer – is so totally awesome!

"Let the weak say I am strong, let the poor say I am rich" as the song goes...from God's perspective... which is the only true and right perspective we should be focusing on. When you focus on self and all you see is poverty, pain, or xxx fill in the blank, then you will see yourself as a victim of your circumstances. Your thoughts create your reality! You are not a victim... you are victorious... in Christ Jesus. Whatever has been taken or defrauded or withheld from you in this life, if you remain faithful and obedient to Jesus, will be rewarded double in recompense, and get this... our Judge knows about every penny ever taken from us.

How do you "spiritually" perceive yourself? Perhaps our greatest bondage is "the perception of self" that keeps us captive to irreverent worldly thoughts regarding "who" we think we are. Ask the Father who you are... because Jesus came to "set captives free" from the tyranny of this world and the lies of the enemy.

Your commission is not based upon what you do, but rather... who you are!

> "Let the lowly brother glory in his exaltation, [10] but the rich in his humiliation, because as a flower of the field he will pass away" (James 1:9, 10).

The subject we need to spiritually grasp is less about defining poor, or what it means to be poor, or discerning the difference between '*ptochos*' or '*anav*', but rather – taking care of our spiritual brethren, the host of earth, who were placed alongside us – some that happen to be relegated by God – as poor. The goal is not to redefine poor or implement a socialist methodology whereby everyone becomes equal in class or status because... the poor you will always have with you!

It's not about classification... it about compassion! By showing mercy to all of God's children without distinction, we honor the Lord because... they are His children and He loves them. And get this: the Lord will return honor to us because "whatsoever you do" you honored His children.

The Psalmist observed an injustice: the rich persecute the poor. The prophet Micah observed the same thing (read the first five chapters). One of my favorite passages in scripture is:

> "He has shown you, O man, what is good; and what does the LORD require of you, but to do justly, to love mercy, and to walk humbly with your God" (Micah 6:8).

Are you concerned about the things God is concerned about?

This question should stimulate a paradigm shift in your perception and understanding of life on earth, and what the Lord requires from all of us. Are you caring for your brethren (His kids)?

> "I would rather feel compunction, than know its definition." (Thomas A. Kempis)

We should be concerned about "*ptochos*" that are regarded as the weak, the poor, the destitute, the brokenhearted, the maligned, the abused and discarded, the invisible, those who have been denigrated and forced into lowly positions often of poor reputation and ill repute; those in slavery, bondage, those that are homeless, motherless, fatherless, illegitimate, beggarly, lepers, orphans, mentally unstable and those without any social standing or redeeming social value. These are all "strangers" on this earth that we must have a care toward. These are the "poor" of this world that Jesus came to save… who have little or nothing except the slightest essence of the indomitable human spirit that God gave them that keeps them alive day by day for the sake of their soul… and a willingness to glorify the Lord through their spirit.

> "For the poor will never cease from the land" (Deut. 15:11a).

Jesus quoted Deut. 15:11(a) nearly word for word, thus we have a comparable understanding what He meant (as well as "poor in spirit)… when He said:

> "For you have the poor [*ptochos*] with you always, **and whenever you wish you may do them good**; but Me you do not have always" (Mark 14:7).

"The poor will never cease from the land" and "you have the poor with you always." Jesus continues, "and we may do good to them whenever we wish" but this rarely happens, especially in regard to health and wealth gospel preachers and faith merchants because it contradicts their message of building up your personal finances and assets with abundance without understanding your spiritual obligation and need to pass it down to bless less-fortunate brethren – even strangers in your midst.

God created both rich man and poor man equal in His eyes and He does not show partiality or favoritism based upon earthly criteria or possessions (both are held accountable for their stewardship of what God has given them either directly through their labors or indirectly through the benevolence of others). Both are here for God's reason according to His purposes under heaven – and both have been placed and positioned as He determines. The highly esteemed and affluent man and the lowly estate and impoverished man are here on earth for the same reason: for the testing their hearts and the sanctification of their soul. The rich person and the poor person are being tested by the Lord to see what they will do *in* their soul and *through* their spirit – either to glorify God – or rob God of the glory He is due.

This test is not about producing earthly assets and kingdoms, but about manifesting spiritual attitudes of the heart regarding thanksgiving and praise toward the Lord. The question is: will you magnify and produce glory for God in your soul – or not? Will you rejoice and give praise to God through your spirit – or not?

What you have – or have not – is irrelevant from a glory perspective! Regardless of how little or how much you have… are you glorifying God with the life He gave you? Are you glorifying God through the provision He gave you? Are you giving thanks in all circumstances? This last point is key to understanding the kingdom: what is your attitude regarding your place and position in life that God apportioned to you? Did you earn it and thus you have a right to use it however you want? Do you foster an attitude of entitlement whereby any gifts by others is something you were entitled to receive and use however you want? Do you have a right to be angry for what you did or did not get – or are you angry about the beggarly things which you were given – or are you jealous of others and covetous of their things which you did not receive?

Regardless of who you are or what you have, everything we have

COMMISSION

received belongs to God – yet how we regard "His things" is how we regard Jehovah Jireh – the Lord our Provider (Gen. 22:14). "Our things" is an illusion; "all things" belong to the Lord... we are merely stewards of "His provision!"

If you do not honor God in your abundance or your poverty... then you dishonor God and you hold God in contempt!

> "... in everything give thanks; for this is the will of God in Christ Jesus for you" (1 Thess. 5:18).

Our testing and proofing on earth has more to do with attitudes – than faith-based aptitudes.

What you think and perhaps purpose in your heart to do – is well and good, and our knowledge of the scriptures is to be commended, but how you respond to this test concerns the proofing of your heart and soul. What comes out of you when you are being tested and proofed ... is the attitude of your heart toward God.

[This next point took me by surprise] God positioned the rich and poor to live alongside one another to be a test for the other – and to be a testimony for one another. The rich man needs the poor person to keep his soul and spirit in check... and vice versa. This is another layer in the mystery of man upon the earth whereby the rich and poor help sanctify one another – by grace!

> "There was a certain rich man who was clothed in purple and fine linen and fared sumptuously every day. [20] But there was a certain beggar [*ptochos*] named Lazarus, full of sores, *who was laid at his gate,* [21] desiring to be fed with the crumbs which fell from the rich man's table. Moreover the dogs came and licked his sores. [22] So it was that the beggar died, and was carried by the angels to Abraham's bosom. The rich man also died and was buried. [23] And being in torments in Hades, he lifted up his

eyes and saw Abraham afar off, and Lazarus in his bosom. [24] "Then he cried and said, 'Father Abraham, have mercy on me, and send Lazarus that he may dip the tip of his finger in water and cool my tongue; for I am tormented in this flame.' [25] But Abraham said, 'Son, remember that in your lifetime you received your good things, and likewise Lazarus evil things; but now he is comforted and you are tormented. [26] And besides all this, between us and you there is a great gulf fixed, so that those who want to pass from here to you cannot, nor can those from there pass to us.'" (Luke 16:19-26).

The beggar named Lazarus (not the Lord's friend) was laid at the rich man's gate (Luke 16:20), which creates an interesting image of *close proximity* between the rich and the poor; therefore, it is important that we take care of those who are within our family, our community, within the house of God and within our sphere of influence to act as gateways of grace and gateways of provision that honors Jesus.

When Jesus said, "For you have the poor (beggars) with you always" (Mark 14:7), He knew what He was talking about! Some people on this planet are simply being tested to trust the Lord in their lowly estate and others are being tested in their abundance of many things… to see if they hoard riches to their own peril (Eccl. 5:13) or if the lowly curse God on account of their poverty to their own peril. Consider this: if the Lord has given you a natural or supernatural gift to make a lot of money... then ask yourself – why? Did He bless you with this ability so that you could store up insidious piles of wealth that would take generations of descendents to squander foolishly… or perhaps this gift you possess is to accomplish a kingdom purpose?

Are you perhaps able to see the larger plan of God in this moment whereby both small and great, weak and strong, rich and poor (even husband and wife) have been ***strategically*** placed alongside one another by God to test both ***and*** to sanctify one another to see if we are going to be good stewards of His things in this life and foster an attitude of gratitude... before He reveals His commission that He predestined for you in this life? Even our spirit and flesh were placed alongside one another (as strength and weakness – or perhaps strength in weakness – or perhaps power under restraint; i.e. humility) to sanctify our soul (which we learned in the previous chapter).

> "For the unbelieving husband is sanctified by the wife, and the unbelieving wife is sanctified by the husband; otherwise your children would be unclean, but now they are holy" (1 Cor. 7:14).

Sanctification tests our allegiance, and proofs our resolve – whereby the temptations we endure by our adversary in this life within this worldly wilderness will sharpen our reliance upon the Lord who saves.

Sanctification, then, as one explanation for man's reason on earth, is done:

- By other people, oftentimes by our polar opposites, as "grace increasers" to either weaken us in our strength... or strengthen us in our weakness
- By circumstances, situations and events that are out of our immediate control that reminds us... we are not in control of anything except our own soul
- By the Spirit, to test us and buffet our pride by humility (i.e. humiliation)
- By the Lord, to remind us who the Lord is who governs creation – and us
- By our adversary, who tempts us so we are perfected through patient endurance

What we think we are being held down by – is oftentimes holding us back from the complete destruction of "self" – or it redirects our foolish efforts from going down the wrong road. In this regard, the ego (self) has a God-given purpose: to glorify God in our weakness rather than the congratulatory success of self… but we need to be constantly reminded since pride is cunning.

> "For everyone will be *seasoned* with fire, ~~and every sacrifice will be seasoned with salt~~" (Mark 9:49; *halizo*-233-sprinkled; omitted ~~words~~ not found in Greek).

> "You are the salt of the earth" (Matt. 5:13)

If you are a person blessed with abundance… give the Lord all praise, thanksgiving and glory, but you must also be willing to see the needs of others less fortunate and bless them with the abundance of "the Lord's resources He has given you to steward for Him" … or do you say… "It is their choice to live that way." Well, my friend, I am living this way, not by choice as many in my own family and within the church have accused, but because this is my current lot and portion which the Lord has relegated to me during this season of writing for Him… and I rejoice in this! I have been given a commission to write and I depend entirely upon God's grace and His daily provision. I have learned contentment living in tents and vehicles because it has opened my eyes to an infinite understanding of who God is (as I host His presence), who I am (as I live out of His presence) – and what I am supposed to be doing on this planet. Extreme heat and cold and rain have been my constant companions along this sojourn; my worldly needs are very minimal, and yet I see many that are living within the invisible realm of homelessness within our communities that are contending daily with spiritual matters far beyond brokenness and despair; they are destitute, lost, downtrodden, under constant demonic attack and without hope of ever getting out of the situation they are in. "The *ptochos* you will always have with you."

Yes, this is my choice, and yet… it is by God's grace and His election that I live in this manner and endure my current lot. "My grace is sufficient for you, for My strength is made perfect in weakness. Therefore most gladly I will rather boast in my weaknesses, that the power of Christ may rest upon me" (2 Cor.

12:9).

God helps those who help themselves……….. is _not_ found anywhere in the scriptures!

God helps those who cannot help themselves!!!

Many have resorted to alcohol to take the edge off this deep spiritual pain they cannot reconcile within them… and have since gotten addicted to alcohol as well as other things. In this, they have become bitter, resentful, critical, negative, disparaging, and belligerent (toward God and man) because they are unable to reconcile the goodness of God within them that has become enslaved within an earthly body within a sinful world that torments them. A hand-up, not a hand-out… is what they wanted most… yet no longer do they wait in hope anymore. They beg for what they need... and their greatest need is a safe place to sleep. How do I know this? Because every night I, likewise, go to sleep not knowing if someone (good or bad) is going to rob me of my peace and safety. Yes, even good people, like police, will knock on your window and tell you to move because you cannot park (or tent) there… but where, then, is a homeless person to go? Does any such place truly exist? Homelessness is very much a condition of placelessness. Where do you belong and where is your God-given place? Most of us have an address; I have a license plate.

Consider this test: cause a wealthy man to lose his wealth or give great wealth to a poor person and you will see the true nature (the spiritual heart attitude) of the person within them come out. Attitudes of the heart will emerge within the midst of great testing… and my sojourn has proven this to be true in my own life. Cause – and effect!

If you are content with what you have and are able to give God glory, then you are honoring God with your life. Thanksgiving is what we do despite what we have – or have not.

If you are _not_ content with what you have, then you will never be content with what you want. Contentment, in this respect, is about having an attitude of gratitude *with* thanksgiving.

If what is in your hand is not what you need, then it is <u>not</u> your harvest... it is your seed!

Society, with its exceedingly liberal skew and skeptical view on spiritual realities, has turned a blind eye and then callously labeled beggarly individuals as irredeemable and deplorable because they are not able "to pick themselves up by their bootstraps." Well, my friends, this is not how sons and daughters of God's kingdom were created to think. Saints of God... we need a paradigm shift of enormous magnitude in order to cause a shift within our spirit... and save *our* wretched soul from the very judgment fire with which we have judged the poor of this earth.

Beggars needing resources need makers with ability to produce resources. Beggars need makers... and makers need beggars... to sanctify one another.

> "Better to be of a humble spirit with the lowly, than
> to divide the spoil with the proud" (Prov. 16:19).

The rich may have received their reward in this life, yet the poor in spirit will receive the kingdom of heaven... but fire awaits those who withhold mercy from the poor and oppressed.

Mercy, in this regard, is not feeling bad for another person... but feeling their pain enough to be moved to act on their behalf – by offering mercy with compassion to ease their distress.

> Jesus said: "Give to everyone who asks of you. And from him who takes away your goods do not ask them back. [31] And just as you want men to do to you, you also do to them likewise. [32] "But if you love those who love you, what credit is that to you? For even sinners love those who love them. [33] And if you do good to those who do good to you, what credit is that to you? For even sinners do the same.

> ^{34} And if you lend to those from whom you hope to receive back, what credit is that to you? For even sinners lend to sinners to receive as much back.
> ^{35} But love your enemies, do good, and lend, hoping for nothing in return; and your reward will be great, and you will be sons of the Most High. ***For He is kind to the unthankful and evil***" (Luke 6:30-35).

The rain falls on the just and the unjust alike (Matt. 5:45) and the Lord is kind to the unthankful and evil... and therefore, He is worthy of praise and thanksgiving... and therefore, He alone is worthy to be admired and exemplified! This is the example Jesus taught and, by His sacrificial life, modeled for us how we must also personify this heavenly pattern if we desire to become His disciple as we establish His dominion and His kingdom upon the earth.

> "To the end *that my glory* may sing praise to You and not be silent. O Lord my God, I will give thanks to You forever" (Psa. 30:12).

> "Praise the Lord! Oh, give thanks to the Lord, for He is good! For His mercy endures forever" (Psa. 106:1).

His mercy and goodness and lovingkindness toward us... is praiseworthy! He who showed great mercy toward us exemplified this great mercy to us through Christ Jesus. Aught not we imitate His glorious example and show mercy toward others? Indeed, we are commanded to.

> "Blessed are the merciful, for they shall obtain mercy" (Matt. 5:7).

Mercy, may I remind you, "does not mean only to sympathize with a person in the popular sense of the term; it does not mean simply to feel sorry for some in trouble. *Chesedh* [sic], **mercy, means the ability to get right inside the other person's skin until we can see** *things with his eyes, think things with his mind, and feel things with his feelings"* (Copied from page 56).

Mercy and meekness – are godly attributes of the Lord's disciples – and New Earth residents!

Tithing To Remind Us

Thousands of promises within Old Testament scriptures testify of God's goodness and blessing being poured out upon those who desire to live according to God's plan. Consider, now, one of the most popular messages about giving within the church today:

> "Bring all the tithes into the storehouse, that there may be food in My house, and try Me now in this," Says the Lord of hosts, "If I will not open for you the windows of heaven and pour out for you such blessing that there will not be room enough to receive it" (Mal. 3:10).

The Lord intended us to live as His faithful ones being generous in giving, and the tithe was instituted as "the minimum standard" of giving (or returning) that acknowledges "all" of it belongs to the Lord, so let me ask you this: is the tithe intended to put food in God's house for His consumption? What four things did the Lord specifically designate the tithe be used for?

> "I have brought the firstfruits of the land which you, O LORD, have given me.' "Then you shall set it before the LORD your God, and worship before the LORD your God. [11] So you shall rejoice in *every good thing which the LORD your God has given to you <u>and</u> your house, you and the Levite and the stranger who is among you.* [12] "When you have finished laying aside all the tithe of your increase in the third year—the year of tithing—*and have given it to* **[1]** *the Levite,* **[2]** *the stranger,* **[3]** *the fatherless, and* **[4]** *the widow, so that <u>they</u> may eat within your gates and be filled,* [13] then you shall say

before the LORD your God: 'I have removed the holy tithe from my house, and also have given them to the Levite, the stranger, the fatherless, and the widow, according to all Your commandments which You have commanded me; I have not transgressed Your commandments, nor have I forgotten them. [14] I have not eaten any of it when in mourning, nor have I removed any of it for an unclean use, nor given any of it for the dead. I have obeyed the voice of the LORD my God, and have done according to all that You have commanded me. [15] Look down from Your holy habitation, from heaven, and bless Your people... " (Deut. 26:10-15).

The Old Covenant tithe was carried forward into Christianity as New Covenant offerings; they were intended to provide for: 1) ministers of the gospel, 2) orphans, 3) widows, and 4) strangers.

Can you see a problem in how we (the church) redirect the offering? How are we supposed to use it? Do we benefit the people that God intended us to help (even Abraham tithed to Melchizedek – a priest – before there was a Law), or do we use it based upon the dictates of deacons and elders? And yet the church (being apart from the Law) is not obligated to continue the tithe, but if we didn't have some obligation to giving... the church today would say: "My offering is dedicated to God" (Matt. 15:5) just like the Pharisees did, yet deny the greater requirements of the commandment. Hello, everyone, this is our tendency when we live apart from the Spirit: we gratify the good intentions of our self-directed life and adopt traditions and doctrines to support our agenda. The minimum standard that God expects for the church, in caring for PLOWS (the poor, lost, orphan, widow, stranger) – may be disregarded and then rendered as "unprofitable" by those with abundance and affluence in high estate... even within the church. The Lord put us alongside one another to take of one another!

Do we use the church offering for programs, utilities, insurance, the building fund and whatnot? Salaries for paid staff is permissible (i.e. do not muzzle the ox), but what about everything else? Do we implement a one-third budget as a dedicated offering toward these five people groups and then a two-third budget for whatever pleases us? The purpose of these questions is not to restrict our giving... but to influence church rules, laws and governance in keeping with God's original intent: assist those in need within the community, especially those "in the house" of God.

Let's turn our swords – into plowshares (Isa. 2:4). Sharing with PLOWS is what God intended we do... as we sojourn on earth.

"Abel thoroughly understood and comprehended that it was the Lord's doing that allowed him to create abundance to begin with; he also recognized that it was the Lord's creation, and therefore it was the Lord's increase, not his. He was the created vessel the Lord used to produce this increase – and thus – he gave God glory in all that he produced whereby... he returned to Him "a portion" with glory attached to it.[139] Cain, on the other hand, gave an offering that gave himself the credit and the glory for the increase – and God called it wicked. ***Anything that robs God of His glory is wicked.***" [140] I wonder how much of our tithe actually glorifies God – or even – if the time spent collecting the offering during "worship" by calling it "a form of worship" is merely a rouse in itself to glorify giving rather than the Giver. Selah.

The Spirituality Test

---

[139] This portion is not the precursor to the tithe; this portion is the precursor to righteousness through faith. The tithe was just a legal instrument that was implemented by God to teach Israel to remember the Lord and acknowledge the Lord as the Creator, Provider, and the Source of all increase – and the tithe was merely the minimum return that acknowledges the Lord God is worthy to receive ALL increase! Not just a 10% return, but all of it – 100% belongs to the Lord! The tithe, in this respect, is not a form of worship... but ***an act of obedience*** to return glory to God that rightfully belongs to Him! If you want to regard tithe as a ***voluntary act of worship***, then return 100%!
[140] Excerpt from "Dominion" section titled "My Glory Will I Give."

Now, let's take a test. If I presented you with a scale from one to one-hundred with one being abject poverty with anguish and despair... and one-hundred being wealth beyond comprehension yet with enormous accountability to God for proper stewardship of His resources, where along this numeric scale would you select a number? Ok, pick a number before reading further and remember it (write it down).

Now I want you to consider the spiritual responsibilities and consequences associated with these numbers which includes maintaining your love and trust relationship with God, promoting an attitude of grace with thanksgiving, fostering goodwill with generosity toward your fellow man and giving God all the glory with what you have been entrusted... whereby your success or failure to manage these duties and responsibilities and giving glory to God through this process will directly affect your kingdom placement, true riches and eternal reward in the next life. Ok, what number would you pick?

Was the second number lower than the first? For nearly all of us – it usually is. Now I want you to think how other people from other countries would answer this test. Now I want you to think how the first century church would have answered this? Now I want you to think how apostles, prophets, evangelists, teachers, preachers, and devoted disciples and followers of Jesus would answer this? How would the giants of faith answer this... like John the Baptist, Mary, Abraham, Elijah, Jeremiah, Ezekiel? Was their concern monetarily focused... or kingdom of God focused?

Truly, we (the church) need a spiritual paradigm realignment that is consistent with the teachings of Jesus Christ... to establish His dominion upon the earth.

Money or the lack thereof is not the problem... our "attitude" toward God either in abundance or lack is the issue. It is just as hard to praise God and give Him glory in great abundance as it is in abject poverty.

And now we shall learn the meaning of: "Blessed are the poor in spirit." Those persons that are poor, in anguish and despair – and yet are still able to rejoice and be glad in the Lord in their soul – and are able to praise Him through their spirit – are very precious to the Lord. They are blessed! Most people would give up and become bitter, cynical, resentful and hostile toward God, but those who are able to rejoice through their spirit are very, very rare and precious to God. Few are those who are able to endure and persevere… and those that do will receive a very great reward.

Can a person be poor "in spirit" but exceedingly rich toward God? Yes! Can a person be exceedingly rich in material wealth and exceedingly rich toward God? Yes, however...

> "And again I say to you, it is easier for a camel to go through the eye of a needle than for a rich man to enter the kingdom of God" (Matt. 19:24).

The eye of the needle is not a certain door leading into a city or a small door within a gate, as modern preachers often say; the eye of the needle is the smallest orifice (5169+4476) through which something may barely pass through. In this case… literally nothing!

Oh, how foolish our spiritual teachers have been. And Oh, how wicked are the health and wealth faith merchants who manipulate truth and trick the Lord's sheep out of their true riches in Paradise to support their self-exalted worldly ministry. Woe to sheep merchants!!! You have defrauded the sheep of their rightful inheritance in the New Earth by deceiving them to build a perishable kingdom you tricked them into building. You have been selling heaven with wide gates that anyone with the smallest of faith may enter in, but this contradicts Christ's message:

> "Because narrow is the gate and difficult is the way which leads to life, and there are few who find it" (Matt. 7:14).

And what better reproof for faith merchants than these words from the Apostle Paul:

> "But in all things we commend ourselves as ministers of God: in much patience, in tribulations, in needs, in distresses, [5] in stripes, in imprisonments, in tumults, in labors, in sleeplessness, in fastings; [6] by purity, by knowledge, by longsuffering, by kindness, by the Holy Spirit, by sincere love, [7] by the word of truth, by the power of God, by the armor of righteousness on the right hand and on the left, [8] by honor and dishonor, by evil report and good report; as deceivers, and yet true; [9] as unknown, and yet well known; as dying, and behold we live; as chastened, and yet not killed; [10] as sorrowful, yet always rejoicing; as poor, yet making many rich; as having nothing, and yet possessing all things" (2 Cor. 6: 4-10).

I could write an entire book at this precise moment regarding all the thoughts the Lord is washing through my mind right now concerning the spiritual state of the church which makes a good show of helping the poor with glossy marketing brochures and flashy heart-wrenching commercials to give-give-give and sow abundantly into their do-gooding ministry ...

"But your heart is far from Me" says the Lord of mercy and compassion.

> "From the Jews five times I received forty stripes minus one. [25] Three times I was beaten with rods; once I was stoned; three times I was shipwrecked; a night and a day I have been in the deep; [26] in journeys often, in perils of waters, in perils of robbers, in perils of my own countrymen, in perils of the Gentiles, in perils in the city, in perils in the wilderness, in perils in the sea, in perils among false brethren; [27] in weariness and toil, in sleeplessness

> often, in hunger and thirst, in fastings often, in cold and nakedness— ²⁸ besides the other things, what comes upon me daily: my deep concern for all the churches. ²⁹ Who is weak, and I am not weak? Who is made to stumble, ***and I do not burn with indignation?*** " (2 Cor. 11:24-28)

Is your plush recliner getting a little hotter? Consider, also, this message regarding Jesus:

> "But the Lord is the true God; He is the living God and the everlasting King. At His wrath the earth will tremble, ***and the nations will not be able to endure His indignation***" (Jer. 10:10).

We have forgotten who we are and what we are supposed to be doing on earth, and yet the church has been teaching and selling a false heaven doctrine so we may attain heaven while ignoring our heavenly mandate to have dominion on earth – and take care of one another – in the name of Jesus. Indignant is how the Lord shall return… and with a great powerful angelic army!

The reason I am able to teach this word is because I have nothing to gain, and since I have surrendered it all… I have nothing to lose either! I can't be voted out by deacons, I cannot lose my tenure at a university, I cannot be forced to resign my position by a board, and I am most certainly not intimidated by a defeated foe that lost his teeth *and* his dominion on Calvary. I would rather write a hundred books in the wilderness that gives all glory to Jesus – rather than forfeit my heavenly peace that surpasses all understanding upon the altar of complacency and compromise. Jesus is my all in all, and I am not ashamed of Jesus or the message of the gospel.

Back on topic… the poor have been placed on this earth with a lowly commission and told to simply "Believe and trust in the Lord your deliverer." In the day of salvation, He will be your Savior and Deliverer. If you acknowledge Him, then He will acknowledge you.

The "***poor in spirit***" represent any persons that can only get what they need from begging. These persons are so brokenhearted they may not be able rejoice in the Lord with their spirit, having become so spiritually exhausted and depleted by the enemy and by negligent "neighbors and friends" that should have helped them in their time of distress… whereby they are unable to sing praises unto the Lord.

However – "***Blessed are - the poor in spirit***" represent those persons that continue to rejoice *despite* their brokenness and despair… for they have not forgotten the reason they were placed on earth to worship the Lord and give all glory unto Him through their spirit. They are blessed and highly favored because they "remembered to praise" and continued to rejoice greatly in the Lord who will one day reward them and put them in charge of His kingdom to steward His things in righteousness and truth in the New Earth. "Blessed are the poor in spirit" because they continue to bless the Lord in their soul and through their spirit *despite* their circumstance or condition!!! This world will call them wretched, but in the Day of Christ, they will be called blessed and highly favored because they overcame all adversity and strife and oppression in order to cling to the hope that dwells within them, and in doing so… they will be richly rewarded by Jesus in the New Earth (aka the kingdom of heaven).

> "For the needy shall not always be forgotten; the expectation of the poor shall not perish forever" (Psa. 9:18).

Is there any among the rich with such a glorious hope as this? Those who are wealthy in this life have already received their reward, yet the poor in spirit "will be blessed" when their Savior stands before them and says, "Enter into the joy of your salvation. Rejoice and be glad, for you overcame the temptation to forget Me and bring a charge against Me; thus, you honored Me with the spirit I gave you and did far more than mighty kings and princes were able to accomplish – but didn't. You glorified Me and rejoiced in your spirit – to glorify Me. Enter into everlasting joy and enjoy your salvation."

> "He raises the poor from the dust and lifts the
> beggar from the ash heap, to set them among
> princes ***and make them inherit the throne of glory***.
> "For the pillars of the earth are the Lord's, and He
> has set the world upon them" (1 Sam. 2:8).

When this message was given to me... I myself was not prepared for the conclusion... which is yet to come.

Blessed Are The Beggars

As I stated before, the phrase by Jesus "Blessed are the poor in spirit" had me perplexed for quite a while. Even after receiving much Spirit-guided wisdom and understanding regarding the terms "poor" and "spirit" there was another little connective word between these words that helps to clarify the message Jesus meant. Here is what appears in the Greek:[141]

"Μακάριοι οἱ πτωχοὶ **τῷ πνεύματι**, ὅτι αὐτῶν ἐστιν ἡ βασιλεία τῶν οὐρανῶν" (Matt. 5:3)

Μακάριοι (Blessed) οἱ (the) πτωχοὶ (poor/beggar) **τῷ** (-) **πνεύματι** (spirit), ὅτι (for) αὐτῶν (of them) ἐστιν (is) ἡ (the) βασιλεία (kingdom) τῶν (of the) οὐρανῶν (heavens).

The word 'τῷ-3588' oftentimes translated (this, that, the, of the, that of)[142] is a connective word that associates with the word following immediately after, which typically has the same ending as the word associated with it. A classic example is found within this same passage: "of the heavens" (**τῶν** οὐραν**ῶν**). While this is usually the case, the pattern is inconsistent at times whereby translators are allowed some latitude with interpretation. This exact same word 'τῷ' occurs in Matt. 4:21 (ἐν τῷ πλοίῳ μετὰ Ζεβεδαίου – in ***the*** boat with Zebedee) and also Matt. 4:23 (πᾶσαν

---

[141] Greek scriptures (in all books) are from the SBL Greek New Testament.
[142] Strong's Concordance.

μαλακίαν ἐν τῷ λαῷ - every illness among *the* people). However, the word in question (Matt. 5:3) has an ending that does not associate with the word "spirit." The most glaring point at issue amidst these word diagnostics is the absence of one word (ἐν) which translators typically translate "in."

Blessed the beggar (τῷ –this, that, the, of the, that of) spirit.

And thus, my perplexity continued, so I waited upon the Spirit to bring additional understanding. There are 29 exact matches in the New Testament for these two words: "**τῷ πνεύματι**"[143] and here are some notable verses to consider.

Mark 8:12 – "καὶ ἀναστενάξας **τῷ πνεύματι** αὐτοῦ λέγει· Τί ἡ γενεὰ αὕτη ζητεῖ σημεῖον; ἀμὴν λέγω ὑμῖν, εἰ δοθήσεται τῇ γενεᾷ ταύτῃ σημεῖον"

> "But He [Jesus] sighed deeply *in His spirit*, and said, "Why does this generation seek a sign? Assuredly, I say to you, no sign shall be given to this generation."

Mark 12:36 – "αὐτὸς Δαυὶδ εἶπεν ἐν **τῷ πνεύματι** τῷ ἁγίῳ· Εἶπεν κύριος τῷ κυρίῳ μου· Κάθου ἐκ δεξιῶν μου ἕως ἂν θῶ τοὺς ἐχθρούς σου ὑποκάτω τῶν ποδῶν σου"

> "For David himself said *by the Holy Spirit*: 'The LORD said to my Lord, "Sit at My right hand, till I make Your enemies Your footstool."

Luke 4:1 – "Ἰησοῦς δὲ πλήρης πνεύματος ἁγίου ὑπέστρεψεν ἀπὸ τοῦ Ἰορδάνου, καὶ ἤγετο ἐν **τῷ πνεύματι** ἐν τῇ ἐρήμῳ

---

[143] Matt. 5:3; Mark 2:8; 8:12; 9:25; 12:36; Luke 2:27; 4:1; 8:29; 9:42; 10:21; John 11:33; 13:21; Acts 6:10; 7:51; 15:28; 16:18; 18:25; 19:21; 20:22; Romans 8:16; 12:11; 1 Cor. 5:3; 6:11; 7:34; 14:15; Eph. 1:13; 4:23; Col. 2:5; and 2 Thess. 2:8.

"Then Jesus, being filled with the Holy Spirit, returned from the Jordan and was led *by the Spirit* into the wilderness."

Luke 10:21 – "Ἐν αὐτῇ τῇ ὥρᾳ ἠγαλλιάσατο **τῷ πνεύματι** τῷ ἁγίῳ καὶ εἶπεν

"In that hour Jesus rejoiced *in the Spirit* and said, "I thank You, Father, Lord of heaven and earth, that You have hidden these things from *the* wise and prudent and revealed them to babes.""

John 11:33 – "Ἰησοῦς οὖν ὡς εἶδεν αὐτὴν κλαίουσαν καὶ τοὺς συνελθόντας αὐτῇ Ἰουδαίους κλαίοντας ἐνεβριμήσατο **τῷ πνεύματι** καὶ ἐτάραξεν

"Therefore, when Jesus saw her weeping, and the Jews who came with her weeping, He groaned *in the spirit* and was troubled."

John 13:21 – "Ταῦτα εἰπὼν ὁ Ἰησοῦς ἐταράχθη **τῷ πνεύματι** καὶ ἐμαρτύρησεν καὶ εἶπεν·

"When Jesus had said these things, He was troubled *in spirit*, and testified and said, "Most assuredly, I say to you, one of you will betray Me.""

Acts 16:18 – "διαπονηθεὶς δὲ Παῦλος καὶ ἐπιστρέψας **τῷ πνεύματι** εἶπεν

"But Paul, greatly annoyed, turned and *to the spirit* he said, "I command you in the name of Jesus Christ to come out of her." And he came out that very hour."

Acts 18:25 – "οὗτος ἦν κατηχημένος τὴν ὁδὸν τοῦ κυρίου, καὶ ζέων **τῷ πνεύματι** ἐλάλει καὶ ἐδίδασκεν ἀκριβῶς τὰ περὶ τοῦ Ἰησοῦ

"This man [Apollos] had been instructed in the way

of the Lord; and being fervent *in spirit*, he spoke
and taught accurately the things of the Lord, though
he knew only the baptism of John."

Acts 19:21 – "Ὡς δὲ ἐπληρώθη ταῦτα, ἔθετο ὁ Παῦλος ἐν **τῷ πνεύματι**

"When these things were accomplished, Paul
purposed *in the Spirit*." (Note: it is perhaps more
accurate to say Paul purposed "in (the/his) spirit")

Romans 8:16 – "αὐτὸ τὸ πνεῦμα συμμαρτυρεῖ **τῷ πνεύματι** ἡμῶν ὅτι ἐσμὲν τέκνα θεοῦ.

"The Spirit Himself bears witness *with our spirit*
that we are children of God." (Note: it is more
accurate to say the Spirit witnesses *with the spirit* of
us")

Romans 12:11 – "τῇ σπουδῇ μὴ ὀκνηροί, **τῷ πνεύματι** ζέοντες, τῷ κυρίῳ δουλεύοντες,

"… not lagging in diligence, fervent *in spirit*,
serving the Lord."

1 Cor. 7:34 – "καὶ μεμέρισται. καὶ ἡ γυνὴ ἡ ἄγαμος καὶ ἡ παρθένος μεριμνᾷ τὰ τοῦ κυρίου, ἵνα ᾖ ἁγία καὶ **τῷ σώματι** καὶ **τῷ πνεύματι**"

"There is a difference between a wife and a virgin.
The unmarried woman cares about the things of the
Lord, that she may be holy both *in body* and *in
spirit*."

1 Cor. 14:15 – "τί οὖν ἐστιν; προσεύξομαι **τῷ πνεύματι**, προσεύξομαι δὲ καὶ τῷ νοΐ· ψαλῶ **τῷ πνεύματι**, ψαλῶ δὲ καὶ τῷ νοΐ

> "What is the conclusion then? I will pray **with the spirit**, and I will also pray with the understanding. I will sing **with the spirit**, and I will also sing with the understanding."

It seems the Apostle Paul tee-d it up perfectly: "What is the conclusion then?" Do everything on earth "in the spirit" and "with the spirit" in partnership with the Holy Spirit who enables our spirit with spiritual understanding (John 3:3) and with supernatural power ... to rejoice and be fervent "in spirit" in service to Jesus our Lord. Our spirit is the means whereby our soul is able to manifest the goodness and glory of God into this world – from the inner (spirit-minded) spiritual man to manifest it through the outer (flesh-constrained) man.

> Jesus said: "It is the Spirit who gives life; **the flesh profits nothing**. The words that I speak to you are spirit, and *they* are life" (John 6:63).

"The spiritual state of the soul is normal for the believer, but to this state all do not attain, nor when it is attained is it always maintained."[144] The spirit, in this regard, is given by God to assist our soul and to attain and maintain our spiritual state of communion – to live in divine relationship and oneness with Him! God's commission for every believer is to become a disciple of Jesus Christ so as to continue the Lord's work – in us and through us – and establish the kingdom of heaven – here and now.

Eph. 1:13 – "ἐν ᾧ καὶ ὑμεῖς ἀκούσαντες τὸν λόγον τῆς ἀληθείας, τὸ εὐαγγέλιον τῆς σωτηρίας ὑμῶν, ἐν ᾧ καὶ πιστεύσαντες ἐσφραγίσθητε **τῷ πνεύματι** τῆς ἐπαγγελίας τῷ ἁγίῳ,

> "In Him you also *trusted,* after you heard the word of truth, the gospel of your salvation; in whom also, having believed, you were sealed **with the Holy Spirit** of promise"

---

[144] Strong's Concordance, notes on 4152-*pneumatikos*.

The Holy Spirit sealed you, not just for redemption and salvation, but also as ambassadors of the Living God to operate in the similitude of Jesus according to His example. In order to accomplish this, we (our soul) is given a new heart and a new spirit... along with the indwelling Holy Spirit... to complete the spiritual transformation process by renewing our mind... to have a sound mind... so we think like Jesus.[145]

Eph. 4:23 – "ἀνανεοῦσθαι δὲ **τῷ πνεύματι** τοῦ νοὸς ὑμῶν

"... and be renewed *in the spirit* of your mind"

We have been exhorted to be renewed in the spirit of our mind (soul) through the Spirit's transformational process of sanctification to renew our mind (Rom. 12: 2) and thus be changed and conformed into the image of Christ. This is a "spiritual" renewal process of the mind and soul, and not an intellectual program that involves our spirit, so keep this in mind.

In conclusion: do these examples help us understand what Jesus meant by "τῷ πνεύματι"? There are numerous translation possibilities that allow us to select any of these options, yet the Spirit did not stop my research at this point. The Spirit reminded me that Jesus often began a phrase or teaching by quoting an Old Testament verse which He then proceeds to build upon[146] which we will explore in a little while.

Thus far, various words have been used to describe the inherent meaning of poor, such as meek, lowly, depressed, humble, broken, despairing... and then understanding came to me: when we are poor, we are near-or-at zero. Zero becomes the state when we have been completely emptied of whatever – and now we are ready

---

[145] I think it would have been easier if the Lord replaced our mind rather than our heart and spirit.
[146] Such as "My God, My God, why have You forsaken Me" is in reference to Psalm 22. The same is true for us if we begin saying: "The Lord is my shepherd..." we pick it up by adding... "I shall not want" (Psalm 23).

to be replenished by God's Spirit "in our spirit."

> "I have been crucified with Christ; ***it is no longer I who live***, but Christ lives in me; and the life which I now live in the flesh I live by faith in the Son of God, who loved me and gave Himself for me" (Gal. 2:20).

We have all attempted to infill our lives with a multitude of many things wherein the flesh was gratified and glorified; however, once our soul becomes thoroughly depleted and our spirit becomes unable to strengthen us any more, this, then, is when we come to the end of ourselves. And regardless if we have been rendered destitute, emotionally depressed or if we lack nothing physical this world has to offer, we are still faced with the poverty of our soul – longing once again – for the things "of the spirit." This, then, is when the Lord can change us the most... because we are holding onto one thing: hope. And this, then, is when the Lord can use us the most... because we are least in the kingdom "of this world."

> "Whoever receives this little child in My name receives Me; and whoever receives Me receives Him who sent Me. For he who is least among you all will be great" (Luke 9:48).

> "But he who is greatest among you shall be your servant" (Matt. 23:11).

The majority of the people who are reading these words have no understanding of poverty or begging, and the minority that do understand... will never see or read these words. So, how can I communicate the essence of "beggar-*ptochos*" that you might possibly understand? Well, let me introduce to you a friend of mine whose new name the Lord gave him is "Zero." Yes, this is a real person and that is his real name. The best way to describe my friend is according to his status within society: he is a zero (by his own admission). He has no earthly possessions except a tent that is pitched near a swamp on unusable private property... with enough supplies to take care of his daily needs. He describes his situation with modest affection as "being in the world but not of it." His heart is completely and totally focused on Jesus and doing His will... and since he has barely anything to take care of or defend from thieves, his approach to living for Jesus is unencumbered by worry or worldly cares or any need to accumulate "stuff." What some people might spend on a barbeque grill will supply his needs for an entire year. Zero emptied himself and has forsaken everything in this life in order to focus on Jesus and follow Him without reservation. He is a sojourner living in the wilderness. Does this sound like anyone you know? Consider the prophets of old... and the Lord Himself!

What did Jesus teach us about the care of many things?

> "Do not lay up for yourselves treasures on earth, where moth and rust destroy and where thieves break in and steal; [20] but lay up for yourselves treasures in heaven, where neither moth nor rust destroys and where thieves do not break in and steal" (Matt. 6:19, 20).

What did Jesus teach us about trying to save our life?

> "For whoever desires to save his life will lose it, but whoever loses his life for My sake and the gospel's will save it" (Mark 8:35).

How did Jesus teach us to be concerned about today?

> "Therefore do not worry about tomorrow, for tomorrow will worry about its own things. Sufficient for the day is its own trouble" (Matt. 6:34).

Are we supposed to worry about what to eat or what clothes to wear?

> "Therefore I say to you, do not worry about your life, what you will eat or what you will drink; nor

about your body, what you will put on. Is not life more than food and the body more than clothing? ^{26} Look at the birds of the air, for they neither sow nor reap nor gather into barns; yet your heavenly Father feeds them. Are you not of more value than they? ^{27} Which of you by worrying can add one cubit to his stature?" (Matt. 6:25-27).

Blessed the beggar τῷ spirit – who understands that everything he needs he is able to get according to what the Lord will provide – according to His riches in glory. Regardless whether we have great wealth or extreme poverty, the beggar archetype is attributed to everyone on this planet because – whether we recognize it or not – **we are all beggars in the presence of a King**! We are all "lost" – "utterly destroyed ones" in need of Savior. All things we need are provided to us by our heavenly Father… for your Father in heaven knows you need these things" (Matt. 6:8). You have… because the Lord provided it (not because you earned it)… and the beggar understands this kingdom truth better than most.

This manner of living requires a paradigm shift in order to see our purpose in life on this earth as being summed up by this phrase:

> "But seek first the kingdom of God and His righteousness, and all these things shall be added to you" (Matt. 6:33).

You are the light of the world (Matt. 5:14). Do you want to exist merely by maintaining status quo – or do you want to change the world from darkness to light? Do you want to establish the kingdom of heaven on earth as you were commissioned by Jesus? Great, then imitate Jesus… and be the light of the world He created you to be. Advanced training in righteousness makes disciples do extraordinary things because of their intense love for their Lord and King. They surrendered all the cares of this life to establish the kingdom of heaven on earth – in the name of Jesus Christ – for His honor and glory.

How much will it cost you to live this way? "All it costs… is all you've got." If you think this is an unrealistic expectation to live this way, well so did I... when I wore a suit and tie. We are all the same, you and I, yet each of us must calculate the cost of being obedient to the Lord's voice... so I surrendered everything to attain that which I shall never loose.

"He is no fool who gives what he cannot keep to gain what he cannot lose." Jim Elliot

The disciple no longer lives to gratify their worldly needs (by seeking to satisfy the flesh-man), and before a disciple does anything, they seek their Lord to ask Him what the will of the Lord is... in every situation. How, you wonder, is a disciple able to do this for every little thing? The answer is four-fold: 1) the disciple is always listening to hear the Lord's voice, 2) the disciple walks according to the Spirit with his spirit, 3) the disciple has been taught and trained to think and know and understand the ways of the Lord, and 4) the disciple knows the heart of the Lord and does not travail over trivial matters. When "your spirit" is led by the Spirit... small stuff doesn't matter, like what you will eat or what you will wear.

The root word for disciple is not discipline – it is "learner" (3101). A disciple is a pupil who will learn the ways of His Master, adhere to His teachings, and imitate His example – and thus, a disciple will also discipline their spirit and body to seek the kingdom of God and pursue righteousness... which gratifies the deep spiritual longing of their soul to be pleasing to the Lord.

For example: a soldier does not get caught up in trivial civilian matters.

> "No one engaged in warfare entangles himself with the affairs of this life, that he may please him who enlisted him as a soldier" (2 Tim. 2:4).

Much like a soldier operating with a commission under a commander, a disciple will only do what they know is pleasing and proper and godly and right in the eyes of their Commander. This point is most important: do everything as unto the Lord, for it is "in" His name you do it – and it is His reputation that is on display for the world to see whereby the world either believes in the Lord... or mocks Him on account of your attitudes and fleshly living. A true disciple is under the authority of the Lord to do "His" will and has laid aside their personal agenda in order to accomplish perfectly the will of the Lord.

The Lord told us to make disciples of believers, but sadly... it seems the church is more interested in turning believers into members rather than disciples.

Disciples of Love

> "You have heard that it was said, 'You shall love your neighbor and hate your enemy.' [44] But I say to you, love your enemies, bless those who curse you, do good to those who hate you, and pray for those who spitefully use you and persecute you" (Matt. 5:43, 44).

When we operate according to this model of heavenly love and heavenly grace, our earthly focus shall accomplish heaven's objectives in us and through us. When was the last time you prayed to Jesus to hear His voice regarding what car or house you should buy? Did He answer you? Or "if" you should take a vacation? Or "if" you should purchase a luxury item to make dwelling in your McMansion easier and more worry free? Did you ever ask Him if you are working the job that He assigned to you? Listen to Jesus and hear the Voice of the Spirit! Stop listening to commercials and TV ads tell you what the worldly system can do for you because it is a giant fat lie from the enemy that gratifies the flesh to live in the alternate reality[147] that is violently opposed to Christ. And stop running to sheep merchants that have bought into the worldly system and are controlled by the spirit of religion.

---

[147] Read "Understand" section titled: "Alternate Reality."

The problem with being "poor in this life" is that we bristle at the thought of poverty and any struggling to acquire basic necessities; we like our creature comforts, plasma TV's with 1,000 channels, every kitchen appliance, newest handtool, ice cube dispensers on fridges and every toy imaginable for one reason: to embellish this life with every convenience, and yet... our soul within us becomes impoverished by our many worldly cares because we prefer to gratify the body of flesh upon us rather than allowing the Spirit of God to empower our spirit through sanctification and training in righteousness. The hunger we feel in our stomach – is the hunger of our soul for more of Jesus, so stop the merry-go-round... and seek the Lord.

It is easy to gratify and glorify the flesh in this world... but this is not who you are – and certainly not who you were created to be! You are a sojourner sent from heaven. You are a spiritual being having a human experience. You are an ambassador that represents the kingdom of heaven. You are here to glorify the Lord "through your spirit" in His kingdom.

Your commission is not "what" you do or the purpose you accomplish – it is all about "who" you are... and "Whose" you are. Our identity and our commission are found "in Christ."

If your spirit within you has become impoverished, weak, emaciated, poor and starving for spiritual food to fortify your soul, then perhaps the exhaustion you feel every day is not physical... but spiritual!

When was the last time you fed your soul and strengthened your spirit by reading the scriptures, or renewed a steadfast spirit within you through prayer and meditation to hear God's voice, or fanned a burning fire of zeal in your spirit for righteousness' sake by fasting? There are 10,080 minutes in every week, yet getting a fifty minute dose of God on Sunday morning and expecting it to spiritually feed you for an entire week is foolishness. In fact, you should be getting your spiritual feeding during the week (night and day) by your own daily devotions, personal bible study and listening to the Voice of Truth... and then celebrate the Lord on Sabbath or Sunday in communion with your brothers and sisters in fellowship with Christ – in the unity of the Spirit!

Who do you worship on Sunday? Ok, that's great, now... who do you worship the other 6.92 days of the week? ***Worship is the imitation of that which we admire most. Think about that!***

Many of us are familiar with the unbiblical concept of Lent whereby we sacrifice something during the month leading up to Easter as a form of spiritual hardship in remembrance of Christ's crucifixion, but how many of us are willing to offer our entire "self" as a living sacrifice upon the altar of obedience and lay aside our will and self determination entirely to do the Lord's will? Are you willing to render yourself a zero in order to become a disciple of Jesus?

> "I beseech you therefore, brethren, by the mercies of God, ***that you present your bodies a living sacrifice***, holy, acceptable to God, which is your reasonable service. ^{2} And do not be conformed to this world, but be transformed by the renewing of your mind, that you may prove what is that good and acceptable and perfect will of God" (Rom. 12: 1, 2).

The flesh craves the weak and beggarly elements of this world (Gal. 4:9)... yet our soul craves the lowly, meek and beggarly status in the presence of our beloved Lord and King. Our soul is oftentimes rendered powerless to discipline the flesh because our spirit is not being nurtured with God's truth by His Spirit. Your soul's best friend is your spirit that is steadfast in affection and admiration of Jesus Christ and is being strengthened and tutored by the Spirit (Gal. 3:16)... and yet... we partner with a multitude of worldly, demonic and familial spirits with our spirit at the expense of our eternal soul. Ask yourself... is it really worth it? This manner of living is causing you to forfeit true riches in eternity. Again, I ask.... is it worth it?

The soul, in this regard, is the seat of reflective consciousness (*nous*)[148] – that operates the mind and will of the spiritual person, and the heart is the center of emotion and affections. When we are born anew, the Lord will give us a new heart and a new spirit (Ezek. 36:26)… because they were intended to operate in oneness… and they can be upgraded and supercharged by the Holy Spirit once the Lord has been exalted upon the throne of our heart – through repentance. Our emotions are supposed to be governed by our heart that is managed by the will and intellect of our mind – in oneness of our soul (mind and heart), but what happens so often these days are drama-driven spirits calling attention to the self (and flesh) rather than giving glory to God. In this case, a large dose of humility is all that is needed to keep this spirit in check, that is, *if* it desires to be subordinate (in submission) to the Lord.

Consider, now, how Jesus expressed His emotions through His spirit:

- "In that hour Jesus ***rejoiced in the Spirit*** and said, "I thank You, Father" (Luke 10:21)
- "But He ***sighed deeply in His spirit***" (Mark 8:12)
- "He ***groaned in the spirit*** and was troubled" (John 11:33)
- "When Jesus had said these things, He ***was troubled in spirit***." (John 13:21).

Our spirit is the spiritual instrument whereby our soul is able to release emotions that are consistent with the thoughts and attitudes of our soul (mind and heart). And our spirit is the spiritual means whereby we talk to God – and manifest the goodness of God – from the depth of our soul.

---

[148] "'Nous' (3563) the intellect, i.e. the mind, seat of reflective consciousness, comprising the faculties of perception and understanding, and those of feeling, judging and determining[148] (Luke 24:45; Rom. 1:28; 14:5; 1 Cor. 14:14, 15 (twice), 19; Eph. 4:17; Phil. 4:7; Col. 2:18; 1 Tim. 6:5; 2 Tim. 3:8; Titus 1:15; Rev. 3:18; 19:7). Having been born anew, "this new nature belongs to every believer by reason of the new birth (Rom. 7:23, 25)." Excerpt from "Understand" by the author pertaining to word study on "mind" in Vine's Expository.

Your soul is who you are… with your spirit… in order to manifest the reality of Christ in you and release the grace of God through you into a world of darkness that is desperate for the love of God – and your soul desires to be restored in communion with Him… where He sits exalted upon the throne of your heart as the Governor of your soul (mind and heart).

"There are some who can see a conflict in the manner in which they were taught about the soul as being mind, will and emotion. Well, the soul is the mind and heart – and the spirit is the enabling. Apart from the spirit, the soul is unable to express itself in spiritual realities – and apart from the body, the soul is unable to associate itself in earthly realities."[149] Apart from the spirit, the soul ceases to express itself in spiritual terms – and dies (enters death)… and this is the condition of man when he fell from grace in the Garden of Eden (to gratify and glorify the flesh). Unless this soul is converted and reborn by the Holy Spirit – through repentance – this person is destined to reside in Death until the Day of Judgment… and then be cast into Hell for eternity.

> "… but of the tree of the knowledge of good and evil you shall not eat, for in the day that you eat of it you shall surely die" (Gen. 2:17).

Every soul has suffered a spiritual disconnect from the spirit when the will of man focused its rebellious attention and affection on the desires of the flesh instead of glorifying the Lord of Glory through their spirit. The soul is *required* to make a conscious decision every time it is presented with any opportunity that either allows our spirit to be strengthened by the Spirit of God – or our spirit to be compromised by the desires (lust) of the flesh and the cares of this world. This is why true discipleship is rare in the church, because it has the same effect on people today as it did when Jesus preached 5,000 disciples down to twelve… whereby Jesus then asked His disciples: "Do you want to leave also?"

---

[149] Copied from Chapter 1; Soul With Spirit, section titled: "Soul Explanation."

> "But Simon Peter answered Him, "Lord, to whom shall we go? You have the words of eternal life" (John 6:68).

And this is why Jesus said:

> "For many are called, but few are chosen" (Matt. 22:14).

Everybody wants to go to heaven, but nobody wants to die to get there.

> "That which is born of the flesh is flesh, and that which is born of the Spirit is [*of the*] spirit" (John 3:6; *italics* by the author).

Your soul is the vessel (i.e. a spiritual sanctuary) that contains the pearl of great price (a seed of God's glory) and your spirit is the instrument of worship whereby you give glory to God.

God is soul with spirit – and we were created in His image according to His likeness.

Ratio and oratio – will and intellect. The thoughts of God (the expression) always precedes the manifestation… and we, likewise, also operate according to this spiritual pattern. "For as he thinks in his ~~heart~~ nephesh/soul, so is he" (Prov. 23:7). Our soul acts as the gatekeeper for our gateway; whatever we allow to pass through our gateway, we become… and likewise, whatever we release through our gateway by means of our spirit will either testify to the reality of God's light and presence in us – or we will testify to the darkness. Our spiritual construction and its operation is very simple, and yet… we have believed a great many errors to justify our sinfulness… with heavy, burdensome religious doctrines.

> "Truly, this only I have found: that God made man upright, but they have sought out many schemes" (Eccl. 7:29).

We are heavenly gardeners that are cultivating the garden of our earthly heart; whatever we decide (allow) to grow in the garden of our heart will produce a crop. As spiritual gatekeepers, our soul must never allow worldly things to pass through our spirit (gateway) to compromise our earthly commission. We were given a commission to "keep, guard and protect from loss or injury" (*tereo*-5083) the seed of glory placed within our garden, and it is imperative that we do so! Under NO circumstance are we to compromise this commission… or we risk forfeiting our soul to the Pit.

Blessed Are The Poor

At this point, there are many astute bible students and teachers that have been waiting for me to bring up the other "Beatitude" in Luke's Gospel… which omits "in spirit." So, here it is:

> "Then He lifted up His eyes toward His disciples, and said: ***Blessed are you poor***, for yours is the kingdom of God. [21] Blessed are you who hunger now, for you shall be filled. Blessed are you who weep now, for you shall laugh. [22] Blessed are you when men hate you, and when they exclude you, and revile you, and cast out your name as evil, for the Son of Man's sake. [23] Rejoice in that day and leap for joy! For indeed your reward is great in heaven, for in like manner their fathers did to the prophets" (Luke 6:20-23).

Why Matthew added "in spirit" (or perhaps Luke omitted it) is still the work of the Holy Spirit to teach us spiritual truth layer by layer to birth disciples for Lord Jesus. What Jesus taught at the beginning of the Sermon – about poor and rich – sets the tone for the entire Sermon.

"Blessed are the poor, for theirs is the kingdom of God (heaven)." Blessed are the impoverished, the meek, the humble, the hungry, the downcast, the depressed, the lowly; blessed are the excluded, castigated and denigrated ones that are hated, reviled, rejected and labeled as evil.

Blessed are you... seems like such a contradiction by worldly standards, yet indeed... that is exactly what it is! Jesus is repudiating the standards of the worldly system that is based upon the operating system of sin that seeks to crush, kill and destroy ALL humanity at both ends of the poor-rich spectrum by fostering attitudes of condemnation, unforgiveness, and thanklessness by merciless pride that separates us from one merciful thing we were commanded by Jesus to uphold:

Love one another, for love is of God

[Note: I am still unprepared for the messages being revealed to me at this time.] One morning, I observed a homeless person (through my van window) for 10 minutes while I prepared cantaloupe for breakfast. I typically keep plenty of prepared food on hand to pass out to anyone in need (which I was getting prepared to do), then the Spirit said to me: "Ask what he needs." And then the Spirit brought understanding: "The poor and hungry and homeless that Jesus mentioned weren't begging." How true! It is incumbent upon us to see the need – and meet it!

The difference between poor and beggar is: one asks... while the other doesn't. Both have the same need, both are destitute, and both were created by God upright and dignified by His indwelt goodness, but how they get what they need is either – seen and acknowledged by those with eyes to see because the attitude of their humble heart enables them to see – or they are not seen by others because hardened hearts are deaf, dumb and blind to spiritual (and physical) matters.

So, I went to the man and asked him if he needed food. "No" is all he said. So, I asked him if he needed anything. A stern "No" was his only response.

What impact the Sermon on the Mount has on you is predicated by the attitude of your heart.

Many of us (myself included) have turned a blind eye from helping the poor and needy because of a bad heart attitude toward them, as if it is their choice to be that way. All I can say is… "Here but by the grace of God go I." It may be their choice, it may be the result of poor choices or it may be their lot in life, but who am I to judge! From my own personal experience, it doesn't take much for our house of cards to "Humpty Dumpty" come crashing down upon us.

There are many preachers and teachers that have come from hard places, and there are others who have gone through difficult times and places, and while many have written and preached about these times in their past, I am writing them currently – in present tense – as I experience them and feel them as one living this life with homelessness, hunger, placelessness and depression (by others) all around me.

For example, I typically have several pounds of cooked and uncooked meat in my cooler (on hand) that must be eaten within a couple days (from frozen to thawed in 1-3 days > from thawed to cooked in 2-4 days > from cooked to eaten (or re-frozen) in 3 days). Thus, I am able to get frozen meat and maintain it in my cooler with ice for as long as 6-10 days; however, homeless people may not have access to a cooler – or ice.

Then the Spirit taught me: "Consider food storage 100-4,000 years ago." They did not have ice, insulated coolers, canned goods or even plastic bags to keep bread fresh. Their daily bread was good for one day – which was perhaps the most durable food source they had. The same is true with many homeless today; they get the food they need "this day" or else they go hungry. (A word of caution about tent camping with food: raccoons are midnight terrorists with a keen sense of smell that are smart enough to open zippers yet prefer to use their claws to rip a tent wide open to get at any stored food, especially peanut butter.)

"Give us this day our daily bread."

Humility is needed at both ends of the poor-rich spectrum; one with the humility to receive benevolence with thanksgiving without expectation or entitlement – and the other with the

COMMISSION

humility to perceive the need and take action to be a blessing unto others that gives glory to God.

What does the face of poverty look like? What does the face of homelessness look like? Well, most of us are familiar with those images of people sleeping overtop city grates to keep warm or holding messages on a piece of cardboard with some phrase begging for assistance (though rarely asking for money because panhandling is against the law in most communities), but I still encounter many along my journey that are destitute and in great financial need that you would never perceive because they (like me) stay well-dressed, clean-shaven and bathed. From McDonald's managers to store clerks to ladies sitting in the pew next to me – people are surprised to learn that I am homeless... because I don't look the part. If you want to see the homeless and hungry, then you have to perceive the homeless and hungry with spiritual eyes!

Hardened hearts are unable to perceive this reality, and therefore, their hearts rob God of the glory He desires to manifest through them.

We are "all" children of God, but we only become adopted sons and daughters of the kingdom through faith in Jesus Christ... which means that all you have to do is believe, right? Wrong! We need to act like Jesus – and say and do what He said and did. Faith without works is not empty faith – it is unbelief.

> "What does it profit, my brethren, if someone says he has faith but does not have works? Can faith save him? (James 2:14) "Thus also faith by itself, if it does not have works, is dead" (James 2:17).

If you see your brother in need and do nothing, then your faith is considered faithlessness in unbelief. Since Jesus taught us and commissioned us as His representatives, by grace through faith, to love one another and be faithful stewards of His things... how, then, shall we live? What manner of spirit are ye of? (Luke 19:55)

Are you the critical and condemning type of spirit (which is of this world) or are you the sacrificial generous giving spirit (of the kingdom)? What attitude do you have toward the lowly and less fortunate?

This is one of my favorite personal philosophies: I will not partner with any attitude that is inconsistent with Christ's character.

As for me, I am wearing the other person's shoes, and likewise, some of them are wearing mine.

What we have does not really belong to us; everything belongs to God... we are merely stewards and caretakers of His things for one season of eternity on earth. Another season has been apportioned (eternally) for those who understand how the kingdom of God operates, and for this reason Jesus came: to teach us how the kingdom operates... on earth as it is in heaven. The Sermon on the Mount represents the best sermon ever preached on earth (this takes 25 minutes to read aloud, so I encourage you to read Matt. 4:27 – 8:1 in one sitting every day for a week, which will certainly produce a paradigm shift in your thought process regarding how the kingdom of God operates in you vs. how the kingdom of darkness has infiltrated the church).

Sermon on the Mount

The crowds (multitudes) followed Jesus because He captured their attention. Jesus taught the good news and He "healed every disease and sickness among the people" (Matt. 4:23). If such a person were to perform similar deeds as Jesus today, multitudes would likely follow them also; however, there is one significant difference: Jesus healed many physical conditions – and now He will console and heal their spiritual condition by ministering to their soul.

The point is... "the people" mentioned within this large biblical passage are "the poor" that Jesus is about to reference. "Blessed are the poor" are the first words the multitudes heard, and I imagine they were delighted to hear it; however, the poor were not the only persons in attendance listening to Christ's words. Multitudes came from the entire region... and they were likely joined by synagogue leaders, as well as affluent and rich, to see what Jesus may teach, as well as perform more miracles their inquisitive (yet unbelieving) eyes might happen to observe.

Imagine if you can, as you read the Sermon, that Jesus is looking toward (facing) the multitudes throughout this very long sermon and He is encouraging them with very intimate, life-giving words of truth... and then He shifts His glance to the wayside to focus His words toward another group that is too righteous and pious to stand among the poor:

> "Do not think that I came to destroy the Law or the Prophets. I did not come to destroy but to fulfill. ^{18} For assuredly, I say to you, till heaven and earth pass away, one jot or one tittle will by no means pass from the law till all is fulfilled. ^{19} Whoever therefore breaks one of the least of these commandments, and teaches men so, shall be called least in the kingdom of heaven; but whoever does and teaches them, he shall be called great in the kingdom of heaven" (Matt. 5:17-19).

The religious leaders that heard this message must have bristled with incredulity that a poor man without any formal training is teaching well-educated leaders about the kingdom of heaven.

Jesus shifts His gaze back toward the multitudes and continues His teaching: "For I say to you, that unless your righteousness exceeds the righteousness of the scribes and Pharisees, you will by no means enter the kingdom of heaven" (v.5:20). Q: Is this a challenge by Jesus for the poor to become more righteous like scribes and Pharisees, which they could never achieve based upon the manner in which the Law was taught to them that kept them in bondage to the Law – as unrighteous sinners – or can you imagine Jesus leaning forward in His seated position to become intimate with the multitude again to say something that perhaps delighted them... and may have been flavored with sarcasm as a snide remark aimed at the religious elite listening nearby.

We cannot see this subtle nuance in Matthew, but turn to see what Luke recorded next as Jesus returns His gaze toward the religious gatekeepers of that day:

> "But woe to you who are rich, for you have received your consolation. ^{25} Woe to you who are full, for you shall hunger. Woe to you who laugh now, for you shall mourn and weep. ^{26} Woe to you when all men speak well of you, for so did their fathers to the false prophets" (Luke 6:24-26).

If you cannot say Amen, then say "Ouch." There is a wonderful spiritual drama being revealed by Jesus to encourage the poor and lowly to believe in Him, believe His message, continue to faithfully endure this life in obedience to God – and God will take care of you in the hereafter. The poor will receive the kingdom of heaven, and yet somehow, this does not cause the rich to live according to this manner. Why? Because they don't believe this part of the gospel message by Heaven's Messenger! They didn't believe it then... and they certainly don't believe it today!

Kingdom Opposites

The kingdom of heaven does not operate like the kingdom of this world. What you believe does not determine your eternal destination! How you live in obedience to the gospel that is... i.e. according the gospel of truth not to the gospel you want... determines your eternal outcome.

Quite often, Jesus uses familiar terms but applies them in unexpected ways. Why is that? Because Jesus is reorienting the applecart of faith to point in the right direction. The books I've been commissioned to write are no different in this regard, as many religious leaders will reject these words because they are inconsistent with the doctrines they've been taught by religious elite for centuries. For example: do we embrace the Lord's teaching of persecution leading unto death, or do we embrace the pastor's message of prosperity and abundance?

> "Blessed are those who are persecuted for righteousness' sake, for theirs is the kingdom of heaven. [11] "Blessed are you when they revile and persecute you, and say all kinds of evil against you falsely for My sake. [12] Rejoice and be exceedingly glad, for great is your reward in heaven, for so they persecuted the prophets who were before you" (Matt. 5:10-12)

> "Precious in the sight of the Lord is the death of His saints" (Psa. 116:15).

Back on point: Jesus begins His sermon again by speaking aloud to everyone, yet His attention turns toward the religious elite...

> "You have heard that it was said to those of old, 'You shall not murder, and whoever murders will be in danger of the judgment.' [22] But I say to you that whoever is angry with his brother without a cause shall be in danger of the judgment. And whoever says to his brother, 'Raca!' shall be in danger of the council. But whoever says, 'You fool!' shall be in danger of hell fire" (Matt. 5:21-22).

Let's key in on two terms the Lord used: raca and fool. "*Raca*-4469" literally means "empty-headed" intellectually as a term of utter contempt often applied by elite to uneducated poor; and "fool-*moros*-3474" meaning "blockhead; a godless, moral reprobate"[150] as another form of contempt with disdain typically heaped upon the minds of the poor seeking to please God under the Law – yet apart from official training in righteousness in the Law. Jesus, however, has turned the table and is using these terms

---

[150] Strong's Concordance; terms contained in 4469.

against the religious leaders who have become the very things they themselves attributed to the poor and beggarly masses, as *"raca* – a morally worthless scoundrel, which scorns a man's mind and calls him stupid; and *moros* – which scorns his heart and character; hence the Lord's more severe condemnation."[151]

Does this help us see what Jesus meant by this sermon? Absolutely! Jesus was comforting the poor and downcast (multitudes) *and* He was rebuking (heaping disdain upon) the rich, affluent and educated establishment that have placed heavy legalistic burdens on people that they themselves were unwilling to carry. Not only are the religious leaders unable to hear the Lord's message, but the multitudes have become "deaf" by listening to their toxic doctrines as well.

> "But if you had known what this means, 'I desire mercy and not sacrifice,' you would not have condemned the guiltless" (Matt. 12:7).

There are two types of people listening to Jesus: those who cannot understand – and those who refuse to understand. Jesus explains why neither of them is able to understand in Matt. 13.

"Then Jesus said, "Therefore I speak to them in parables, because seeing they do not see, and hearing (191) they do not hear (191), nor do they understand" (Matt. 13:13). The word "hearing" is '*akouo*' meaning "to hear, listening" – but the operative word here is "understand." They are hearing (listening with the sense of sound), but they do not spiritually hear, nor do they spiritually *understand* (4920 – *suniemi*, to put together mentally, to comprehend, understand).

'Why can't they understand? The Lord Jesus answered this question for us 2,000 years ago when He gave the answer to Isaiah (Isa. 6:9, 10; Matt. 13:14): their hearts are hardened and stupefied!

---

[151] IBID; terms contained in 3474.

- "Hearing (189) you will hear (191) and shall not *understand* (4920 - *suniemi*),
- And seeing you will see and not *perceive* (1492 – *oida*: completely comprehend);
- ¹⁵ For the hearts of this people have *grown dull* (3975 – *pachuno*: dull, waxed gross, to thicken, to fatten, stupefy or render callous; with the idea of being fixed, "pegged" like a pitched tent); "For this people's heart is waxed gross" (KJV)
- Their ears (of their mind) are *hard* (917 – *bareos*: heavily, weighed down, burdened) of *hearing* (191 – conveying the sense of having heard many religious sounding, weighty words that have become weary, burdensome); "and their ears are dull of hearing" (KJV)
- And their eyes (of their heart) they have closed," (Matt. 13:14, 15)."[152]

Throughout His Sermon on the Mount, Jesus was resetting the spiritual timeline on earth by teaching about the kingdom of heaven that He established by His parousia (visitation). Within one sermon, Jesus is rendering obsolete the Old Covenant and instituting a New Covenant with a new spiritual code of living... by living according to the spirit rather than the letter which kills!

Jesus is also resetting the terms and conditions of living by the spirit back to a previous operating system whereby anger toward a brother shall render a person in danger of judgment and the fire of hell. The attitude of anger toward a brother is just as reprehensible as the act of killing them, which in this case is the attitude of the establishment that denigrates the poor as "raca and fools" whereby religious leaders do nothing to help the less fortunate – as somehow deserving their impoverished and unintelligent existence. [Please keep in mind another significant point: Jesus was considered poor and uneducated by the establishment and religious elite... much like the very poor He preached to.]

---

[152] Excerpt copied from: "Listen" section titled "Another Reason."

Jesus begins again (in verse 22) to teach the multitudes in very simple terms children could comprehend... "But I say unto you" establishes a new code for living that is based upon living according to the spirit (by the empowering of the Spirit) and not according to the letter of the Law. This, therefore, is the sublime magnificence of the Gospel! This, perhaps, is more to the essence of the teaching than anything else... *while the multitudes are powerless to live according to the law, the gospel is being preached to cause a spiritual shift from the letter of the Law to the human spirit enlivened, enlightened and empowered by the Holy Spirit*.

> "But now we have been delivered from the law, having died to what we were held by, so that we should serve in the newness of the Spirit and not in the oldness of the letter" (Rom. 7:6).

> "... who also made us sufficient as ministers of the new covenant, not of the letter but of the Spirit; for the letter kills, but the Spirit gives life" (2 Cor. 3:6).

Does this put into better context the message Jesus taught regarding the Beatitudes? The problem we have understanding the meaning of the beatitudes and the scriptures is because:

- Words have been interpreted by religious men educated in such a manner that often segregates and disassociates "them" from poor and beggarly multitudes as being "above" them rather than alongside them. Sometimes, it takes a poor homeless person to see the light of truth in the scriptures... that others reluctantly refuse to consider.
- Doctrines have been developed from these translations to teach multitudes about the kingdom of God from man's perspective, including the false heaven doctrine.

By His example, Jesus taught the truth and exemplified the truth.

> "For you know the grace of our Lord Jesus Christ, that though He was rich, yet for your sakes He

became poor [beggarly], that you through His
poverty might become rich" (2 Cor. 8:9).

By Paul's example, he demonstrated the archetype of living as the Lord's disciple:

"... to the weak I became as weak, that I might win
the weak. I have become all things to all men, that I
might by all means save some" (1 Cor. 9:22).

Jesus knows how difficult it is here on earth, as He was also treated with contempt and disdain; however, those who continue to praise the Lord through their spirit and are faithful even unto death will be given a crown of life.

"These things says the First and the Last, who was
dead, and came to life: [9] "I know your works,
tribulation, and poverty (but you are rich); and I
know the blasphemy of those who say they are Jews
and are not, but are a synagogue of Satan. [10] Do not
fear any of those things which you are about to
suffer. Indeed, the devil is about to throw some of
you into prison, that you may be tested, and you
will have tribulation ten days. Be faithful until
death, and I will give you the crown of life" (Rev.
2:8-10).

Our attitude toward the things in this life must never superimpose the promises we have been promised (through obedience) by being faithful to Jesus despite tribulation, poverty, persecution and imprisonment. The Holy Spirit was given to us to strengthen our spirit and comfort our soul to patiently endure, persevere, remain steadfast and remain faithful to Jesus – and praise Him despite whatever circumstance or situation we are in.

Blessed are the poor in spirit, for as their spirit continues to be strengthened from above, their soul continues to live eternally… to the glory of God who dwells within them.

It's all about Jesus – and God gets the glory!

Hannah's Prayer

When you live life with the proper perspective, which is from God's perspective, your life is no longer encumbered by a multitude of false expectations, unrealistic agendas or entitlements – wherein the sound mind is able to operate in the manner of your true nature – through your spirit – in the similitude of Christ. We would all do well to learn from Hannah, this mighty woman of faith… who had the right posture and perspective that was revealed "through" her prayer.

"And Hannah prayed and said: "My heart rejoices in the LORD; My horn is exalted in the LORD.
I smile at my enemies, Because I rejoice in Your salvation. [2] "No one is holy like the LORD,
For there is none besides You, Nor is there any rock like our God.
[3] "Talk no more so very proudly; Let no arrogance come from your mouth, For the LORD is the God of knowledge;
And by Him actions are weighed. [4] "The bows of the mighty men are broken, And those who stumbled are girded with strength.
[5] Those who were full have hired themselves out for bread,
And the hungry have ceased to hunger. Even the barren has borne seven, And she who has many children has become feeble. [6] "The LORD kills and makes alive; He brings down to the grave and brings up. [7] *The LORD makes poor and makes rich; He brings low and lifts up.* [8] *He raises the poor from the dust And lifts the beggar from the ash heap, To set them among princes
And make them inherit the throne of glory.* "For the pillars of the earth are the LORD's,
And He has set the world upon them. [9] He will guard the feet of His saints, But the wicked shall be silent in darkness. "For by strength no man shall prevail. [10] The adversaries of the LORD shall be broken in pieces; From heaven He will thunder against them. The LORD will judge the ends of the earth. "He will give strength to His king, And exalt the horn of His anointed" (1 Samuel 2:1-10).

COMMISSION

While in this world,
we are captives to our perspectives,
and our condition is but temporary,
yet our soul shall continue to live eternally,
in the kingdom you are building now,
in the sanctuary of your heart.

Change us, Lord, by the renewing of our mind, to operate from your perspective,
according to newness – through truth, change and oneness.
Change the way we think,
To think the way You think,
To see things as You see them and
To imitate You
And do Your will on earth – as it is in heaven

Go in grace and mercy, and peace be yours in abundance.

Love one another!

It's all about Jesus – and God gets the glory!

Amen and Amen.

Chapter 5: Disciples

Every Easter, Christians celebrate the resurrection of our Lord and Savior, Jesus Christ. While this foundational truth is embraced by all those who profess themselves as being a Christian with faith in Christ, the most astonishing thing is this: God came to earth and became a Man.

God came to earth – and – became a Man. It sounds blasphemous every time I ponder it.

When we consider the most significant reason that Jesus came to us – to teach men how to live like Him within earthen vessels – the repercussions of this realization should send shock waves through our soul to embolden us to become what He created us to become: His disciples.

Sadly, the church spends more time making believers into members – instead of disciples.

> "But he who is joined to the Lord is one spirit with Him." (1 Cor. 6:17).

The topic of discipleship is one of the most important messages that I was commissioned to write about – second only to listening to the Voice of the Holy Spirit, understanding the message, and being guided by Him into newness – through truth, change and oneness.

The word disciple '*mathetes*-3101' means: "a learner, pupil, disciple… indicating **thought accompanied by endeavor**." Disciple, from the root '*mathano*-3129' implies: "to increase one's knowledge," frequently "to learn by inquiry, or observation."[153] Disciples are not merely learning the doctrines of their Lord as "followers of His teaching"… they are also imitating Him so as to think like Him and **endeavor to become like Him**!

---

[153] Strong's Concordance.

> "Then Jesus said to those Jews who believed Him, "If you abide in My word, you are My disciples indeed"" (John 8:31).

> "I am the vine, you are the branches. He who abides in Me, and I in him, bears much fruit; for without Me you can do nothing. ⁶ If anyone does not abide in Me, he is cast out as a branch and is withered; and they gather them and throw them into the fire, and they are burned. ⁷ If you abide in Me, and My words abide in you, you will ask what you desire, and it shall be done for you. ⁸ By this My Father is glorified, that you bear much fruit; ***so you will be My disciples***" (John 15:5-8).

Jesus is not content that we merely believe in the truth; He wants us to abide in the truth and for Christ to abide in us! Jesus is delighted when we do all things according to His will – yet more so, Jesus wants us to be imitators of Him. Jesus wants disciples that think like Him, perceive and '*oida*' understand like Him, do like Him and thus… become manifest expressions of Him on earth. The core of our being as disciples is not merely to be doers of the word, but be imitators of the Word Made Flesh! Think like Jesus! Act like Jesus!

When I see televangelists on the glowing amusement box, I am instantly repulsed by the hypocrisy; they talk the words of Jesus, but they look and sound nothing like Him. When crocodile tears come during prayer to invite people to salvation, do they not appear fake and worldly to the world? Does not the tone of their voice change at the onset of their emotional plea for souls – and donations? Your donations are not sowing into the ministry of Christ – you are sowing in their ministry of deceit! Believers are supposed to, according to the spiritual nature within them, be generous givers – and faith-merchant wolves in sheep clothing fully comprehend this spiritual nature within believers… and they exploit it to achieve their own kingdom agenda.

Likewise, believers are supposed to have the spiritual gift of discernment, yet it seems few do.

Disciples, however, are more than believers and followers – they are imitators of Christ. Disciples are manifest representatives – as Christ's body – upon the earth. Disciples are His offspring...

> "... for in Him we live and move and have our being, as also some of your own poets have said, 'For we are also His offspring.' [29] Therefore, since we are the offspring of God, we ought not to think that the Divine Nature is like gold or silver or stone, something shaped by art and man's devising" (Acts 17:28, 29).

Disciples willingly desire to be shaped and conformed into the image of Christ.

> "For whom He foreknew, He also predestined to be conformed to the image of His Son, that He might be the firstborn among many brethren" (Rom. 8:29).

We were created in His Own image and likeness... to become a likeness of His Image.

> "Grace and peace be multiplied to you in the knowledge of God and of Jesus our Lord, [3] as His ***divine power*** has given to us all things that pertain to life and godliness, through the knowledge of Him who called us by glory and virtue, [4] by which have been given to us exceedingly great and precious promises, ***that through these you may be partakers of the divine nature***, having escaped the corruption that is in the world through lust" (2 Per. 1:2-4).

Are you in the habit of being conformed into the image of Jesus? Do you ask Him for guidance and instruction before you make a decision? Jesus is God Incarnate, and the reason He always consulted His Father was in order to teach us "how" to live according to the divine nature (spirit) that He placed within us. He taught us according to this manner and demonstrated this pattern for our benefit.

Let me share a recent event with you. While purchasing an ink cartridge for my printer, I was faced with a choice: purchase the factory one or purchase a recycled one. The factory cartridge had a 20% rebate, but the recycled cartridge (which does not work as well) was $10 cheaper. In that moment, I asked the Holy Spirit: "should I purchase the factory or the other?" Immediately, the Spirit said, "The other." When I took the cartridge to the cash register, the cashier looked at me and said, "Would you like to get $10 off?" She had a special coupon that allowed her to take another $10 off – instantly. When I told her about my prayer, she grinned and indicated she was a believer and appreciated the testimony. Not only did I get a great deal on an ink cartridge, but the light of Christ was shared between two strangers that were now united by the Spirit.

This example may seem extremely small and trivial within the larger scheme of things, and yet I ask: do you want to live according to this manner? This is how the Lord Jesus taught us to live and how to ask for the things we need. If you are making all decisions without any input from the Lord, then "who" is the Lord of your life?

Ten bucks or ten million is irrelevant! Do not act independently or take initiative, but before doing anything, ask the Lord and seek Divine guidance first and foremost (not afterward to get out of any self-inflicted mess). Furthermore, not all events are designed to produce a positive financial benefit in your favor. The issue is: how are you choosing to live your life (which is actually His life that He gave to you) – and what is the pattern you are following that guides your decision-making if, that is, you desire to be a disciple of Jesus?

Are you living according to the kingdom of self… or the gospel of grace?

The Gospel of Grace

When suffering happens, we often think, "What did I do to deserve this?" Well, my friend, it isn't about you and never was. You will encounter trials and tribulations and suffering and persecution because you believe in Jesus – nothing more, nothing less. It isn't about you! Pride will tell us it's all about you, but pride is an enemy of grace.

Pride is an enemy of grace! It's all about Jesus – and you are suffering on account of Christ in you. Pride would have you believe otherwise. Let me explain what I mean from a military perspective (because we are in a spiritual war): when an army of ten thousand is coming against your army of five thousand, do you consider the merit of any individual soldier that is coming against you? No! You shoot to kill every soldier you see before they get you because they are an enemy combatant. From their perspective, you are an enemy combatant and they are not interested in the least if you have a college degree, a wife, two kids, a Golden Labrador, a leadership position in a church or alphabets after your name. You are merely a person they have been ordered to kill indiscriminately. Our adversary, the devil, has an army that has been ordered to kill and destroy every human being, indiscriminately, but they have a problem: the Lord has prevented them from doing it themselves, so they must recruit other humans to do their evil killing.

Because the enemy cannot kill, it resorts to those means allowed by the Lord (study the message of Job, especially the first two chapters and you will have a better understanding what I mean). God does not cause us to suffer, but God has allowed it for a reason that we often take personally. Well, I repeat myself… IT ISNT ABOUT YOU! Get over it. Suffering isn't personal to you (unless you think it so)… but your suffering is personal to God! The Lord, in His infinite wisdom, grace, and mercy has elected this means of sanctifying us wherein you are the one that either sits in judgment of "you" – or the Lord will make you a judge over armies and demons that did not succeed in their mission to get you to deny your faith in Jesus.

You are not alone! Let the Spirit of grace empower you as an overcomer… by grace.

Pride is an enemy of grace. Pride exalts your thoughts higher than God's thoughts, and your plans higher than God's purposes, which the bible calls: foolishness. God has given every one of us "grace upon grace" so that we may endure and overcome the onslaught of the enemy against us, so stop running away from adversity – and start running toward it – in the name of Jesus. When you encounter the enemy, the Lord gave us an arsenal of tools to combat them, chiefly: the Word of truth. Use this sword to vanquish your adversary… and ask the Holy Spirit to guide you in righteousness and truth as a soldier in the army (host) of earth.

Our biggest problem is pride, because pride tricks us into thinking, "It's all about me" and "I've got this." Grace, on the other hand, convinces us, "It isn't about you" and "It's all about Jesus" and "You can put your trust in Jesus."

Suffering is to be expected, especially toward disciples engaged in ministry.

Let me tell you about an inspirational message from my pastor who was praying for his wife while he was mowing the yard regarding her leadership in hosting a woman's conference "for her burden to get lighter," then the Spirit's response stopped him in his tracks: "Don't pray for the burden to go away or get lighter… pray for more grace to endure." This is the message we need more than ever: we need more grace to endure and to help us persevere.

Our spirit is strengthened by grace. Our commission is strengthened by grace.

Grace is not about our failure – it's about our surrender. It's all grace from beginning to end. Your faith is actually a work of God's grace in you. God is doing it – in you, with you, to you, through you and for you – as a work of Grace. God created you, formed you, inserted you onto earth at just the right time, appointed people to write the word of truth for you, appointed people to share the word of truth with you, appointed ministers to guide you into the truth and has appointed pastors to encourage you in faithfulness to the Lord... so where along this path did you do anything to earn grace? It is by grace and God's election you were saved and are being saved... and none of this was accomplished by you... except your initial and sustained surrendering of your soul in submission to Jesus as your Sovereign Lord and King.

> "For by grace you have been saved through faith,
> and that not of yourselves; it is the gift of God"
> (Eph. 2:8).

Grace enables us to endure persecution and suffering for the sake of Christ. Grace helps us stay focused on Jesus... despite whatever situations or circumstances we find ourselves in. Pride is a deceitful miscalculation that makes us think it's personal. You are special... but that's not the point. It's not about you! Bear your cross and follow Jesus! Jesus promised us suffering and persecution, so then, what were you promised when you came to faith? Happiness?

In this life you will have sufferings and trial and tribulations – on account of Christ in you.

Three times the Apostle Paul prayed, and the Lord said... "My grace is sufficient!"

Grace is sufficient! If you think you need anything other than grace, then you did not enter into faith by the gospel of grace. You cannot do it alone and you are not getting off this planet alive. You will never be worthy of grace and there is nothing you can do to earn it. Grace is what Jesus did because you (and all of us) were completely unable, but the spirit of religion will have you believe otherwise. The interesting thing is: Jesus created us with weakness to become vulnerable, so when we turn away and stray from Him in an effort to accomplish anything in our own strength, fortitude, creativity, determination and human effort – our failure is predetermined. Pride relies upon self reliance and fortitude. Perseverance relies entirely upon grace!!!

Pride is an enemy of grace! God is exalted when we humble ourselves – by grace.

God's Attributes Given To Mankind

Grace represents all the attributes of God's character that He has given to mankind. Grace is more than just the power to endure and persevere; grace is the manifest presence of God abiding in us that enables us to endure anything "this world" throws against us by operating according to His character being manifested in us and through us. Grace is the miraculous power and divine wisdom we need to operate like sons and daughters of God in this world. Grace is what we claim and credit to God when we succeed, and grace is what we pray for when we encounter adversity, suffering and persecution.

> From beginning to end, it's all about Grace – and God gets the glory!

Jesus is "grace personified" which He manifested for us – and we should imitate His example. When someone attacks you or insults your character, then ask: "What Would Jesus Do?" If you intend on reacting to every assault, insult or false accusation against you, then know this: the enemy is more than happy to keep you busily consumed in your defense of "you" rather than you doing good that gives glory to God. If someone slaps you or defrauds you, then turn the other cheek. Keep this in mind: God dwells in you. That person is defrauding God and they are slapping God. By doing good and not retaliating, you are operating according to grace… and they are heaping burning coals upon themselves.

Are you courageous enough to live like this? Say "Yes" to Jesus in a "no" world because cowardice is also an enemy of grace.

Stop trying to fix this world. Be the agent of change the Lord predestined that you become – and be a gateway of God's grace! Grace is power perfected in weakness.

The fruit of the Spirit is love – the power of the Spirit is grace.

Amazing Grace

Over the years, grace has been redefined to mean many things which seem contrary to God's attributes being manifested in man and through man – by God Himself. When we create acronyms that teach us grace represents God's riches at Christ's expense, we erringly focus our attention on attaining riches rather than mercy and grace. The acronym I prefer is:

God's Righteousness and Christ's Example

Grace enables us to forgive others and show mercy; and grace enables us to receive mercy – and also forgive ourselves.

Grace helps us remember the good things of God; grace helps us forget offenses committed against us by others.

Grace empowers us to live courageously; grace enables us to make ourselves a living sacrifice for the sake of Christ. Any suffering in our flesh is perfecting the work of God's grace being manifested in us and through us (soul and spirit).

Grace challenges us to discredit timidity – yet do all things with humility.

Grace is not to be limited by definition as getting something we don't deserve, nor is mercy to be limited by not getting something (wrath) that we do deserve. God has poured grace upon grace upon us – so that we may become more like Jesus – and be extensions (gateways) of His grace and mercy to others (Micah 6:8).

Grace isn't about giving or getting... grace is about becoming!
Grace constitutes the attributes of God's character being manifested and perfected in us – as something God initiated in us since before the foundation of the world and is being consummated and perfected through us – to the praise of His glory.

Lord, may the Spirit of Grace fill us with Your character – so that we become more like You.

Grace Commands Obedience

Remember this: when Jesus asks you to do something, these words are not suggestions... they are commands.

On October 27, 2014, I experienced an encounter with the Lord in which I saw His eyes. He began teaching me about His dominion for several days, and then He said: "I am going to ask you to go where you are not accustomed to going, to do something that is outside of your understanding." Even now, I do not know if the sojourn I am on pertains to this request or if a greater challenge is to be expected. My response remains the same: "Yes... even before you ask, Lord! If you make your will perfectly clear to me, I will never disobey You!"

There are times when Jesus asks us to do things to see what our response will be – because He has given us free will to say yes or no. Within this context, there are three dynamics:

1. He asks to see if we will readily accept
2. He will "wait and see" what our response will be
3. He will consider our concerns when we respond

During training, the Teacher is instructive and verbal, but during the test, the Teacher is often silent... waiting to see if we learned the lesson. We need to pass the test... and life is a test! If the Teacher is silent, then be encouraged... a Tutor has been assigned to help you pass, but you must be willing to listen to the quiet Voice of the Holy Spirit and you must obey His instruction.

Jesus demonstrated uncompromised obedience to the Father while on the earth, yet on one occasion He asked the Father to "take this cup" from Him. Jesus is God and He knew all things, and He knew He was going to experience inhumane torture and a violent death on a cross. Jesus knew this in advance! Jesus did not say these words because He was trying to back out of that which He was purposed to accomplish; He knew His disciples were listening and, thus, Jesus taught us that we can petition God to see if there may be another means to accomplish the task set before us. Abraham did the same thing regarding Sodom and Gomorrah.

We do not enter into negotiations with God; however, we can ask the Lord if other options exist, and if there aren't, then we must petition the Lord as a "*ptochos*" poor in spirit for the grace necessary to endure the cross set before you.

> "... though He was a Son, yet He learned [taught us] obedience by the things which He suffered" (Heb. 5:8).

The Spirit of Grace is teaching us by the power of grace how to live by grace to become sons and daughters of grace so that we can stand boldly before the Throne of Grace. Who you are becoming is what the gospel of grace – and transformation by the Spirit – is perfecting in us.

Grace and glory – in love – and the peace of God – is what the gospel of grace is all about.

We will all experience pain and suffering; however, when we focus on these things, we erringly allow our focus to shift away from Jesus and consequently these things appear to become larger than God's ability to help us. Magnify God in you… not the circumstance.

Magnify the Lord in your soul – until there is no problem larger than CHRIST – in you!

We live within a culture that embraces a "victim mentality" because: A) we have been inculcated to believe we get more out of society and others by being a victim; B) we don't have to take responsibility for our actions; and C) we resist the need to change when we can blame others for our failure. Rather than playing the part of a victim, become victorious over your circumstances. If there is a mountain or a problem in your life, stop complaining about the problem, call upon God's grace and then ask God what you both should do about it.

> "So Jesus said to them, "Because of your unbelief; for assuredly, I say to you, if you have faith as a mustard seed, you will say to this mountain, 'Move from here to there,' and it will move; and nothing will be impossible for you"(Matt. 17:20).

Either we magnify the Lord – or we magnify our problems and woes. When we magnify the Lord in our soul, He becomes bigger than any problem we encounter. Set your sights on things above – and not on things below.

We must start our walk in Christ from a position of victory… rather than as victims in defeat.

The Crucible Called Life

> "Normal Is A Dryer Setting."

The Lord placed me upon a path beginning in 2012 to remember and understand what the kingdom of God is about. During this time (nearly five years thus far devoted entirely to writing and research), I have learned a simple truth: Jesus is our example. Everything that Jesus endured and went through – was done in order to teach us more about who we are… and why we are here. Jesus became our Example to teach us who we are – and demonstrate (exemplify) what we should be doing on earth. "As he is, so are we in this world" (1 John 4:17). At this juncture, very few question-marks remain… yet many exclamation-marks abound in my sojourn to remember who we are, to comprehend many mysteries... and understand!

For example: Jesus is the Lamb of God. Our doctrines accurately teach this, but how exactly does this relate to us (mankind)? As He Is, so are we, and likewise, we are like lambs led to slaughter. If this contradicts your closely-guarded doctrine for man's reason for existing on earth, then try explaining why people suffer on earth and why God allows it.

> "For to this you were called, because Christ also suffered for us, leaving us an example, that you should follow His steps" (1 Pet. 2:21).

This sojourn of mine has relied exclusively on the Holy Spirit to guide me into all truth. Book #8: "Here: The Kingdom of Heaven Is" was initiated by the Spirit's question to me, "Do men go to heaven?" Many problems have been created by our doctrines teaching heaven-only as God's predetermination to explain man's future and eternal habitation, yet Jesus never promised us heaven, the apostles never preached it and our creeds don't teach it. If you go to heaven after you die, how wonderful, but what will you be doing after that? If your doctrines cannot explain that, then perhaps you should read what the Spirit told me as to where we go and what we will be doing for all eternity. We were promised "life eternal" in "the place prepared for you" of which there are fourteen. While I was utterly amazed by the truth being taught to me in book #8, I was woefully unprepared for the wisdom the Spirit revealed to me in book #3 about Jesus... and understanding who He is from His perspective (which is a game-changer for the church). These books reach different conclusions than those doctrines taught by the institutional church, yet they are supported entirely by scriptures given to me by the Holy Spirit... not for building an institutional body of believers into a new church religion called Christianity 5.0, but rather, for building Christ's Body, His church, comprised of disciples according to the gospel of grace and truth – yet not according to works, legalism, sacrifices, guilt manipulation, fear or whatnot. There are times when the deception in the institutional church is so blatantly obvious to me that the enemy has certainly played a significant role in creating doctrines that muddy the pure, clean waters of truth. Search the scriptures for the truth! For starters: we are spiritual beings having a human experience for one season of eternity on earth. Remembering who we are is necessary in order to remember what we are supposed to be doing – on earth as it is in heaven.

The Holy Spirit started me on a path to discover all mysteries. If your doctrines include teachings that are mysteries which no one can explain, then they are not divine in origin… but demonic. God's mysteries, which are temporarily concealed, are intended to be revealed by Him to earnest seekers of truth (Prov. 25:2).

The New Earth conclusions documented within these books answer nearly every question I ever had, yet the institutional church must reject it in order to defend its preexisting prejudice of heaven as our eternal home, their limited understanding of Jesus, and their denominational kingdoms as well. If your doctrines leave you with more question-marks than exclamation marks, then read these books to learn about the truth the institutional church refuses to acknowledge or teach you. As the famous dictum of Sherlock Holmes says:

> "When you have eliminated the impossible, whatever remains, however improbable, must be the truth."

Since we are like Jesus, having been created in His image according to His Own likeness, and since Jesus is the Lamb of God, how then are we like sheep? "The Lord is my shepherd" (Psa. 23) is one of numerous instances in the scriptures wherein even Jesus refers to us as sheep.

> "My sheep hear My voice, and I know them, and they follow Me" (John 10:27).

We are lambs of God. And since we are like sheep being led to slaughter, then what is our purpose for living and being on earth?

That is the million dollar question! The mystery of man is sanctification. That is what this book (Commission) and all Image Bearer books are about: understanding sanctification – having been created on purpose for a purpose. The Lord put us on earth – and we were placed in harm's way as soldier-servants taking part in a human army in the midst of a war against a demonic army, and yet, we were given the option of becoming His disciple and coming against powers and principalities– or forfeiting life eternal by choosing to live according to our will. It is "we" who judge ourselves worthy (or not) based upon the manner in which we choose to live this life, either in subordinate obedience to Jesus as Lord of our life – or as His opponent in league with the demonic kingdom of darkness.

"In this life, you will have trouble." "In this life, you will be persecuted on account of Christ" (Matt. 5:10-12). In this life, you will have suffering. In this life, you will have grief, sorrow, and many woes including life's final enemy: death. If anyone told you life was going to be easy once you accepted Jesus as Lord – they were selling you something they could never deliver. Faith in the sovereignty of Jesus makes life in "this world" infinitely more difficult and painful with trials, persecutions, suffering and great tribulations by an unseen enemy. Life in this world is full of suffering, but if you are fortunate enough to be in the very small category of people that does not struggle with famine, oppression, undrinkable water, oppressive dictators and a myriad of diseases, then count your blessing as you consider why the Lord blessed you rather than someone else (perhaps to be a blessing to others). We suffer, not always because of what we've done (though we reap what we sow), yet rather... always because of who we are (sons of men in transition of becoming sons and daughters of God – again).

Suffering is not a popular topic, but it is paramount in importance for disciples to know.

> "For I will show him how many things he must suffer for My name's sake" (Acts 9:16).

The Lord has allowed Satan to sift us in order to sanctify us, but only under certain conditions. Take, for example, what Jesus said to Peter:

> "And the Lord said, "Simon, Simon! Indeed, Satan has asked for you, that he may sift *you* as wheat" (Luke 22:21).

Satan cannot destroy or kill Peter (which Satan is not allowed to do), and Satan was not allowed to sift his faith… but Satan was given permission to sift Peter, to challenge his faith and draw him into closer intimacy with Jesus. Satan has been given permission to sift us, and yet, even though the sifting process of wheat to remove chaff to purify the wheat is painful, the sifting process also works to Satan's disadvantage: we become more valuable in service to the Lord in this life… and life eternal in glory.

We (mankind) are like wheat seed cast upon earth to produce more glory and honor for Jesus and to fill the earth with the glory of the Lord. We were cast as seed in the midst of much adversity – or more accurately – we were placed in the midst of a cosmic spiritual between goodness and evil for dominion of this earth. Earth is your eternal home and rightful habitation which Satan stole from us (courtesy of Adam and Eve) and we have been sent here to redeem the land and come against the kingdom of darkness with the light of truth abiding within us. Whatever you have sacrificed for this cause – to establish the kingdom of heaven on earth –will be rewarded and recompensed at least double (like Job) or perhaps 30, 60, 100-fold. Every time we sacrifice our will and agenda to accomplish the will of the Lord shall be regarded as deeds of righteousness for the sake of Christ that shall be forwarded into our heavenly bank account when we get to the other side… as true riches. All worldly riches acquired in this life account for less than nothing (I say this because they have a negative effect on the final disposition of your soul) unless you steward them and use them to advance the gospel of grace.

Life is not fair. Life is painful. Life is lived within a sea of adversity. Life will experience rejection and hardship. Life will feel the onslaught of evil against us to prevent us from claiming our rightful inheritance called "Earth." Jesus experienced every pain we will ever experience and He was tortured beyond what nearly any of us will ever experience in order to exemplify who and what we really are: sheep led to slaughter.

> "Ought not the Christ to have suffered these things and to enter into His glory?" (Luke 24:26).

> "For it was fitting for Him, for whom are all things and by whom are all things, ***in bringing many sons to glory***, to make the captain of their salvation perfect through sufferings" (Heb. 2:10).

> "…and if children, then heirs—heirs of God and joint heirs with Christ, if indeed ***we suffer with Him, that we may also be glorified together***" (Rom. 8:17).

> ***"For I consider that the sufferings of this present time are not worthy to be compared with the glory which shall be revealed in us"*** (Rom. 8:18).

Suffering is not new to anyone living on earth, but why we suffer – is. Our salvation is made perfect through suffering – in this spiritual process called sanctification.

> "Yes, and all who desire to live godly in Christ Jesus will suffer persecution" (2 Tim. 3:12).

We are admonished to "present ourselves as living sacrifices, made holy and acceptable to God" (Rom. 12:2). Whatever any other reason may be, it is important for us to thoroughly comprehend this: God is in us and is with us… throughout all of it. Just as the Father was in Jesus the entire time He was being tortured and then brutally executed on a cross for doing nothing wrong, likewise, God is in us even when we are led to slaughter up to and including the moment of our death. God who dwells in us knows our pain and feels our pain, and in this regard, "He was acquainted with" every manner of physical and emotional torment in His own body such that "He knows what we are going through." God sent us here, but God did not send us here to suffer alone… God dwells within us and suffers along with us whether we choose to acknowledge Him and love Him – or not. His love for us is unconditional, yet our response to that love will never negate His love for us. "God is love." We may be able to create a false (alternate) reality where we pretend He does not exist, but that doesn't change the fact: God is with us and dwells in us.

Let Jesus help you. You were never intended to do this on your own… or do it alone!

No one would willingly choose to suffer, yet some choose to suffer alone. Grace upon grace enables us to endure patiently, with the Lord dwelling in us, and with the Spirit empowering us to overcome every trial and tribulation.

There is honor among men when you do what is right. Bear your cross… in whatever that happens to be which the Lord has allotted to you – bear your cross. Adversity happens. Suffering happens. The question I propose to you is: do you want glory attributed to it – or not?

> "For as the sufferings of Christ abound in us, so our consolation also abounds through Christ. [6] Now if we are afflicted, it is for your consolation and salvation, which is effective for enduring the same sufferings which we also suffer. Or if we are comforted, it is for your consolation and salvation. [7] And our hope for you is steadfast, because we know that as you are partakers of the sufferings, so also you will partake of the consolation" (2 Cor. 1:5-7).

Trust In The Lord Jesus

A dear friend of mind had a dream encounter with the Lord. In this dream, the Lord showed him a specific man that He wanted him to help in ministry about 80 miles away. Then the Lord told him: "I want you to leave your church and go right away. If you don't do this, then I can't trust you anymore." This was a very specific request and such specific requests... are non-negotiable! My friend did as directed and resigned from many important church duties to which he was assigned. It didn't matter to him if his actions were misunderstood; obedience doesn't care what other people think or perceive. Obedience is done in service to the Lord of Heaven and Earth.

Disciples hear the voice of Jesus – and obey! "Who, having heard, *disobeyed*?" (Heb. 3:16; also translated *rebelled*).

Disciple Sons and Daughters

Perhaps the most important task we will ever undertake on earth is to pass along the truth of God to the next generation that was entrusted to us by Jesus. This seems like a simple and straightforward task, and yet, not many of us have actually been discipled past basic doctrine and mentoring or have discipled someone else? The problem, I perceive, is that we (the church) have produced a great many "believers" that are standing on first base, but they have not yet been instructed to yield to the Spirit's process of sanctification (second base) nor embraced the gospel message to abandon the cares of this world to become a disciple of Jesus Christ (third base). Members and believers have been produced and reproduced by the billions, but disciples? Very few, it seems.

A healthy church will have a vibrant discipleship program with training geared toward transforming believers into disciples with deep spiritual truth into deep spiritual growth, yet many church programs seem more interested in plugging new members into service functions of that church while discipleship training is largely nonexistent.

Today, it is no longer cool to refer to yourself or anyone else as a disciple because it now implies you belong to a cult that inculcates weak-minded followers with brainwashing techniques to go all-in and dedicate their life in full submission to a worldly-minded spiritual leader with very narrow interpretations of select prophetic biblical messages. When the subject comes up, I am not ashamed to tell people I am a disciple of Jesus… and I often see them recoil. This is who I am because Jesus told me on November 1, 2014… "You are My disciple." I am not ashamed to say this about myself; it has become a badge of ownership as I am also the Lord's bondservant.

Jesus did not tell his disciples to "go ye therefore" into the world to make believers or converts as if to become members of a Christian club or fraternity; Jesus said… make disciples! If every disciple was to mentor and teach two people in a discipleship manner, this world would have been converted to the truth a long time ago.

Over the past thirty years, I have submitted myself to many pastors, several teachers, and even a mentor (for one brief moment), but there was only one person in my life that guided my steps with advanced training in righteousness who became a type of spiritual mother to me. Her advanced training in discipleship happened in the same as mine: under the tutelage and guidance of the Holy Spirit. Rather than teach me to hear her point of view and adopt it, she would simply ask me one question: "What did the Spirit tell you?" If the message I received wasn't clear, then I was advised to go back and wait until the answer became clear. She was training me to be a disciple that listens to the Spirit of the Lord's voice because – no other voices matter!

For some people this seems spiritually dangerous, so let me ask you this question: where did most of the Old Covenant prophets live? Were they not living in wilderness areas away from all formal teaching and free advice? So then, where did they get their formal teaching and tutoring? The answer is not "where" but from "Whom"!

Take for example John the Baptist who lived in deserted areas for thirty years under the tutoring and guidance of the Holy Spirit; he spoke the message he was prepared to speak as the forerunner for the Messiah for perhaps only six months before he was beheaded for the truth he proclaimed. There are countless stories of people living in desolate areas that have a deeper understanding of God than most people sitting in cushioned pews listening to awesome sermons by preachers with doctoral distinction. Don't misunderstand what I am saying… I love to hear good sermons and I like to tell pastors what awesome messages were commissioned through them, but I would rather hear five words from the Holy Spirit that motivates me to host God's presence and imitate Christ than 50 minutes of great exposition that stays in my head long enough to get to Cracker Barrel or Olive Garden… but never makes it to my heart.

Being an intelligent believer is easy… but living like a disciple of Jesus that hears and obeys – is what the King of Heaven and Earth is looking for. During most of my Christian life (post Spirit baptism) I have uttered this simple prayer and meant every word of it: "Lord, if You make your will perfectly clear to me, I will never disobey You!"

Again, I say… "Who, having heard, rebelled" (Heb. 3:16).

It takes a disciple to pass along the discipleship mantel… because calm seas never make a skillful sailor! A true disciple is able to hear God's voice – and will always do what the Lord tells them to do. ALWAYS – WITHOUT DOUBT – and without hesitation!!! You cannot call yourself a disciple unless you have dedicated your life to hearing and obeying the Voice of Truth! Every morning, I begin the day in total silence and stillness – seeking the Lord and asking Him what He wants me to do. The day does not belong to me – I belong to the Day! I am not on earth to do my will and satisfy my agenda. The Lord commissioned me as His writer in 2013 and this is all I've done ever since – living entirely by grace. I have experienced many hardships along the way and the Lord has used these to deepen my trust in Him and deepen my understanding regarding spiritual matters. Apart from grace – I am nothing. If a disciple claims to have had a smooth and blessed path without any hardship or rejection, then I question it... because when you get closer to Jesus, the world will hate you and come against you. This is not my opinion – this was promised by Jesus that His disciples will follow His example, will carry a cross... and share in His suffering.

> "If the world hates you, you know that it hated Me before it hated you" (John 15:18).

Sell Everything, Then Follow Me

The hardest thing a believer being trained as a disciple will ever do – is to give it all away when Jesus tells us to (not by the voice of any pastor or even by these words which you are reading). Disciples are listeners of Jesus only! Do what He tells you!

Why is giving it all away the hardest thing? Because we do not trust Jesus works in this manner, and because we have been taught to trust the worldly system. We have been taught the truth about faith, but not the whole truth... especially in regards to discipleship and giving it all away. They say, "Jesus would never tell you to sell your house – and then give all that money away. Jesus wants us to be happy and prosperous. Those bold preposterous words cannot be from Jesus, but rather... from the enemy." How intriguing are these words as coming from people embracing the worldly paradigm of Satan to get... rather than give?

Be not encumbered by the things of this world.

> "Now these are the ones sown among thorns; they are the ones who hear the word, [19] and the cares of this world, the deceitfulness of riches, and the desires for other things entering in choke the word, and it becomes unfruitful. [20] But these are the ones sown on good ground, those who hear the word, accept it, and bear fruit: some thirtyfold, some sixty, and some a hundred" (Mark 4:18-20).

The health and wealth gospel panders to believers that have no skin in the game. If Jesus tells you to give it all away, do not consider it a suggestion; it is a command. Every word that Jesus speaks is not open for debate – it is a command. The worlds were created by His Word and raging storms became peaceful by His Voice, so why do we think the Lord's words are an invitation we may debate and take under advisement? If Jesus does give you an option, it is because you must freely sacrifice… because mandatory sacrifice is not worship – it's obligation.

When the Lord began preparing me for the journey He preordained me to walk according to, I struggled against it. You see… I had become a very pompous, proud, smug, arrogant, successful, self-righteous jerk that needed to die. I am not just talking about the metaphorical dying to self… my entire way of living and thinking had to come to a complete end. I (the self)… needed to thoroughly die!!!

> "I have been crucified with Christ; it is no longer I who live, but Christ lives in me; and the *life* which I now live in the flesh I live by faith in the Son of God, who loved me and gave Himself for me" (Gal. 2:20).

This was the most painful thing I have ever experienced in my life. The process began in 2006 with a failed marriage, then I got cancer in 2009 and then I lost an excellent job in 2010. For the next two years, I suffered from post traumatic stress disorder which I carefully tried to hide from my children and my friends. After having been unemployed for the majority of two years, I lifted my eyes to heaven and shook my fist at God and said, "Fine! If you are so intent on taking everything from me, then just take it all!"

The Lord heard my prayer… and heaven rejoiced. He didn't need my permission, but I gave it nonetheless. Friends, the Lord doesn't need your permission to take everything away from you (because it all belongs to Him anyway), but it is actually less painful to us when we surrender it all at once rather than doing it piecemeal by having the Lord pry our fingers from "stuff."

By 2013, I was completely out of money and four credit cards were maxed. During this time, the Lord was teaching me "not to worry." His word to me one particular morning was… "Worry is idolatry." Every time we take our eyes off Jesus to focus on something else other than Him… is a form of idolatry. Months later, Jesus commissioned me as His writer on September 27 and by November 1st the mortgage was in default and it was only a matter of time before the foreclosure and eviction process began. By grace, I applied for and was given forbearance on any mortgage payments for a year… which the Lord used to teach me to trust Him in all things as I faithfully wrote His messages that I heard from Him every day.

Bliss… is not how I would describe living in debt with credit card companies calling you nearly every day while unemployed without any form of income. Twenty months later (having lived in that house mortgage free and rent free – by grace), the day finally came to move out of the house whereby I established four Saturdays to garage sale all my stuff. And then I heard the soft voice of the Lord say: "Give it away." Well, this is my confession: I went ahead with the garage sale. The first Saturday came and went and not one piece of furniture sold, so I went to the Lord in prayer on Monday and asked Him what we were going to do about it, and the Spirit said, "Missionaries coming to town will need it." I asked everyone I knew if they were aware of any missionaries coming to town with a furniture need. No after no after no was all I heard. Then on Saturday, with a good crowd in attendance, a couple came up to me to see what I had – and the wife became excited by my "stuff," so I gave her a piece of paper to make a list of all items with the price tag. Meanwhile, the husband and I continued to chat wherein small talk turned to God talk and then he said, "We are missionaries from China and we just bought a house that needs everything." So, I turned to him and said, "You're the man." The dazed expression on his face became more perplexed when I told him the Lord told me that "Missionaries coming to town will need it" and that I was to give all my furniture to him. Seeing the expression on his face was well worth being obedient to the Lord. (chuckling) Then his wife came out with the list of stuff and it included all furniture, four appliances and even lawn furniture.

When she handed me the list, I flipped it over to the blank side and said, "It all belongs to you." They were very polite with a shell-shocked look on their face, and said they simply couldn't take it without paying anything, so I explained... "I must be obedient! The Lord told me to do it – so I must do it!"

Little did I know the journey I was embarking on would need very little "stuff." Several weeks later, on July 7, 2015, as I awoke in a hotel room on my first morning without house, without furnishings, without job, no finances, tons of credit card debt and little more to my name except the laptop with which I continue to write and whatever else I could fit into a sedan, I sought the Lord that morning as I always do... and then I heard Him say, "Your are My son. Today I have delivered you." Wowza! The Lord Jesus called me "son!"

There are many messages that serve as take-aways from my experience to encourage many, but the one that means the most to me is "sonship." One year earlier He called me "His disciple" and a year earlier He called me "Beloved." This is the Godly heritage the Lord desires to have with each and every one of His children – by hearing His voice and following Him on the path He has predestined for you. The Lord is walking ahead as your leader and the Holy Spirit is alongside as your Paraclete for help and strength. You are not alone!!! The Lord is in you, with you, for you and will never leave you or abandon you. If you are one of the few who said "Yes" without any preconditions, then it is only a matter of time before you are also able say, "I am greatly blessed and highly favored. I am blessed going in and going out! Blessed be the name of the Lord!" You are the Lord's beloved and He desires to teach you all the mysteries of the kingdom when you "Seek first the kingdom of God and His righteousness" i.e. Jesus Christ.

My story is to encourage you – and yet – the journey of a disciple isn't easy.

Don't expect anyone to recognize you according to the gift or the calling the Lord placed upon you. Don't expect anyone to ask you to preach or give a testimony or take a leadership position. From personal experience (and the experience of others), recognition and notoriety are not outcomes of discipleship; obedience is! If the Lord has called you to do something, then get started. Don't calculate... just get going, don't stop, and keep at it. **Recognition not required**!

Fanfare rarely happens. Acceptance rarely happens. Accolades rarely happen! It may be years before anyone even recognizes let alone accepts what the Lord has done through you (and that is the key – it is God doing it in you and through you). Let me attach my response to a dear brother who cautioned me about the messages I was writing along the journey I was on:

> "Thank you for your words of counsel. I am ever mindful of the gravity of the commission committed to me; these are not my books... they are His books! Like David, who wrote out of his experience with the Lord, likewise... I host the Lord's presence and write under the inspiration, anointing and tutoring of the Holy Spirit. I establish His kingdom, not mine; His will, not mine; His agenda, not mine. "My life is not my own" (1 Cor. 6:19; Gal. 2:20).
>
> "And like the Apostle Paul (my role model and mentor in absentia), he wrote many things under the tutoring of the Holy Spirit to establish the church - in grace and truth, being rooted and established in love, yet without any understanding his letters would constitute the majority of New Testament canon 300 years later... and I continue with that understanding yet from a reformation perspective.
>
> "Isaiah wrote many things that were unfavorable to Israel and Judaism, and he also wrote prophetically about our Lord 750 years before His parousia, and yet he wrote what he was inspired to write without needing or seeking validation or the encouragement of others; his steadfast devotion to the Lord

encourages me even now.

"My writings will never contradict the word – and they are compatible with His word, and the understanding the Spirit has taught me is within the written word itself, but our doctrines have blinded us from seeing the bigger picture in many aspects of faith in Christ, who we are and what man should be doing on earth. We have forgotten – and we need to remember!!!

"And yet, we need to be looking forward, not backward!

"I have embraced the scripture you sent me (1 Cor. 16:13, 14). Thanks for remembering me in your prayers. You are very dear to me as a true brother in Christ and I am blessed to call you my eternal friend." [END]

My friend was cautioning me about the words I write, which he never read, to be consistent with the Word of God because "All He wants us to know for now is what is IN His Word now." Incredibly, everything I write is in His Word now, yet few are paying attention to the message. My true, unedited, emotional response that I wanted to say... but withheld from sending is:

"I bristle at your comment: "All He wants us to know for now is what is IN His Word now." If this was the attitude in the first century church, then Paul's messages about grace would have been rejected. The reason it was accepted is because they asked the Holy Spirit for guidance. The church has become oblivious to any word from the Lord that may come to us from the Spirit Himself (i.e. outside of the word of God) because... we trust in the bible as the complete and infallible word of God and boldly declare it as "the final authority" concerning

> God's word, yet Jesus is the Word of God... and His Voice has never stopped speaking to His children (unlike the 400 years before His parousia 2,000 years ago). The OT scriptures were mostly silent on the resurrection of the dead, as well as the manifestation of the Messiah; however, the truth was in His word, but it was veiled from understanding until after Christ's resurrection whereby the Spirit (sent by Jesus) began tutoring and instructing men who dedicated their life as the Lord's disciples."

Jesus is the Word of God... and He has never stopped speaking to us about His kingdom!

> "For the kingdom of God is not in word but in power" (1 Cor. 4:20).

Jesus Himself operated in silent obscurity for 18 years before His earthly ministry began, and the Apostle Paul spent 17 years making tents before he presented his gospel of grace to the leaders in Jerusalem. So then, if you are expecting to get an instant emotional rush or some spiritual recognition or goose-bump gratification for the work that Jesus has commissioned you do for His sake, then perhaps you are not doing it for His sake.

Several days after the Lord commissioned me to be "His writer" the Spirit told me to "Wait for it." Would I be waiting forty days, perhaps fifty? Perhaps 1260 days (3.5 years)? Well, that time period also came and went without fanfare... and yet I continue to "wait" upon the Lord joyfully and faithfully to do all that He is instructing me to do. I write every day – under grace.

Most of the promises with blessings in the bible apply to those who surrendered all for the sake of serving Christ – yet they will not receive their reward (or any recognition) until they get to the other side. Persevere! Patient endurance is one of the hallmark qualities of disciples.
Surrendering everything to be a disciple of Jesus is what was

required of me, and I rejoice in the work He has done in me – and through me. Rejoice, and again I say – rejoice!

Endurance is an attribute of grace operating within you – to persevere – for the sake of Christ!

Timothy, My Son

I encourage everyone to read about Paul's mentoring and discipling of Timothy, His true son in the faith. May we all take sufficient time to be properly trained and mentored in this manner through the Spirit and by the person whom the Spirit appoints, and, likewise, train another generation to walk in faithful obedience to Jesus. Train them – to remember all things!

Millennial Servants and New Earth Residents

What will those saints participating in the first resurrection be doing on earth as they rule and reign with Christ for a millennia? And what will you be doing on the New Earth after the second resurrection and the regeneration of all things? What things will glory-bearers be doing while dwelling in glory with Christ Jesus? Disciples are able to answer these questions…

Beloved Disciple, Abide In Me

> "Abide in Me, and I in you. As the branch cannot bear fruit of itself, unless it abides in the vine, neither can you, unless you abide in Me. I am the vine, you are the branches. He who abides in Me, and I in him, bears much fruit; *for without Me you can do nothing*" (John 15:4, 5).

Read the entire Image Bearer series!

Grace and peace be yours in abundance, paul.

Made in the USA
Columbia, SC
11 November 2018